CONCISE COURSE

Green and Henderson: Land Law

OTHER BOOKS IN SERIES

Baker—Tort, C. D. Baker
Brave—Law for Retailers, J. Brave
Brown—GCSE Law, W. J. Brown
Davies on Contract, R. Upex
Dobson Sale of Goods and Consumer Credit, P. Dobson
Eddey—The English Legal System, P. Darbyshire
Field—Hotel and Catering Law in Britain, D. Field
Gill—The Law of Arbitration, E. A. Marshall
Green and Henderson—Land Law, F. J. Harcup
Grime—Shipping Law, R. Grime
Hogan, Seago and Bennett—"A" Level Law, B. Hogan, P. Seago and G. Bennett
Hogan, Seago and Bennett—"A" Level Law: Cases and Materials, B. Hogan, P. Seago and G. Bennett
Seago—Criminal Law, P. Seago

AUSTRALIA
The Law Book Company
Brisbane • Sydney • Melbourne • Perth

CANADA
Ottawa • Toronto • Calgary • Montreal • Vancouver

AGENTS
Steimatzky's Agency Ltd, Tel Aviv;
N.M. Tripathi (Private) Ltd, Bombay;
Eastern Law House (Private) Ltd, Calcutta;
M.P.P. House, Bangalore;
Universal Book Traders, Delhi;
Aditya Books, Delhi;
MacMillan Shuppan KK, Tokyo;
Pakistan Law House, Karachi, Lahore

CONCISE COURSE TEXTS

Green and Henderson: Land Law

Sixth Edition

by

Joy Harcup, LL.B.,

Senior Lecturer in Law, College of Law

LONDON
SWEET & MAXWELL
1995

First Edition 1965
Second Edition 1970
Third Edition 1975
Fourth Edition 1980
Fifth Edition 1988
Sixth Edition 1995

Published in 1995 by
Sweet & Maxwell Limited of
South Quay Plaza
183 Marsh Wall
London E14 9FT
Phototypeset by LBJ Enterprises Ltd. of Aldermaston and Chilcompton
Printed in England by Clays Ltd., St Ives plc

No natural forests were destroyed to make this product;
only farmed timber was used and replanted

A CIP catalogue record for this book is available from the British Library

ISBN 0-421-52300-X

Preface

As with previous editions, it is the aim of this sixth edition to provide an introduction to modern land law, whilst providing some insight into its historical roots — background knowledge that is fundamental to a full understanding of the development of land law today. The initial chapters, charting the historical progress of land law, have therefore been retained, but are balanced with an explanation of practical modern developments. In particular, because of the implementation of compulsory registration of title in all regions of England and Wales, the introductory section on registration of title has been expanded. This provides an opportunity for a preliminary comparison of the procedure for proving title under the registered and unregistered title system. However, the main discussion of this topic is still reserved for the final chapter of the book, as the procedure, in the main, has not altered substantive land law principles.

In the seven years since the last edition, not surprisingly, there has been considerable landlord and tenant legislation. Chapter 13 (perhaps aptly numbered because of the horrendous complexity of this area of the law) has been extensively rewritten to cover the Housing Act 1988, governing security of tenure for short-term private residential tenancies, and the Leasehold Reform, Housing and Urban Development Act 1993, which gives long leasehold flat owners the right to collective enfranchisement. Nevertheless, in this constantly changing subject, yet further changes are afoot. In the case of agricultural tenancies, we have the Agricultural Tenancies Act 1995 and the Landlord and Tenant (Covenants) Bill which proposes the abolition of privity of contract also for leases created in the future (which has not been enacted at the time of going to press).

Another significant piece of legislation is the Law of Property (Miscellaneous) Provisions Act 1989, which alters the law relating to contracts for the disposition of land. The chapter on contracts has therefore been amended to incorporate both this legislation and the latest cases on the interpretation of these provisions. These have a wide reaching effect on varying types of land contracts, ranging from mortgage contracts to options to purchase land.

There has also been activity in the development of case law in other land law topics since the last edition. In particular, the House of Lords has considered, in respect of leases, the requirement for certainty of term *(Prudential Assurance Co. Ltd. v. London Residuary Body)* and also the extent of a tenant's right to relief from forfeiture, where a landlord re-enters for breach of covenant *(Billson v. Residential Apartments Ltd.)*. It also addressed the thorny problem of resulting trusts *(Lloyd's Bank Plc v. Rossett)*. The House however demonstrated its reluctance to legislate judicially. It reassuringly re-confirmed the well established principle that the burden of a positive covenant is not directly enforceable against third parties *(Rhone v. Stephens)*, until such time as Parliament chooses to intervene. It is hardly surprising that, in view of the economic climate of the early 1990s, the other courts have been preoccupied, in particular, with cases involving mortgages and mortgagee's remedies. These cases are explored in Chapter 18 and demonstrate how contract law also applies to land-related cases.

The law is as at May 1, 1995.

On a personal note, I would like to thank my colleagues at the College of Law, Store Street and my friends for their help and patience during the birth of this sixth edition and for their invaluable tips and suggestions. Also many thanks to my family for their support and the supply of chocolate cake, which is so essential when 'living' with a land law book for 18 months.

Joy Harcup
May 25, 1995

Extract from Preface to First Edition

This book is intended to give a practical outline of the land law, or, as it is otherwise known, the law of real property. Its primary purposes is to meet the needs of the many students who are now studying law as part of a wider syllabus. It is hoped that it will also be useful as an introductory book to those who require a more detailed knowledge of the subject: experience has shown that there is much advantage to be gained from studying a short book before proceeding to a more comprehensive work, particularly where the subject is as difficult as is the land law.

E.S.G.
March 1, 1965

Contents List

Table of Cases

Table of Statutes

1. The scope of land law

The law of land, or real property, is concerned with the rights, interests and obligations which can exist over land and buildings; how they are created, enforced, assigned and extinguished. Its undoubted complexity is explained by two main factors.

The first lies in the nature of land itself. Land is permanent property, and so lends itself to the creation of a diversity of concurrent and consecutive interests. The same plot of land or the same house may at once be "owned"[1] by A, and let by A to B for a period of, say, 125 years under a lease. In turn it may be sub-let by B to C for a shorter term of, say, 99 years creating a sub-lease. It can be mortgaged by any of them to a bank as security for repayment of a loan; entitling the bank to sell the property, for example, to recover the loan if it is not repaid. The land may also be subject to a right of way in favour of one neighbour allowing him to use the land, for instance, as access from his own property to the main road. In favour of another neighbour, it may be subject to a restrictive covenant (or promise) preventing A and his successors, for example, from building on the land and affecting the neighbour's enjoyment of his property. Another example of simultaneous rights existing in land is under a settlement which creates a succession of interests in land. Again, by his will A may direct that the land is to be held for his widow during her life, and then for his eldest son during his life, followed by all his grandchildren absolutely in equal shares.

The nature and the validity of these diverse interests are determined in accordance with rules and principles established over a long period by the courts and by statute. In contrast, other forms of property, such as goods and company shares, are normally the subject of absolute ownership only. Although goods may be let by the owner under a contract of hire or hire-purchase, and personal property generally may be used as security for a loan or may be included, like land, in a family settlement, the normal transaction with such property is an outright transfer.

[1] We shall see that, properly speaking, ownership attaches not to the land itself, but to an estate or interest in the land.

The second reason for the complexity of land law is historical. The foundations of the law of land were laid at a time when land was virtually the sole form of wealth, and formed the basis of the feudal system established after the Norman conquest. The doctrines and rules then developed were appropriate to a feudal society, but they soon acquired a rigidity and formalism which hampered their adaptation to meet the needs of a changing social and economic structure. Although the deficiencies of the common law[2] were in some respects made good by the system of law called "equity"[3] administered by the Court of Chancery, and in others by legislation, the result was seldom to simplify, but almost invariably to complicate, the law.

No serious attempt was made to reduce the complexity and obscurity of the land law until the 19th century, when many statutory reforms were introduced. Finally, sweeping changes were effected by the 1925 property legislation, which came into operation on January 1, 1926. The effect of this legislation, and in particular of the Law of Property Acts 1922 and 1925, the Settled Land Act 1925, the Land Charges Act 1925[4] and the Land Registration Act 1925, will be considered in due course. As a whole it constitutes a watershed in the land law; it is natural, therefore, to speak of the old law and the new law, or the law before 1926 and the law after 1925.

[2] The common law is the basic, judge-made law of the country.
[3] See Chap. 6.
[4] Now repealed and largely re-enacted by the Land Charges Act 1972.

2. Tenure and estate

TENURE

At common law the ownership of all the land in the country is vested in the Crown. No one other than the Crown can own land. However, other persons may be *tenants, i.e. holders*, of land and have rights in the land which the law will protect even against the Crown. Originally, under the system called feudalism, every such person held his land as tenant of some superior feudal lord (who might be the king himself, or someone holding from the king), to whom he owed certain feudal services. Failure to perform these services would cause a forfeiture of the tenant's rights *i.e.* the superior feudal lord had the right to take back the land. In addition to these services certain obligations called *incidents* were owed by the tenant to the superior feudal lord.

There were different *tenures* in the land, *i.e.* different methods of land holding, each of which had its own characteristic services and incidents. Thus, if a tenant held by the tenure of knight service he rendered military services to his superior feudal lord, whereas if he held by socage tenure he rendered agricultural services to his lord. By 1925, however, the number of tenures had become so reduced that only two tenures of any importance remained. These were *socage* tenure, otherwise known as freehold, and *copyhold* tenure, formerly known as villeinage. For all practical purposes, by 1925 freehold tenure existed in name only: it had lost its old feudal incidents, and the freehold tenant no longer rendered services to a superior feudal lord. By 1925 freehold tenants almost always held directly of the Crown because it was a rule of the common law that in the absence of evidence of an intermediate lordship (and such evidence was rarely available in 1925) the tenant held directly of the Crown.

Copyhold tenure, on the other hand, remained a living tenure until 1926. The services of this tenure had originally been agricultural, but these services had long since been commuted for annual money payments, known as quit-rents. All copyholds were converted into freehold tenure, by the Law of Property Act 1922, as from January 1, 1926. Some of the incidents of this tenure have been permanently preserved, and in particular as a general rule the ownership of any minerals beneath the surface of the land is vested in the former lord or his successor in title—a point that sometimes needs to be watched when buying land even today.

To sum up, there is now only one common law tenure, namely freehold tenure, and this has been shorn of its old feudal incidents, except that former copyhold land is still subject to those few incidents which have been permanently preserved.

ESTATE

The doctrine of estates developed as a consequence of the doctrine of tenure. Since a tenant was not regarded as owning the land itself, it was necessary to determine what it was that he did own, *i.e.* the nature and extent of his interest in the land. The answer to this question is that he owns an *estate* in the land and the type of estate depends upon the terms on which the land was granted to him or to some predecessor in title of his.

The doctrine of estates has two principal features. First, estates are classified according to the length of time for which they are limited to endure; secondly, several persons may simultaneously own distinct and separate estates in the same piece of land.

Before considering these features, we may notice that the word estate is also used in two other senses namely; a) as referring to a particular plot of land, *e.g.* the Blackacre estate, and b) as referring to the assets or property of a deceased person. The sense in which the word is used in any particular case will appear from the context.

The estates classified

Broadly there are four estates in land. These are (1) the fee simple, (2) the fee tail, (3) the life estate and (4) the leasehold estate.

1. The fee simple

The word "fee" denotes an estate of inheritance, *i.e.* one that will not necessarily come to an end with the death of the individual tenant, but is capable of being inherited by another. The word "simple" indicates that the fee is the ordinary or normal fee, in contrast to the fee tail (see below). Before 1926 on the death intestate (*i.e.* without leaving a will) of a tenant in fee simple the land passed or devolved upon his heir. The heir was ascertained by applying a series of rules known as the canons of descent. Under these rules the heir might be found among descendants, ancestors, or collateral relatives (*e.g.* brothers). If there was no heir the land passed to the superior feudal lord by a process known as *escheat.* On a death intestate after 1925 the land will no longer devolve upon the heir, but will be held on trust for those next of kin entitled to inherit under the Administration of Estates Act 1925. Those so entitled are called the *statutory next of kin*.

As will be seen later, the fee simple owner has for long been in the position of absolute owner of land for all practical purposes.

2. The fee tail

A fee tail resembled a fee simple in that on the death of the tenant in tail the land devolved upon his heir, but the fee tail differed from the fee simple in that the heir had to be found amongst *descendants* of the original tenant in tail. The land could not be inherited by an ancestor or a collateral relative of the original tenant in tail. The position is the same today—this is one of the few cases in which the old canons of descent still apply after 1925.

If upon the death of a tenant in tail it is found that there are no living descendants of the original tenant in tail, the fee tail comes to an end. The consequences of this are considered below.

3. The life estate

This explains itself. Land may be granted to a person for his life and his estate then determines with his death. The estate is not one of inheritance. Another form of life estate, known as an estate *pur autre vie*, arises whenever a tenant is entitled to land during the life of another (called the *cestui que vie*). For example, if X leaves Blackacre to "A for the life of B", B is the cestui que vie. Such an estate determines on the death of the cestui que vie, not of the tenant *i.e.* it ends on the death of B.

4. The leasehold estate

This is the estate enjoyed by a tenant under a lease, *i.e.* a tenant under the modern relationship of landlord and tenant, where a person, the tenant, is entitled to exclusive possession of land for a certain period of time, in return usually for paying rent.[1] The person who grants a lease is called the *lessor* or landlord; the person who receives the lease is called the *lessee* or tenant. This relationship is historically distinct from the earlier feudal relationship of lord and tenant, and is based on contract rather than status. Originally leasehold was not recognised as an estate, but today the law recog-

[1] See Chap. 12.

nises it as both an estate and a tenure. It is an estate because it tells us the duration of the tenant's interest in the land. It is a tenure because it is a method of land holding.

Reversions and remainders

The law allows the owner of an estate in land to confer a lesser estate on another person, and a *reversion* then arises. For example, if S, the fee simple owner of Blackacre, grants the land to A for life, S is said to have a reversion because on the death of A the land will revert to S or, if S is then dead, to his personal representatives[2]. His personal representatives will either be called his *executors*, if appointed by his will, or his *administrators* if he dies without expressly appointing executors or where a purported appointment fails.

The law also allows a fee simple owner to create a succession of estates in the land, and this is called a *settlement.* For example, S, the fee simple owner of Blackacre, may grant the land to A for his life and thereafter to B for a fee simple estate. B's estate is then said to be a *remainder,* because upon the death of A the land will remain away from the grantor instead of reverting to him. If, at the death of A, B is already dead the fee simple estate will vest in B's personal representatives. It will be noticed that, whereas a reversion arises by operation of law, a remainder is created by the express terms of the grant.

As a further illustration, S, the fee simple owner of Blackacre, might grant the land to A for life, with remainder to B in tail, with remainder to C in fee simple. In this illustration if, at the death of A, B is already dead the fee tail will devolve upon B's heir, found amongst his descendants. If and when the fee tail comes to an end the land will pass to C or, if he is already dead, his personal representatives.

Both remainders and reversions are future interests, or *reversionary interests* (a much wider and looser expression than reversion in the strict sense). A reversionary interest is any interest in property which will fall into possession at some future time.

Reversion has a different meaning in the context of leaseholds: the lessor's reversion on a lease signifies his estate in the land subject to the lease. For example, if L, the lessor and an owner of a fee simple estate, grants a 10 year lease to T, the lessee, L's fee simple estate, still subsists, but it is a reversion and is commonly referred to as the *leasehold reversion*. This, unlike a reversion under a settlement, is an interest in possession[3], not a future interest.

[2] The person in whom a deceased's property automatically vests on death and who administers the deceased's estate *i.e.*, pays off the debts of the deceased and distributes his assets to the beneficiaries. Estate in this sense means all the assets and liabilities of the deceased rather than an estate in land.

[3] See pp. 32–33.

3. Classification of property

The fee simple, the fee tail and the life estate are known as freehold estates, *i.e.* estates of fixed but uncertain duration. They are fixed, in that they are limited to endure for the life of a person, or for the lives of a person and his heirs. They are uncertain, in that the duration of those lives is uncertain. The leasehold estate is a non-freehold estate, *i.e.* an estate of certain duration, being either for a fixed term *e.g.* five years or determinable by notice.[1] (In practice the word "freehold" is generally used, even by lawyers, in another sense, as a synonym for the fee simple estate. Thus, if a man is asked whether he owns the freehold of his house, what is meant is whether he owns a fee simple estate, rather than a mere leasehold.)

Most systems of law divide property into immovables (*i.e.* interests in land) and movables, which comprise all other property, including goods and chattels, and stocks and shares. The English classification, however, is into *realty* and *personalty*. Realty comprises those forms of property which in the early days of the common law would support a real action, *i.e.* an action by which, if he were wrongfully dispossessed, the owner of the property could recover the property itself (the *res*). Only the freehold estates in land would support such an action and therefore, they alone, are realty. All other forms of property are personalty[2]. Even the leasehold is personalty, because in the early law a tenant under a lease was not regarded as having an estate at all, his rights being merely contractual and personal. If he was wrongfully dispossessed by anyone except the landlord himself he had no remedy, and even against the landlord his remedy was subject to fulfilling certain conditions. Although by the sixteenth century the action of ejectment enabled the tenant to recover the land from anyone who dispossessed him, and his rights came accordingly to be recognised as constituting an estate in land, the same terminology persists to this day, and leasehold estates are technically still personalty (or otherwise referred to as *chattels real*).

This confusion of terminology cannot be regarded with much satisfaction; indeed it constitutes a serious obstacle in the way of

[1] Periodic tenancies are determinable by notice, see Chap. 12.
[2] As to "fixtures," see pp. 14–16.

understanding English land law. Before 1926 the distinction between realty and personalty had important practical consequences, in relation particularly to devolution on intestacy, but the 1925 legislation assimilated the two forms of property in certain respects. Nowadays both can be entailed,[3] both can now be mortgaged by the same method[4] and both now devolve on intestacy under the same rules. Any remaining problems of classification or definition[5] can and usually will be minimised in practice by avoiding abstract expressions such as "realty" and "personalty" in the drafting of any instrument.

[3] See p. 19.
[4] See p. 184.
[5] See also the doctrine of conversion, see pp. 56, 73.

4. Words of limitation

The expression "words of limitation" means the words that are necessary to transfer or create a particular estate in land, such as the fee simple or the fee tail. For example, if the fee simple owner of Blackacre wishes to transfer the fee simple to A by deed,[1] the question arises whether the deed should say that the land is conveyed to A "in fee simple," or "absolutely," or whether some other form of wording is necessary to pass the fee simple estate.[2]

GRANTS BY DEED

Before 1926 in order to transfer a *fee simple* estate in land the grant had to be made to A "and his heirs" or "in fee simple" (the latter expression being first allowed by the Conveyancing Act 1881). No other expressions would suffice, no matter how clear the intention might be, and if the correct expressions were not used then only a life estate passed to the grantee. It is important to note that where a grant was made to A *and his heirs*, the words italicised were words of *limitation* not words of *purchase, i.e.* they operated merely to limit the estate which A was to take, rather than to grant any estate to his heirs.[3] If A died without having disposed of his estate, the heir or heirs would succeed to the land under the old canons of descent; but until then they had no estate, merely a *spes successionis, i.e.* a hope of inheriting the fee simple if A did not dispose of it prior to his death.

The Law of Property Act 1925, s.60, provides that after 1925 a conveyance of land shall pass the whole estate of the grantor to the

[1] A document used to pass the legal estate in land, other than by will, is called a *conveyance* in the case of unregistered land or a *transfer* in the case of registered land, see Chap. 21. A conveyance or transfer of land must generally be made by deed. For the definition of a deed see p. 27.

[2] The problem is confined to the fee simple and fee tail estates. No particular form of words has ever been required to create a life estate or a lease.

[3] Under the rule in *Shelley's Case* (1581) 1 Co. Rep. 93B, this applied even where the grantor's intention plainly was to grant an estate to the heirs, *e.g.* where a grant was made to A for life with remainder to his heirs. This rule was abolished by the LPA 1925, s.131, and the word *heirs* may now operate as a word of purchase if so intended.

grantee unless the deed shows a contrary intention. Thus, assuming that the grantor has the fee simple estate in the land, a simple conveyance of the land to A without any words of limitation will pass the fee simple estate to him, unless the deed shows a different intention.

The rules varied for a conveyance to a 'corporation', which is an individual or group of individuals who are regarded in law as a separate legal entity. There are two types of corporation, a *corporation aggregate* and a *corporation sole*. No words of limitation have ever been necessary in order to transfer a fee simple estate to a corporation aggregate[4], such as the ordinary limited company. However, before 1926 in order to transfer a fee simple estate to a corporation sole,[5] such as a bishop, the words "and his successors" had to be used; otherwise only a life estate passed to whoever was the holder of the office at the date of the grant. The Law of Property Act 1925, s.60, provides that after 1925 the whole estate of the grantor shall pass to the corporation sole, unless the deed shows a contrary intention.

Before 1926 in order to create a *fee tail* the grant had to be made to A "and the heirs of his body" (or some similar expression incorporating the word "heirs" and restricting the heirs to descendants of the grantee) or "in tail". These words were first allowed by the Conveyancing Act 1881. The same strict rule applies today and it has not been relaxed by the Law of Property Act 1925. The inheritance of a fee tail can be restricted either to male or female descendants of the grantee, *e.g.* where land is granted "to A and the heirs male (or female) of his body" or "to A in tail male (or female)." Further, the inheritance can be restricted to issue of the grantee and a particular spouse, *e.g.* by making the grant "to A and the heirs of his body by his wife B": this is known as a fee tail special.

GIFTS BY WILL

The Wills Act 1837, s.28, provided that a testator's whole estate in the land should pass to a devisee[6] unless the will showed a contrary intention. This rule remains today. Thus a simple gift of Blackacre "to A" will prima facie give the *fee simple* to A, if the testator had that estate.

On the death of a testator before 1926 a *fee tail* could be created by the use of any words in the will which sufficiently showed the

[4] A group of individuals acting under a corporate name.

[5] An individual who holds office under succession *e.g.* the Crown. It is a question of construction whether the grantee is intended to take individually or in his corporate capacity.

[6] A *devise* is a gift of *realty* by will; the *devisee* is the donee. A gift of *personalty* by will is called a *legacy* or *bequest*; the donee is called a *legatee*.

intention to do so, *i.e.* the intention to create an estate of inheritance heritable only by descendants of the devisee; for example, "to A and his issue" or "to A and his descendants" would suffice. However, the Law of Property Act 1925, s.130, provides that on the death of a testator after 1925 the same strict, common law or statutory, expressions must be used as are required for a deed, *i.e.* "and the heirs of his body" (or some similar expression which includes the word "heirs") or "in tail."

FAILURE TO USE THE CORRECT WORDS

Before 1926 if the correct technical expressions required to transfer or create an estate of inheritance were not used in a deed the grantee obtained only a life estate. As has been seen, after 1925 if no words of limitation are used, whether in a deed or a will, the grantee or devisee will prima facie obtain the fee simple estate. But suppose that after 1925, in a deed or a will, words are used which show an *intention* to create a *fee tail*, but fail to do so because they are not the correct technical expressions, what is the result? According to section 130 (2) of the Law of Property Act 1925, the effect of such words is to create the same interest as if the property had been *personalty* before 1926. Entails of personalty could not exist before 1926,[7] and therefore it seems that such words would have created an absolute interest. On that assumption, a gift of realty today "to A and his descendants" would pass the fee simple (equivalent to absolute ownership of personalty) to A. Whether A would take the fee simple solely, or jointly with such of his descendants as were *living at the effective date of the gift*, depends on whether the words "and his descendants" are to be regarded merely as ineffectual words of limitation[8] or, alternatively, as words of purchase.[9]

[7] They can since 1925; see p. 19.

[8] The better view.

[9] Obviously they could not be so regarded without the qualification indicated in italics, since descendants constitute an open and unidentifiable class.

5. Rights of beneficial owners

The principal rights of a beneficial owner[1] of land are (i) his rights of possession or enjoyment, and (ii) his rights of disposition or alienation. The extent of both (i) and (ii) will vary with the duration of the owner's estate or interest. If it is limited, *e.g.* a life interest or a leasehold estate, the law may restrict his enjoyment of the land to the extent that this might prejudice those subsequently entitled; and, under the principle *nemo dat quod non habet,*[2] his power to dispose of the land will generally be confined to his own particular estate or interest.[3] Accordingly it will be convenient to consider these rights and powers separately in relation to the fee simple, the fee tail, the life estate and the leasehold.

FEE SIMPLE

For all practical purposes a fee simple owner is today the absolute owner of the land. Nevertheless there are restrictions both at common law and by statute upon the right of the fee simple owner to do as he pleases with the land. For example, at common law he is restrained by the law of tort from using his land in such a way as to cause a nuisance to his neighbours.

The main statutory restrictions on a landowner's rights are now those imposed by the Town and Country Planning Act 1990 (consolidating earlier legislation). If he wishes to develop his land an owner must generally get planning permission from the local planning authority. "Development" is widely defined by the Act and, besides building operations, includes the working of minerals and the making of any material change in the use to which land (including buildings) is put. For example, it would be development, requiring planning permission, to change the use of a building from that of a dwelling

[1] A beneficial owner is a person who is entitled to an interest for his own benefit and not *e.g.* as a trustee.

[2] No one can give what he has not got.

[3] There are important statutory exceptions to this rule: see particularly Chap. 8.

house to that of offices, even though no building work was involved. By way of exception, the Act provides that certain things are not "development," *e.g.* change of use of buildings if the change is from one purpose to another purpose in the same class specified in the Town and Country Planning (Use Classes) Order 1987. Further, the need to obtain planning permission may be dispensed with by the provisions of a General Development Order; for example, the Town and Country Planning (General Permitted Development) Order 1995 permits the extension of residential premises[4]

Subject to what has been said about planning, a fee simple owner's rights over his land are largely governed by common law, and may be considered under the following heads.

Whoever owns the soil . . .

Cujus est solum ejus est usque ad coelum et ad inferos. Whoever owns the soil owns the airspace above the surface and everything beneath the surface. However, there are exceptions to this principle both at common law and by statute. Thus, at common law the Crown is the owner of any gold or silver found in a mine, and of treasure trove, *i.e.* any gold or silver coin, plate, or bullion found concealed on land (including any building thereon), the true owner being unknown. By statute, aircraft have the right of passage through the airspace,[5] and various minerals, such as coal, have been vested in the state or state agencies.

Whatever is planted in the soil . . .

Quicquid plantatur solo, solo credit. Whatever is planted in the soil accedes to the soil and so at law becomes part of the land. It follows therefore that any building constructed on land is normally regarded as part of the land itself.[6] Objects which are on the land, but which are not part of it, are classed as *chattels.* However, if a chattel is affixed to land, or to a building forming part of the land, it may itself become part of the land, and accordingly cease to be a chattel, and become what is called a *fixture*.

In determining whether a chattel has become a fixture two tests are applied:

1. The degree of annexation

Prima facie if a chattel is securely attached to the land it becomes a fixture, whereas if it merely rests upon the land by its own weight it

[4] Subject to certain limitations.
[5] See, *e.g. Bernstein v. Skyviews and General Ltd.* [1978] Q.B. 479.
[6] LPA 1925, s.205 (definition of "land"). This, however, does not prevent ownership of land being divided, whether horizontally or vertically.

remains a chattel. This, however, is merely the prima facie test and determines the burden of proof. It is the second test that is decisive.

2. The purpose of annexation

If a chattel is brought on or attached to land merely to enable it to be *enjoyed as a chattel* it does not become a fixture, and this is so even if the chattel is securely attached to the land or a building thereon. Thus in one case[7] a tapestry was securely attached to the wall of a house, but it was held to remain a chattel. On the other hand, if a chattel is brought on or attached to land for the purpose of improving that land[8] or as part of a scheme of design or layout, it becomes a fixture, and this is so even if the chattel rests upon the land merely by its own weight. Thus in one case[9] stone statues and seats were placed in a garden as part of a scheme of design of the garden, and were held to have become fixtures although they rested upon the land merely by their own weight.

Since fixtures are in law part of the land, they pass on any conveyance of the land unless a contrary intention is indicated,[10] and if land is mortgaged, any fixtures form part of the mortgagee's security, and cannot be removed without his consent.[11]

There are, however, important exceptional cases in which fixtures[12] may be removed:

(i) At common law a lessee, before the end of his lease, has the right to remove trade, ornamental and domestic fixtures which he has added to the premises *e.g.* trade fixtures include petrol pumps at a garage.[13] Similarly a tenant for life[14] (or his personal representatives within a reasonable time after his death) has a right to remove similar fixtures as between himself and a remainderman or reversioner. Agriculture, it has been held, is not a trade, so that at common law a lessee or tenant for life has no right to remove agricultural fixtures.

(ii) By the Agricultural Holdings Act 1986, s.10 (replacing earlier provisions), a lessee of an agricultural holding has a statutory right to

[7] *Leigh v. Taylor* [1902] A.C. 157.

[8] But not if the purpose is to accommodate *other* land: so where a landowner has the right to lay drains under his neighbour's land, the drains do not become part of the land under which they are laid (*Simmons v. Midford* [1969] 2 Ch. 415).

[9] *D'Eyncourt v. Gregory* (1866) L.R. 3 Eq. 382. *Cf. Berkley v. Poulett* (1976) 120 S.J. 836, C.A.

[10] LPA 1925, s.62.

[11] This applies even to fixtures installed after the mortgage was granted (*Reynolds v. Ashby* [1904] A.C. 466).

[12] Chattels which have been so integrated into the land as to lose their individual identity, *e.g.* bricks and timber incorporated into a building, cannot properly be regarded as *mere* fixtures, and accordingly cannot be removed even under the exceptions noted.

[13] *Smith v. City Petroleum Co. Ltd* [1940] 1 All E.R. 260.

[14] Generally a person entitled to possession under a strict settlement. See Chap. 8.

remove agricultural fixtures before the end of his lease or within two months thereafter. This right is subject to certain conditions, and the landlord may elect to purchase the fixtures at a valuation.

Riparian rights

In the case of tidal water, the foreshore, *i.e.* the seashore below the ordinary highwater mark, belongs to the Crown or its grantee. Above that mark the presumption is that the shore belongs to the adjoining fee simple owner.

When a non-tidal stream flows through land belonging to one person that person is prima facie the owner of the bed of the stream to the extent of his frontage. When a non-tidal stream forms the boundary between two plots of land in the ownership of different persons, the presumption is that the owner of each plot is the owner of the bed up to an imaginary middle line.

The owner of the bed of non-tidal water has riparian rights, *i.e.* rights relating to water, although he does not own the water itself which flows through his land.

These riparian rights include the following:

1. Water rights

A riparian owner[15] has the right to take water from the stream for ordinary purposes connected with his land even if thereby he exhausts the stream. Domestic purposes and watering cattle are examples of ordinary purposes. He also has the right to take water from the stream for extraordinary purposes connected with his land provided that he returns the water to the stream substantially unchanged in quantity and quality. Manufacturing purposes are prima facie extraordinary. A riparian owner has no right to take water from the stream for purposes unconnected with his land. If a riparian owner takes water from the stream in breach of these rules, any lower riparian owner who is injured thereby will have an action against him.

These common law rules are now affected by the Water Resources Act 1991, under which, subject to important exceptions, a licence from the National Rivers Authority is required before water can be abstracted from any source of supply.

2. Fishing rights

The riparian owners have the exclusive right to fish in non-tidal water, and the public cannot acquire such a right by long user.

[15] *i.e.* the owner of land through which water flows.

The Crown is the owner of the bed of tidal water, and the public have the right to fish in such water unless the Crown has granted the exclusive right to an individual grantee by an ancient grant known as a franchise of free fishery. The Crown does not possess the right to grant such franchises today.

3. Navigation rights

The riparian owners have the exclusive right to navigate non-tidal water except so far as they have dedicated a right of way to the public. Such a dedication may be presumed from user by the public to the knowledge of the riparian owners.

Except so far as the right is restricted by statute the public have the right to navigate tidal water.

Right of alienation

At an early date the law recognised the right of a fee simple owner to alienate (*i.e.* transfer or convey) the land *inter vivos* (during his lifetime). Thus, if land was granted to A and his heirs, A could transfer the land to B and his heirs, thereby passing the fee simple to B, with the result that on the death of B the land would devolve upon B's heir, and not upon A's heir. The ordinary mode of alienation today is by deed of conveyance or transfer.[16]

On the other hand, the common law did not recognise the right of a fee simple owner to dispose of the land by will. This rule was evaded by means of trusts[17], and has long since been abolished by statute. Today land can be freely disposed of by will. The formalities of a will are now prescribed by the Wills Act 1837.

The law regards the right of alienation as inviolable, and accordingly a condition purporting to exclude the right, or to impose a forfeiture on alienation, will generally be void.[18]

FEE TAIL

Since the fee tail or entailed interest, like the fee simple, is an estate of inheritance, the owner's rights of enjoyment of the land are

[16] See p. 9, note 1.

[17] See Chap. 6.

[18] A *partial* restraint may be valid (*e.g.* a condition not to sell outside the family) (*Re Macleay* (1875) L.R. 20 Eq. 186). Also a *covenant* (a promise contained in a deed) not to alienate (which would be enforced, not by forfeiture, but by injunction or damages for breach of covenant) may be valid: see *Caldy Manor Estate Ltd v. Farrell* [1974] 1 W.L.R. 1303.

generally similar to those of a fee simple owner, and require no further discussion.[19]

Right of alienation

The fee tail was established as an inalienable freehold estate by the Statute De Donis 1285, which provided that land granted to a donee and the heirs of his body should, notwithstanding any alienation by him, descend to his issue on his death, and revert to the donor when the donee and all his issue were dead. The result was that the fee tail, as such, could not be transferred, although, of course, a tenant in tail in possession of land could transfer to another his own personal right to occupy the land during his lifetime.

Before the end of the 15th century, however, methods had been devised for converting a fee tail into a fee simple, and thus *barring,* or breaking, the entail.[20] Originally this was done by means of contrived court actions which were evolved by lawyers called 'common recovery and fines', but these actions were abolished by the Fines and Recoveries Act 1833. The Act substituted a *disentailing assurance* (*i.e.* a deed of conveyance) as the means of barring an entail. If the tenant in tail wishes to dispose of the land by way of gift or sale he makes the assurance in favour of the donee or purchaser; if he wishes to retain the land he makes the assurance in favour of himself.[21]

The assurance will convert the fee tail into a full fee simple if either (a) it is executed by a tenant in tail in possession, or (b) it is executed by a tenant in tail in remainder with the consent by deed of the "protector of the settlement," *i.e.* the owner of the first subsisting freehold estate created by the settlement.[22] If the assurance is executed by a tenant in tail in remainder without the consent of the protector the fee tail is converted into a base fee, *i.e.* an alienable fee simple which will last only so long as the fee tail would have lasted if it had not been barred (in other words so long as there remain descendants of the original tenant in tail). When the fee tail is converted into a full fee simple any remainder or reversion following the fee tail is extinguished, but when the fee tail is converted into a base fee such interests are unaffected. In neither case are estates preceding the entail affected. A few examples may make the position clearer.

19 As an exception, a 'tenant in tail after possibility of issue extinct' (see p. 20) is impeachable for equitable waste (see pp. 20–21).

20 Another word for a fee tail.

21 Until 1926 it was necessary to convey to a trustee on trust for himself, but by the LPA 1925, s.72(3), a person may now convey land to himself. As to trusts see Chap. 6.

22 Before 1926 a settlor could appoint a "special protector," but this power was abolished by the LPA 1925. As regards remainders and settlements see p. 6.

Suppose that land is settled on A for life, with remainder to B in tail, with remainder to C in fee simple, and that B executes a disentailing assurance with the consent by deed of the protector, A. (A's life estate is a freehold estate and, in the absence of special protectors, he is the protector.) B's fee tail will be converted into a full fee simple. C's fee simple remainder will be extinguished, but A's preceding life estate will be unaffected.

Again, assuming the same settlement, if A has died, B without the consent of anyone may execute a disentailing assurance which will convert his fee tail into a full fee simple. Once again C's remainder will be extinguished. But suppose that A is still alive and that B executes a disentailing assurance without the consent of the protector. B's fee tail will be converted into a base fee. This base fee may be transferred from time to time, but whoever has it will have an estate which will come to an end if at any time B's descendants die out. The land will then go over to C or, if C is then dead, C's personal representatives.

The Act of 1833 remains in force, but the Law of Property Act 1925 has made a number of changes, of which the following may be noticed here:

(i) After 1925 an entail can be created in personalty,[23] such as stocks and shares or leaseholds, as well as in realty.

(ii) Fees tail and base fees can subsist only as equitable interests[24] after 1925.

(iii) After 1925 an entail can be barred by will by a simple gift of the property to a devisee or legatee: the donee will then acquire the fee simple or, if the property is personalty, the absolute ownership. But the Act (in section 176) imposes certain conditions. The will must be made or confirmed by codicil[25] after 1925. The testator must be of full age and at the date of his death he must be tenant in tail in possession—hence a barring by will will always create a full fee simple (or absolute ownership), never a base fee. Further, the will must refer specifically to the particular property or to the instrument under which the testator acquired it or to entailed property generally. Hence a gift of "all my property" to Y will not bar an entail, and Y will not acquire any entailed property to which the testator was entitled.

Enlargement of base fees

A base fee may become enlarged into a full fee simple in any of the following ways:

[23] See p. 8.

[24] See p. 31.

[25] A supplementary document to a will, which must be executed in the same way as a will.

(i) By the former tenant in tail executing a fresh disentailing assurance with the consent of the protector or after the protectorship has ceased (*i.e.* after the estates preceding the former entail have come to an end).

(ii) By the owner of the base fee acquiring the fee simple in remainder or reversion.

(iii) By the owner of the base fee remaining in possession of the land for 12 years after the protectorship has ceased.[26] For this reason a base fee will ordinarily come to an end or become enlarged into a full fee simple within a relatively short period of time.

(iv) By a gift of the property by will made by the owner of the base fee if he could have enlarged it during his lifetime without the concurrence of any other person. This power is subject to the conditions laid down by the Law of Property Act 1925, s.176.

Unbarrable entails

The following entails cannot be barred:

(i) an interest in tail after possibility of issue extinct: this arises where the tenant in tail has a fee tail special,[27] and during his lifetime the spouse specified dies without issue;

(ii) entails granted by the Crown (the reversion being in the Crown);

(iii) entails made unbarrable by special Acts of Parliament, such as those granted to the Duke of Marlborough and the Duke of Wellington.

LIFE ESTATE

The doctrine of waste

The law takes the view that a tenant for life has so limited an interest in the land that special restrictions should be imposed upon his right to use the land as he pleases. The rules in question are known as the doctrine of waste. Waste is of three kinds, namely voluntary, permissive and equitable. Voluntary waste is any positive act which alters the land to its detriment, such as felling timber trees, or opening and working a new mine. Permissive waste is allowing the

[26] Limitation Act 1980, s.27.

[27] See p. 10.

land to deteriorate for want of attention, *e.g.* by failure to maintain buildings in repair. Equitable waste is a special kind of voluntary waste and consists of acts of wanton destruction, such as pulling down or defacing the mansion house or felling trees which have been planted for shelter or ornament.

A tenant for life is impeachable for voluntary waste (*i.e.* he is liable in damages to the remainderman or reversioner if he commits it) unless the settlement makes him unimpeachable. He is unimpeachable for permissive waste unless the settlement makes him impeachable, *i.e.* places him under an obligation to repair. (A tenant for life of a leasehold estate is bound to perform any tenant's repairing covenant in the lease, but this liability is not derived from the doctrine of waste, and the liability is not to the remainderman, but to the landlord[28] and the settlor.) A tenant for life is impeachable for equitable waste unless the settlement makes him unimpeachable, and for this purpose it is not sufficient that the settlement makes him unimpeachable for ordinary voluntary waste. If the settlement made a tenant for life unimpeachable for voluntary waste the common law courts would *not* restrain him from committing acts even of wanton destruction. However, the Court of Chancery, taking the view that the settlor did not intend the power to commit waste to be abused, would restrain the tenant for life from doing so. This is why waste of this kind is called equitable waste as originally it was restrained only by the court of equity.[29]

The expression "impeachable (or unimpeachable) for waste," without specifying the type of waste, by convention refers to voluntary waste.

Timber

Trees may be timber trees or non-timber trees. Timber trees prima facie are oak, ash and elm trees at least 20 years old, but this definition may be varied by local custom, *e.g.* beech trees are timber in Buckinghamshire.

A tenant for life who is unimpeachable for waste may fell timber or non-timber trees and keep all the proceeds for himself, subject to the doctrine of equitable waste. As we have seen, to fell timber trees is voluntary waste, but if a tenant for life is unimpeachable for such waste he is, of course, at liberty to commit it.

A tenant for life who is impeachable for waste may not fell timber trees, subject to the following exceptions:

(i) He may take the customary estovers or botes, *i.e.* house-bote (wood required for household purposes), plough-bote

[28] See p. 115.
[29] See p. 2.

(wood required for the repair of agricultural implements) and hay-bote or helde-bote (wood required for the repair of hedges and fences).

(ii) If the estate is a timber estate (*i.e.* it is used to grow timber commercially) or the custom of the locality permits, he may fell timber in the ordinary course of husbandry and keep all the proceeds for himself. This is not regarded as waste.

(iii) By the Settled Land Act 1925, s.66, he may in any case fell timber trees with the consent of the trustees of the settlement or the court, but if he relies upon this power the tenant for life will take only one-quarter of the proceeds and three-quarters will go to the trustees of the settlement as capital money.[30]

A tenant for life who is impeachable for waste may fell non-timber trees that are ripe and suitable for cutting and keep all the proceeds for himself. This is not regarded as waste.

Minerals

If the tenant for life is unimpeachable for waste he may work the minerals in the land and keep all the proceeds for himself. He may open and work a new mine for the purpose if he wishes: to do so is waste, but as he is unimpeachable for waste he may do it.

A tenant for life who is impeachable for waste may continue to work a mine that is already lawfully open and may keep all the proceeds for himself—he does not thereby commit waste. A mine is lawfully open for this purpose if it was opened before the settlement was created, or it was opened by a previous tenant for life who was unimpeachable for waste. A tenant for life who is impeachable for waste may not open and work a new mine.

By the Settled Land Act 1925, s.41, a tenant for life may grant a mining lease for a period not exceeding 100 years.[31] A lease granted under this statutory power will be binding on the remainderman or reversioner. In general the tenant for life is entitled to three-quarters of the rent which is payable under such a lease and the balance goes to the trustees of the settlement as capital money. However, if the tenant for life is impeachable for waste and the lessee is authorised to open and work a new mine, the tenant for life takes only one-quarter of the rent and three-quarters go to the trustees.

Apart from this statutory power, a tenant for life at common law may grant a mining lease authorising the lessee to work minerals to

[30] As to settlements and the role of trustees see Chap. 8 and in particular p. 47, note 32.

[31] See pp. 43–45.

the extent that the tenant for life himself has the right to do so, but such a lease will not be binding on a remainderman or reversioner.

Right of alienation

As has already been mentioned, the owner of a life estate can at common law dispose of the land only to the extent of his interest, and accordingly can pass only an estate *pur autre vie.*[32] However, this is subject to important statutory provisions governing settlements of land, under which extensive powers of disposition are conferred on a tenant for life.[33]

LEASEHOLD ESTATE

The doctrine of waste, as described above, has a limited application as between a tenant and his landlord under a lease,[34] but in practice the rights and obligations of the parties are governed primarily, in this respect as in others, by the express provisions of the lease itself.

A lessee has in general the same right of alienation as any other estate owner, and accordingly can assign his lease (*i.e.* the remainder of the term), subject to any contractual restrictions contained in the lease[35].

[32] See p. 5.
[33] See pp. 43–46.
[34] See p. 115.
[35] See pp. 117–118.

6. The contribution of equity

TRUSTS

As with the criminal law and the law of contract and tort, the basis of the law of real property is common law, but it is in the sphere of property law that equity has made its most important contribution. Like the common law, equity is judge-made law, but it has its origin in the activities of the old Court of Chancery. Equity supplemented and corrected, in the name of fairness, the common law, the older body of rigid judge-made law, which was administered by other courts. Today the same courts administer both, but it remains necessary to distinguish between law (*i.e.* common law) and equity, especially with respect to land.

The most notable, but not exclusive contribution made by equity to the law of real property is its enforcement of the *trust* (formerly known as the *use*). A trust is an arrangement whereby a landowner (the "settlor") conveys his land to a person (a "trustee") to be held for the benefit of and on behalf of another person (the "beneficiary"). The common law provided no remedy for breach of trust, so that if S, the fee simple owner of Blackacre, conveyed it to T in fee simple, directing him to hold it upon trust for B in fee simple, T at common law was at liberty to disregard the claims of B and to use the property for his own benefit. If a claim was brought by B (the beneficiary), the Court of Chancery, however, would enforce the trust against T (the trustee) and compel T to apply the property to the use or benefit of B. It should be noticed that the Court of Chancery did not deny T's legal, *i.e.* common law title to the land, but merely required T to use his ownership of the land for the benefit of B on the ground that, having undertaken the trust, he was bound in conscience to do so. It was not long, however, before it was realised that the effect of compelling T to account to B for all the fruits of ownership was to make B for many purposes the real owner of the property.

We are now in a position to understand the meaning of some important terms. The fact that the common law recognises T as the owner of the land is expressed by saying that T is the *legal owner* of the land, or that T has the *legal estate* in the land. The fact that B has the benefits of ownership is expressed by saying that B is the *equitable* (or *beneficial) owner,* or that B has the *equitable estate or interest* in the land.

Originally the Court of Chancery would enforce the trust only against the trustee himself, and not against any other person into whose hands the land might come. However, in the course of time equity so enlarged the classes of persons that, for one reason or another, it regarded as bound by the trust that, in the end, the trust became enforceable, not only against the trustee himself, but also against any other person who might acquire the land, *except a bona fide purchaser for value of the legal estate without notice, actual or constructive, of the trust* (or any person claiming through such a purchaser)[1]. Equitable rights under a trust, although originally enforceable *in personam (i.e.* against the trustee personally), thus became virtually rights *in rem,* or rights of property, enforceable against the whole world—subject to the one important exception mentioned above. The reason for this exception, which distinguished legal from equitable rights, can be understood if one remembers that the trust, unlike legal ownership, was enforced as a matter of conscience: a purchaser whose conscience was not affected, *i.e.* who had no notice of the trust, would not be regarded as bound in equity.

At first, trusts were of a simple character, *e.g.* a man going on the crusades might convey his land to trustees for the benefit of his family during his absence. However, in the course of time it became possible to create a succession of estates under the trust, just as such a succession of estates could be created at common law without a trust. For example, as we have seen, S, the fee simple owner of Blackacre, might convey Blackacre to A for life, with remainder to B in fee simple, and A would then have a *legal* life estate and B a *legal* fee simple in remainder. Alternatively, it now became possible for S to convey the land to one or more trustees in fee simple directing them to hold the land upon trust for A for life, with remainder to B in fee simple. A would then have an *equitable* life estate and B an *equitable* fee simple in remainder. The trustee or trustees had the legal fee simple; the beneficiaries had equitable estates.

In developing the equitable (or beneficial) interest under the trust in this way, equity borrowed the common law system of estates. In other words equity allowed the settlor to create as equitable estates those estates, and only those estates, that could be created as legal estates at common law without employing a trust. Moreover, to these equitable estates equity applied nearly all the common law rules governing the particular estates. For example, on the death of the owner of an equitable fee simple, or fee tail, the equitable estate would devolve in the same way as if it had been a legal estate: it

[1] See p. 29.

would devolve upon (or pass to) his heir, ascertained by applying the old common law rules of descent. Only in a few instances did equity decline to "follow the law" in this way.

OTHER EQUITABLE INTERESTS

Apart from equitable interests arising under a trust, equity also recognised and enforced many other interests to which the common law refused to give effect—usually because the correct form had not been observed in their creation or transfer.

In general any estate or interest in land such as a fee simple, a lease, a mortgage[2] or an easement[3] was (and still is) valid at law only if granted by deed.[4] A deed is defined, nowadays, under section 1(2) and (3) of the Law of Property (Miscellaneous Provisions) Act 1989 as a document which a) makes itself clear on its face that it is intended to be a deed and b) is validly executed as a deed. A deed is validly executed if (i) it is signed by the maker in the presence of a witness who also signs (called an "attesting witness") and (ii) it is delivered as a deed, by doing some act which shows that it is intended to be binding *e.g.* by using the words "I deliver this deed".

Traditionally, if a *contract*[5] rather than a deed was used to create an estate or interest in land the contract to create such an interest could still be enforced at law to the extent of recovering damages for its breach. However, this would often be an ineffectual remedy. Firstly, because it is available only against the other contracting party and not against a third party to whom he may subsequently have transferred the land. Secondly because, even as against the other contracting party, monetary compensation is seldom an adequate substitute for the land itself.

The intervention of equity at this point proceeded in two parts. First, the equitable remedy of specific performance could be awarded,[6] compelling the defendant to carry out his promise, *i.e.* to grant the estate or interest which he had contracted to grant. Secondly, on the basis that "equity regards as done that which ought to be done" equity would treat any specifically enforceable contract for the disposition of land as *at once* creating an equitable interest in the land, before any order of specific performance was obtained or even sought. Thus, under a contract for the sale of a fee simple, or for the grant of a lease or a mortgage or an easement, the intended

[2] See Chap. 18.
[3] See Chap. 14.
[4] LPA 1925, s.52 (but, the rule is much earlier in origin).
[5] For the formalities which must be complied with as regards a contract for the sale or other disposition of an interest in land, see Chap. 11.
[6] The remedy is discretionary, unlike the common law remedy of damages.

purchaser, lessee, mortgagee or grantee of the easement was regarded *in equity* as having an immediate interest equivalent to a fee simple, lease, mortgage or easement respectively. His interest, however, being merely equitable, was subject to the same defect as indicated above in relation to interests under a trust,[7] namely that it was not enforceable against a purchaser without notice (as we may call him for short).

An example will illustrate the significance of this doctrine of equity. The normal conveyancing procedure for transferring or creating, for example, a legal fee simple estate in land involves two stages. The first stage is that the parties each sign a contract for sale of land; their respective contracts are then exchanged and, at the same time, the purchaser pays a deposit to the vendor of, usually, ten per cent of the purchase price. At the second stage, usually a month later, the vendor executes a deed of conveyance or transfer to pass the fee simple estate to the purchaser and, at the same time, the purchaser pays the balance of the purchase price. Let us suppose that, V, the fee simple owner of Blackacre, has contracted to sell and convey the land to P. If subsequently, in breach of contract, V fails to execute the conveyance, P can enforce the contract against V *at law* by an action for damages, or in *equity* by seeking an order for specific performance. If V not merely fails to convey the land to P, but (wrongfully) conveys it to Q, P still has his common law remedy of damages against V. Alternatively, however, P can enforce his equitable interest in the land against Q (unless Q is a purchaser without notice), and thereby compel Q to convey the legal estate to him.

Apart from the interests recognised by equity where the proper formalities have not been complied with, three further species of new interests created by equity may be briefly mentioned: first the mortgagor's equity of redemption,[8] secondly, restrictive covenants,[9] the burden of which may in equity (though not at common law) run with the covenantor's land, thirdly a form of interest based upon a principle commonly referred to as equitable or proprietary estoppel.[10]

LEGAL AND EQUITABLE INTERESTS

We may now compare an equitable interest in land with a legal interest. Every legal right is a right *in rem, i.e.* once it attaches to land it binds that land in the hands of everyone who afterwards acquires it, regardless of notice. For example, if A has a legal lease over the land of B, and B sells the land to C, A may still enforce his lease against

[7] See p. 26.
[8] See p. 186.
[9] See p. 173.
[10] See pp. 161–162.

the land, and it is irrelevant that C may have been unaware that the lease existed when he acquired the land. Conversely, as already seen, historically equitable interests bind all persons except a bona fide purchaser for value of the legal estate without notice, actual or constructive, or any person claiming through him. This is commonly referred to as the old *doctrine of notice*. Thus, if A's lease is equitable only, or if A has a beneficial interest under a trust affecting B's land, then, although A's equitable rights will generally be enforceable against the land itself, not merely *in personam*, they will be unenforceable against C (or anyone claiming through C) if he is a bona fide purchaser for value of the legal estate without notice, actual or constructive.

Analysing the old doctrine of notice; a "bona fide" purchaser is a person who acquires an interest in land in good faith, without fraud and the term "purchaser" includes a lessee or a mortgagee. To be a "purchaser for value" he must have given consideration in money or monies worth or marriage. For example, he may have purchased the land in exchange for other land or shares or in consideration of a marriage in the future. Any person who acquires the legal estate by gift or under a will or intestacy will not be a purchaser for value.

The expression "constructive notice" requires a few words of explanation. A purchaser of land has constructive notice of any interest in the land which he would have discovered if he had made the customary investigation of his vendor's title for the full statutory period (which is now 15 years[11]). This investigation of title involves an inspection of the documents of title to the land for the period in question. A purchaser also has constructive notice of any interest in the land which he would have discovered if he had made those other inquiries and inspections (such as an inspection of the land itself) which a prudent purchaser customarily makes.[12] Further, if a purchaser employs a solicitor or other agent to act for him in acquiring the land, the purchaser has constructive notice of any interest that his agent discovers in that transaction, or would have discovered if he had made the proper investigation of title, inquiries and inspections.[13] This form of constructive notice is sometimes called "imputed notice," because the agent's actual or constructive notice is imputed to the purchaser. It follows that if a purchaser fails to inspect the title deeds to the property, and consequently is unaware of a trust imposed by one of the deeds, or if he fails to inspect the land itself, and consequently is unaware of the fact that it is occupied by someone other than the vendor, he will generally be fixed with constructive

[11] Law of Property Act 1969, s.23, replacing the earlier period of 30 years under the LPA 1925, s.44(1).

[12] LPA 1925, s.199(1)(ii)(a).

[13] LPA 1925, s.199(1)(ii)(b).

notice of the rights of the beneficiaries under the trust or of the occupier.[14]

It is still an underlying principle of land law today that legal interests in land bind the whole world and that equitable interests are enforceable against everyone except a purchaser without notice; nonetheless, the 1925 legislation has radically amended this in two major ways. Firstly, the systems of registration under the Land Charges Act 1972[15] and the Land Registration Act 1925[16] mean that certain rights in land must be registered before they will be binding on a purchaser. Secondly, equitable beneficial interests under a trust are now, for the most part, *overreached* on a sale of land *i.e.* become detached from the land itself and attached to the proceeds of sale, provided that certain statutory conditions are satisfied.[17] The old doctrine of notice has retained residual importance and still may be applied in some cases to overcome loopholes in the 1925 legislation. For instance, it has been applied as regards unregistered land to those equitable interests which can be neither registered under the Land Charges Act 1972 nor overreached, as is explained further in the next chapter.

[14] Occupation by a tenant is constructive notice of his rights (*Hunt v. Luck* [1902] 1 Ch. 428): if he had a *legal* lease, this would of course be binding regardless of notice.

[15] Replacing LCA 1925 and applying to unregistered land. See Chaps. 7 and 21.

[16] Which applies to registered land. See Chaps. 7 and 21 as to the distinction between registered and unregistered land.

[17] See Chap. 7.

7. Estates and interests since 1925

The main aim of the 1925 property legislation was to simplify conveyancing by i) reducing the number of estates and interests which could exist at law and ii) extending the systems of registration of rights in land.

REDUCTION OF LEGAL ESTATES AND INTERESTS

Legal estates

It will be evident from what has been said in the previous chapter that until 1926 any of the estates (the fee simple, the fee tail, the life estate and the leasehold) could be created either as legal estates or as equitable estates under a trust. After 1925, however, by section 1(1) of the Law of Property Act 1925 only two estates can subsist as legal estates (*i.e.* without the necessity for a trust), namely:

(i) the fee simple absolute in possession, and
(ii) the term of years absolute.

These two estates may alternatively arise as equitable interests[1], but all other estates, such as the life estate and the fee tail, can be created *only* as equitable interests[2] under a trust. Indeed the term "estate" itself is now confined to the two legal estates, all others being properly called "interests," *e.g.* a life interest or an entailed interest.

The policy behind this radical reform was to facilitate conveyancing by confining legal ownership of land[3] to such forms as are appropriate to dispositions of an ordinary commercial kind, such as the conveyance of a freehold, and the grant of a leasehold. Dispositions of land by way of a family settlement, creating successive life or entailed

[1] *e.g.* if not created by deed, under the principle discussed at pp. 27–28.
[2] LPA 1925, s.1(3).
[3] *i.e.* the legal estates.

or other limited interests, can now be effected only by the machinery of a trust which, combined with the device of overreaching,[4] ensures that legal ownership is both simple in form and effective in operation. The expression "estate owner" means the owner of one of the two legal estates in land. It should also be noted that by section 1(6) of the Law of Property Act 1925, a legal estate cannot be held by an infant.

1. Fee simple absolute in possession

Not every fee simple is capable of subsisting as a legal estate, but only a fee simple absolute in possession. As defined by section 205 of the Law of Property Act 1925, possession includes receipt of rents and profits of the land, or the right to receive the same, if any. Hence, if the ordinary fee simple owner (or freehold owner, as we generally call him nowadays) grants a lease of the land to a lessee, the fee simple remains "in possession" and is a legal estate. This is despite the fact that the lessee acquires the physical possession of the land.

A fee simple which is in remainder or reversion is not "in possession" and cannot, therefore, be a legal estate. For example, if land is settled on A for life with remainder to B in fee simple, B's fee simple remainder is an equitable interest, not a legal estate. Similarly, if the fee simple owner, S, settles land on A for life with remainder to B in tail, S has a fee simple reversion which is merely an equitable interest. The contrast between S's reversion in this case, and the so-called reversion of a landlord who has granted a lease, is so marked that the use of the same word to refer to both can only be regarded as inept. The reversion of a settlor under a family settlement is essentially a *future* interest, entitling him to no present rights whatever of enjoying the property, whether by occupying it or by taking the rents and profits. In contrast, the landlord's reversion on a lease, *i.e.* his legal estate subject to the lease, carries with it all the *present* rights reserved to him by the lease, including the right to receive the rent.

An estate is not "absolute" if either its commencement or its duration is made dependent on some contingency which may or may not occur. If an estate is limited to *commence* on the happening of some future uncertain event, *e.g.* the grant of a fee simple to A when he reaches age 25 and he is currently aged 10, it is neither absolute nor in possession. The grantee has merely a *conditional* interest and the disposition must be effected by way of a trust. Equally, if the grantee has an estate which is limited to *determine* on the happening of some future uncertain event, *e.g.* the grant of a fee simple to A until he becomes bankrupt, it is not absolute, but either *determinable* or (where the provision is expressed as a condition, by the use of the words, *e.g.* "provided that" or "on condition that" he does not

[4] See p. 30 and Chap. 8.

become bankrupt), conditional. The distinction is somewhat technical, but the main difference is that a determinable interest comes to an end automatically in the event stipulated, whereas breach of condition merely gives rise to a right of re-entry whereby, if he chooses to, the grantor may re-enter the land and forfeit the grantee's estate. In either case, land subject to such interests is settled land, and is subject to a trust.[5]

2. A term of years absolute

The expression "term of years" is synonymous with leasehold: it is defined[6] as including "a term of less than a year, or for a year or years and a fraction of a year, or from year to year". For the purposes of the Law of Property Act 1925, a term of years is nonetheless absolute even though liable to determination by notice (as in the case of periodic tenancies) or by re-entry (as where the landlord reserves the right to forfeit the lease for breach of the tenant's obligations)[7] or by cesser on redemption (as in the case of a mortgage term).[8] It should be noted that a legal term of years need not be in possession; a lease to commence at some future time[9] may accordingly exist as a legal estate.

Legal interests

Section 1(2) of the Law of Property Act 1925 reduces to five the number of incumbrances, or rights against the land of another, which can subsist as legal interests. These are—

- (i) an easement, right or privilege in or over land for an interest equivalent to an estate in fee simple absolute in possession or a term of years absolute;
- (ii) a rentcharge in possession issuing out of or charged on land being either perpetual or for a term of years absolute;
- (iii) a charge by way of legal mortgage;
- (iv) certain statutory charges on land;
- (v) rights of entry exercisable over or in respect of a legal term of years absolute, or annexed for any purpose to a legal rentcharge.[10]

[5] See Chapter 8. There are minor exceptions under the LPA 1925, s.7.
[6] LPA 1925, s.205.
[7] See pp. 104–105.
[8] See p. 184.
[9] Not more than 21 years from the grant of the lease (LPA 1925, s.149(3)): see p. 104.
[10] As to equitable rights of entry, see *Shiloh Spinners Ltd v. Harding* [1973] A.C. 691, and p. 172 below. This case affords a valuable insight into the effect of the 1925 legislation in relation to legal and equitable rights in property, and the systems of overreaching and of registration of incumbrances under LCA 1925.

We shall come across most of these rights in due course.

All other interests which could have been created against the land of another before 1926 can still be created today, but they will be merely equitable, not legal, interests[11]. It is not a question of employing a trust in order to create such an equitable interest—the interest will *automatically* be equitable if it is not in the list of five given above.

THE SYSTEMS OF REGISTRATION

Another repercussion of the 1925 legislation was to consolidate and extend the provisions concerning the registration of rights in land. A distinction must be made here between the conveyancing procedure where the whole title to land is registered (commonly referred to as *registered land*) and the procedure where there is no central register of the title to land but, certain encumbrances over the land are registered such as mortgages and restrictive covenants (this system is called *unregistered land*). The two systems are mutually exclusive although, predominantly today, title to land is registered and indeed it is the policy under the Land Registration Act 1925[12] and the Land Registration Rules 1925, as amended, that ultimately all land in England and Wales will be registered. However, for reasons discussed later[13], unregistered title will still survive for some considerable time to come, so that the two systems exist side by side for the time being. The distinction between the two systems is clarified by comparing the conveyancing procedure on the sale of a fee simple estate in land. The actual form of registration is a matter of conveyancing practice and an introductory explanation to this is found in the last chapter.

Unregistered land

This is the traditional method of conveyancing, where the purchaser investigates the vendor's title to the land by examining the various title documents to the property, which have been generated over the years, as the land has passed from fee simple owner to fee simple owner. To ensure that the purchaser obtains good title to the land, under statute he must inspect the title documents relating to the property covering at least the previous 15 years prior to the purchase and commencing with a document which includes the whole legal and equitable interest in the land *e.g.* a conveyance on sale. Legal title to

[11] LPA 1925, s.1(3).
[12] As amended by various Acts including the Land Registration Acts 1986 and 1988.
[13] See Chap. 21, note 1.

the land is conveyed to the purchaser by the vendor executing a *deed of conveyance.*

The traditional rules concerning legal and equitable interests apply[14] so that the purchaser will be bound by all legal rights affecting the property, regardless of notice. Nevertheless, as regards equitable interests, the old doctrine of notice has been modified by firstly, the principle of overreaching and secondly, by the requirement to register certain encumbrances under the Land Charges Act 1972. As mentioned previously[15] beneficial interests under a trust (commonly referred to as *family interests*) can be overreached. This is achieved by paying the purchase monies to all the trustees, being at least two in number or a trust corporation *e.g.* a bank, and by so doing the purchaser of the land takes free from such interests (whether or not he has notice of them), which attach purely to the proceeds of sale.[16] Most other equitable interests (commonly referred to as *commercial interests*) such as equitable leases, equitable easements and restrictive covenants are now registrable under the Land Charges Act 1972 in the Land Charges Register maintained at Plymouth. If the interest is registered, this is deemed to be actual notice of its existence to everyone acquiring the land or any interest in it.[17] Conversely, failure to register the interest renders it void against a later purchaser of the land,[18] even if he does in fact have notice,[19] so registration is of paramount importance.

The old doctrine of notice has retained its application to those equitable interests which can be neither registered nor overreached. These include an interest arising by way of equitable or proprietary estoppel[20] and an equitable right of re-entry,[21] neither of which is referred to in the Land Charges Act 1972. They also include interests arising under a trust which, although capable of being overreached, are in the event not overreached because the statutory conditions are not satisfied[22] *e.g.* because payment is made to only one trustee.

Registered land

Quite different from the system of registration of charges referred to above is that of registration of title to land, which is governed by

[14] See p. 28.
[15] See p. 30.
[16] See pp. 48–49 and 57–58.
[17] LPA 1925, s.198.
[18] LCA 1972 Act, s.4 and see Chap. 21.
[19] LPA 1925 s.199.
[20] See pp. 161–162.
[21] See p. 33 note 10.
[22] See pp. 57, 70.

the Land Registration Act 1925 as amended. This system is much more ambitious, and is designed to replace the traditional method of establishing title to land.

As has been seen, the traditional process of investigating the title of a vendor, normally involves examining and interpreting an assortment of documents, some of them often obscure or inconclusive, and raising requisitions as to matters arising on those documents. The same elaborate ritual will be repeated on each occasion of successive dispositions of the land. The Land Registration Act 1925, without wittingly changing the substantive law of property,[23] seeks to simplify conveyancing by making proof of title easier. Where the title to land has been registered reference need only be made to the register, which is kept at Her Majesty's Land Registry (either in London or at one of the District Registries throughout the country), to ascertain what estate and rights the proprietor has in the land, the nature of his title, any restrictions on his powers of disposition, and any encumbrances affecting the land. Following the Land Registration Act 1988, it is open to any member of the public to inspect the register on payment of a fee.

Instead of executing a deed of conveyance on the disposition of registered land, a *transfer* is used which is a deed in simple statutory form. The title deeds of an estate owner in unregistered land are replaced by a Land Certificate which is issued by HM Land Registry and contains particulars corresponding to those contained in the register itself.[24] The fundamental principle which applies to registered land is that the purchaser of the legal estate takes the land subject to all the incumbrances and other entries appearing on the register and also subject to any *overriding interests,*[25] but free from any other estates and interests. Overriding interests are a category of interests which need not be entered on the register but which nevertheless bind a purchaser of land, whether or not he has notice of their existence.

The traditional rules concerning the enforceability of legal and equitable rights are therefore varied in that all legal and equitable estates and interests must be registered or noted on the title register in order to bind a purchaser (subject to the important exception of overriding interests). This is a crucial difference between registered and unregistered land; for example, under registered conveyancing procedure on the sale of a legal fee simple to a purchaser, not only must the vendor execute a deed, as with unregistered land (although, in this case the deed will be the *transfer*), but the transfer must be

[23] The underlying structure of land law is the same whether the title to the land is registered or unregistered; changes made by the LRA 1925 are ostensibly procedural only, although some important differences of substance have also emerged, see Chap. 21.

[24] See Chap. 21.

[25] See pp. 223–225 and LRA 1925, s.20(1) and s.70(1).

registered, in order to pass the legal estate. Note also that the terminology used in respect of registered land differs somewhat from unregistered land; for example the fee simple estate and the term of years absolute are referred to as the *freehold* and *leasehold* respectively; land is *transferred* rather than conveyed to a purchaser; and the legal fee simple owner or leasehold owner of a term granted for more than 21 years is called the *registered proprietor*.

It is important to bear in mind that the above rules do not alter the application of overreaching to registered land. For example, where registered land is subject to equitable family interests under a trust, which have been noted on the register or which are overriding interests, a purchaser can still overreach those interests and take free from them.[26] On the other hand, it seems that the old doctrine of notice as such has no part to play in registered land.[27] This is because a fundamental principle of land registration states that the only kind of notice which is recognised as valid is that of an entry on the register. This is subject, of course, to the statutory exception in the case of overriding interests, which do not need to be protected by an entry on the register to bind a purchaser. A further exception to the fundamental principle is that the Land Registration Acts cannot be used as a means of committing fraud. Under equitable principles, if a purchaser is fraudulent he may still take subject to rights which are not protected on the register and which are not overriding interests, by the court imposing a constructive trust.[28] Mere knowledge of an unprotected interest which purports to effect land is not sufficient to show fraud.[29] However, an example of when a constructive trust might be imposed on a purchaser, is where a purchaser buys property subject to an unprotected interest and pays a lesser price for the property, because he believes that he is bound by the right.[30] In such a case the courts may take the view that the purchaser's conscience is affected and that he should take subject to those unprotected rights under a constructive trust.

[26] See p. 225.

[27] Lord Wilberforce in *Williams and Glyn's Bank Ltd v. Boland* [1981] AC 487 at p. 504.

[28] See *Lyus v. Prowsa Developments Ltd* [1982] 1 WLR 1044 where a purchaser bought property *expressly* subject to an unregistered proprietary interest in land.

[29] It was sufficient in the first instance case of *Peffer v. Rigg* [1977] 1 WLR 285, but this has been heavily criticised.

[30] An obiter example by the Court of Appeal in *Ashburn v. Arnold* [1988] Ch 1 (at p. 23) from *Binions v. Evans* [1972] Ch. 359. See also Chap. 15 concerning constructive trusts.

8. Strict Settlements and Trusts for Sale

A settlement of property is a disposition of property which creates a succession of interests in it, *e.g.* where property is settled on A for life with remainder to B in fee simple. Settlements of land are of two kinds, namely (i) the strict settlement,[1] which is governed by the Settled Land Act 1925, and (ii) the trust for sale, which is governed by the Law of Property Act 1925. The principal difference between the two is that under a strict settlement the legal estate (*i.e.* the fee simple where the land settled is freehold, or the term of years where it is leasehold), together with the powers of disposition over it, are and must be vested in the tenant for life (*i.e.* broadly, the person who is for the time being beneficially entitled in possession under the terms of the settlement), whereas under a trust for sale it is the trustees who have both the legal estate and the powers of disposition.

Whichever form of settlement is used, it should be remembered that the interests of those beneficially entitled under the settlement (in the example above, A's life interest in possession and B's fee simple in remainder) can only exist under a *trust*. As we have already seen, the fee simple absolute in possession and the term of years absolute are the only legal estates in land since 1925, and the interests of A and B are therefore both necessarily *equitable*. Furthermore, whatever form the settlement or trust takes, the machinery of the Settled Land Act 1925 and of the Law of Property Act 1925 enables the land (*i.e.* the legal estate) to be freely disposed of, and the beneficial interests to be overreached, *i.e.* detached from the land and attached instead to the proceeds of sale or capital money in the hands of the trustees. The detailed statutory provisions governing settlements are thus directed towards the twin aims of protecting first a purchaser of the land and secondly the beneficiaries.

The broad effect of section 1 of the Settled Land Act 1925 is that land is *settled land, i.e.* subject to a strict settlement, wherever it is limited in trust for persons by way of succession or for an infant in

[1] The expression "settlement" is commonly used as referring to strict settlements only.

possession or is subject to family charges (*e.g.* an annuity, an annual sum, paid in favour of the settlor's widow).[2] Land which is held upon *immediate binding trust for sale,* however, is excluded from the operation of the Act. Such a trust for sale will normally be imposed expressly by the settlor, with the specific object of avoiding the provisions of the Settled Land Act 1925, but a trust for sale also arises by statute if two or more persons are entitled *simultaneously* in possession to land in undivided shares,[3] *e.g.*, where the fee simple in land is held by X, Y and Z jointly. A trust for sale is "immediate" if it is operative now and not merely in the future. Thus, suppose land is settled on A for life, with remainder upon trust for sale for the benefit of B for life, with some further remainder or remainders over. During A's lifetime the land will be settled land and subject to the Settled Land Act 1925 because the trust for sale is not immediate. When A dies, however, the trust for sale will become immediate and the land will cease to be settled land and the Law of Property Act 1925 will then apply. The meaning of the word "binding" is a matter of doubt.[4] What is clear, however, is that land will be settled land unless there is a *trust* to sell it (*i.e.* an obligation to sell it), and that if the instrument purports merely to confer a *power* of sale on the trustees this will not take the settlement out of the Settled Land Act 1925.

A trust for sale which otherwise is immediate and binding is not prevented from being so by reason of the fact that the trustees have power to postpone sale, or that they may be required to obtain the consents of specified persons before selling,[5] or that they may be directed to permit a beneficiary to reside on the land.[6] A trust to retain or sell land is to be construed as a trust for sale with power to postpone sale.[7]

SETTLEMENTS OLD AND NEW

Traditionally, the typical settlement was a marriage settlement. If it was desired to keep the land in the family, as far as possible, a strict settlement was used, whereas if the land was regarded as an investment (to provide an income or ultimately to sell and to distribute the proceeds of sale to beneficiaries) a trust for sale was employed (and then the settlement was often known as a trader's settlement).

If the land was brought into the settlement by the husband and a strict settlement was used, the husband would settle the land on

[2] See p. 52. For the position where land is held in trust for a minor: see p. 203.
[3] SLA 1925, s.36(1). See p. 62 note 4.
[4] See M. & W. pp. 368–389.
[5] LPA 1925, s.205.
[6] *Re Herklots' W.T.* [1964] 1 W.L.R. 583.
[7] LPA 1925, s.25(4).

himself for life, with remainder to his first and other sons successively, in order of seniority in tail. Subsidiary provision would also be made for the wife, both during the marriage and during her widowhood, and for any younger sons and daughters of the marriage. When the eldest son came of age, his father would induce him to bar the entail with his consent,[8] thereby converting the fee tail into a full fee simple. This fee simple would then be resettled on the son for life with remainder to *his* sons in tail. The result would be that when the father died and the son came into possession of the land he would do so as a mere tenant for life. This process of re-settlement would be repeated generation by generation, and in consequence the tenant in possession of the land at any given time would have only a life estate and no power to dispose of the land in fee simple. So undesirable were the social and economic consequences of this device for keeping the land in the same family that Parliament felt compelled to intervene and finally, by the Settled Land Act 1882, adopted the drastic solution of conferring upon the tenant for life a statutory power to sell the land or any part of it which no provision in the settlement could exclude or restrict. This provision has been re-enacted by the 1925 Act[9] and in consequence the use of a strict settlement nowadays by no means ensures that the land will be kept in the family even for one generation.

If a marriage settlement was made by the husband by means of a trust for sale, the essential trusts would be for the husband for life, with remainder to the wife for life if she survived him, with remainder to the children or remoter issue of the marriage in such shares as the husband and wife should jointly by deed appoint and, in default of such appointment, as the survivor should by deed or will appoint and, in default, for such of the children of the marriage as should attain the age of 21 or being females marry under that age.

Thus, having regard to the historical difference between the strict settlement and the trust for sale, it is odd that today it is possible by means of the trust for sale to ensure that land is kept in the family at least for a time, whereas this is not possible if a strict settlement is employed. When a strict settlement is used no restriction can be imposed upon the statutory power of sale which is given to the tenant for life; but when a trust for sale is employed the trustees can be required to obtain the consents of specified persons before selling, and a sale that would defeat the true purpose of the trust may be restrained.[10]

Settlements in either form may carry a heavy burden of taxation: if property is settled on beneficiaries in succession, tax (formerly estate

[8] See p. 18.
[9] SLA 1925, s.106 (see p. 45).
[10] See pp. 58–59.

duty, later replaced by capital transfer tax, now in turn replaced by inheritance tax) is payable on the full capital value of the property each time a beneficiary dies. For this reason trusts of a different kind, namely trusts for accumulation and maintenance, are now more commonly used in order to minimise the tax burden. Nevertheless, strict settlements and trusts for sale as discussed in this chapter are still likely to be encountered. In particular it must be noted that a strict settlement may arise inadvertently as where a testator makes a home-made will leaving property to a charity, but indicates that his widow may live in his house if she so wishes for the rest of her life.[11]

STRICT SETTLEMENTS

Vesting instrument and trust instrument

To create a strict settlement *inter vivos*, *i.e.* during the settlor's lifetime, the settlor must employ two documents, namely (i) a *vesting deed*, by which he transfers the legal estate in the land to the tenant for life, and (ii) a *trust instrument*, by which he declares the beneficial interests,[12] *e.g.* to A for life or until she marries, remainder to B. If the settlor, who already has the legal estate himself, is to be the tenant for life the vesting deed will merely declare that the land is vested in him.

If a strict settlement is created by *will*, the will ranks as the trust instrument setting out the beneficial interests. On the testator's death the land automatically vests in the testator's personal representatives. The vesting deed is replaced by a *vesting assent* by which the testator's personal representatives transfer the land to the tenant for life.[13] (Personal representatives have the power to transfer land by a written instrument, which need not be a deed, called an "assent.")

The trust instrument in either case must:

(i) declare the trusts affecting the settled land;
(ii) appoint trustees of the settlement;
(iii) contain the power, if any, to appoint new trustees of the settlement;
(iv) set out any powers intended to be conferred by the settlement in extension of those conferred by the Act;
(v) bear any stamp duty which may be payable in respect of the settlement.[14]

The vesting instrument (whether a deed or an assent) must contain the following statements and particulars:

[11] See *Re Carne's Settled Estates* [1899] 1 Ch. 324 and p. 159, note 4 below.
[12] SLA 1925, s.4.
[13] *Ibid.* ss.6, 8.
[14] *Ibid.* s.4.

(i) a description of the settled land;
(ii) a statement that the settled land is vested in the person or persons to whom it is conveyed, or in whom it is declared to be vested, upon the trusts from time to time affecting the settled land;
(iii) the names of the persons who are the trustees of the settlement;
(iv) any additional or larger powers conferred by the trust instrument;
(v) the name of any person for the time being entitled to appoint new trustees of the settlement.[15]

Tenant for life

The expression "tenant for life" is defined in detail in sections 19 and 20 of the Settled Land Act 1925, and means broadly any person[16] of full age who is for the time being entitled in possession either to the land itself or to the income of the land (*e.g.* when the land is already leased to tenants). The nature of his beneficial interest is irrelevant: whether he has a life interest itself, or an entailed interest, or a conditional or determinable fee, he will be the tenant for life for the purposes of the Act, provided his interest is in possession.

It follows that only in rare cases will it happen that there is no person who satisfies the statutory definition of tenant for life. If, however, there is no such person,[17] or if there is but he is not of full age, the settled land and the statutory powers of disposition will be vested in the "statutory owner." This is defined[18] as the person of full age upon whom the settlement expressly confers the powers of a tenant for life, or, in any other case, the trustees of the settlement.

Powers of tenant for life

The statutory powers of a tenant for life are contained in Part II of the Settled Land Act 1925. They include extensive powers of disposition and management which bind the settled land, *i.e.* the whole legal estate, not merely his own beneficial interest.

These powers may be enlarged by the express terms of the settlement. However, any powers which the settlement purports to

[15] *Ibid.* s.5.
[16] If two or more persons are *jointly* so entitled they together constitute the tenant for life.
[17] For examples, see *Re Frewen* [1926] Ch. 580; *Re Gallenga* [1938] 1 All E.R. 106.
[18] SLA 1925, ss.23(1), 117(1) (xxvi). References throughout this chapter to the tenant for life should be taken as referring to one who is of full age, and as including the statutory owner, except where the context indicates the contrary.

confer on the trustees or on any person other than the tenant for life will be regarded as additional powers of the tenant for life, exercisable by him alone.[19]

The most important of the statutory powers are those of sale, leasing, and raising money on mortgage.

1. Power of sale

The tenant for life may sell the settled land or any part thereof, or any easement, right or privilege of any kind over or in relation to the land.

2. Leasing powers

The tenant for life may grant a building lease or a forestry lease for a term not exceeding 999 years; a mining lease for a term not exceeding 100 years[20]; and any other lease for a term not exceeding 50 years.

3. Power to mortgage

The tenant for life may raise money by mortgage of the settled land for a number of purposes specified in section 71 of the Act, and in particular in order to pay for *improvements* authorised by the Act under provisions which we are now to consider.

4. Improvements

The tenant for life may require capital money, including money raised by mortgage, to be applied in payment for certain improvements, which are specified in the Third Schedule to the Act. This Schedule is divided into three parts. Part I contains a long list of improvements including the construction of drainage, farm roads and farm-houses and other farm buildings. In respect of these the tenant for life cannot be required to repay the cost. Part II contains a much shorter list which includes the building of dwelling-houses generally and the restoration or reconstruction of buildings damaged or destroyed by dry rot. In this case the trustees of the settlement *may* (and shall if so directed by the court) require that the money expended be repaid to them out of the income of the settled land by not more than 50 half-yearly instalments. Part III includes items such as the provision of heating, hydraulic or electric power apparatus for buildings, the installation of artificial light in any building, and the

[19] *Ibid.* ss.108, 109.
[20] *Ibid.* ss. 41–48 and see p. 22.

purchase of movable machinery for farming or other purposes. In this case the trustees of the settlement *must* require repayment by such instalments as have been mentioned.

Personal character of statutory powers

The powers conferred by the Act upon a tenant for life are personal to him and they remain with him notwithstanding any assignment of his beneficial interest, whether express or by operation of law, *e.g.* on his bankruptcy (when his beneficial interest would normally pass to his trustee in bankruptcy for the benefit of his creditors). Further, any contract by a tenant for life not to exercise his statutory powers is void.[21]

An exception to these principles arises when a tenant for life, with intent to extinguish his beneficial interest, assigns it to the person next entitled in remainder or reversion under the settlement. The remainder is then accelerated and the tenant for life loses his statutory powers.[22] For example, if land is settled on A for life with remainder to B for life, and A assigns his life interest to B (who is of full age) with intent to extinguish it, the remainder is accelerated, B becomes the tenant for life under the Settled Land Act 1925 and A must by vesting deed convey the legal estate to him. Had the remainder to B been in fee simple the remainder again would have been accelerated but, in this case, the settlement would have come to an end, as there would no longer be a succession of interests.

If a tenant for life has ceased (by reason of bankruptcy, assignment to a person other than a remainderman or otherwise) to have a substantial interest in the settled land, and either i) he has unreasonably refused to exercise any of his statutory powers, or ii) he consents to an order, the court may make an order authorising the trustees of the settlement to exercise in the name and on behalf of the tenant for life, any of the powers conferred upon him by the Act. To this extent the tenant for life is then precluded from exercising his powers.[23]

Protection of statutory powers

The Act invalidates any provision in a settlement which purports to exclude or restrict the powers conferred by the Act on a tenant for life. Any provision in the settlement is void to the extent that it would

[21] SLA 1925, s.104.
[22] *Ibid.* s.105.
[23] *Ibid.* s.24.

even tend to prevent a tenant for life from exercising the powers.[24] For example, suppose the settlement provides that the tenant for life's interest shall come to an end if he ceases to reside on the settled land. If he ceases to occupy the land for some reason other than the exercise of his statutory powers, this provision will be valid, and the tenant for life will lose his beneficial interest. However, if in exercise of his statutory powers he sells or leases the land and for that reason ceases to reside there, the provision for forfeiture of his beneficial interest will be void, and he will continue to be entitled to the income of the land, either from the proceeds of sale or from the rents under the lease.[25]

The tenant for life as trustee

As we have seen, the legal estate in the land (*i.e.* the fee simple or, if the property settled is leasehold, the term of years) is vested in the tenant for life together with the statutory powers of disposition. The tenant for life is not the beneficial owner of the legal estate—if he were, there could be no settlement because there would be no succession of interests. He holds the legal estate upon trust for all the beneficiaries—including himself—in accordance with the terms of the trust instrument. A tenant for life, therefore, is in a dual position. Under the trust instrument he has whatever beneficial interest is conferred upon him, *e.g.* a life interest, and of this he is absolute owner. Under the vesting instrument he has the entire legal estate, but this he holds as trustee. However, the tenant for life is not as such a "trustee of the settlement." The trustees of the settlement must be expressly appointed by the trust instrument, and they have distinct functions under the Act.[26]

The Act provides generally that a tenant for life shall, in exercising any power under the Act, have regard to the interests of all parties entitled under the settlement, and shall in relation to the exercise thereof by him be deemed to be in the position and to have the duties and liabilities of a trustee for those parties.[27] The effect of this, however, is merely to restrain an improper use of the powers, rather

[24] *Ibid.* s.106.

[25] *Re Acklom* [1929] 1 Ch. 195. See also p. 53.

[26] There is nothing to prevent the tenant for life being expressly appointed as a trustee of the settlement.

[27] SLA 1925, s.107. Further, under SLA 1925, s.64, the tenant for life may, by obtaining a court order, put into effect any transaction (not otherwise authorised by the settlement or Act) if the court is of the opinion that it is for the benefit of the settled land or the beneficiaries interested under the settlement and if it is one which could have been validly effected by an absolute owner. This power is exercisable to vary the terms of the settlement despite provisions to the contrary in the statute creating the settlement, see *Hambro v. The Duke of Marlborough* [1994] Ch. 158.

than to afford a means of directing their exercise. Thus, if one of two joint tenants for life wishes to sell the property, and the other wishes to retain it, the court cannot order sale.[28] The same principle would apply if a dispute were to arise between the tenant for life and a remainderman. The latter might have much the more substantial interest in the land, but he could not compel the tenant for life to exercise his statutory powers,[29] however advantageous it might be to dispose of the land. Neither, on the other hand, could he challenge the exercise of the powers, except where he could prove fraud.[30] The Act thus ensures the autonomy of the tenant for life, but at the cost of providing only limited means of protecting the interests of other beneficiaries under a settlement, which are discussed below.

The tenant for life can make no disposition of the land except such as the Settled Land Act 1925 authorises him to make,[31] and, although the Act gives him wide powers of disposition, it attaches conditions which are designed to protect the interests of the other beneficiaries. Thus, in respect of most transactions he is required to give written notice to the trustees of the settlement. In a few exceptional circumstances, he may be required to obtain their consent or an order of the court prior to a transaction.[32] Again, on a sale or lease of the settled land he must obtain the best consideration in money, or the best rent, that can reasonably be obtained. Further, above all, any capital money arising on a disposition of the settled land must be paid, not to the tenant for life, but to the trustees of the settlement, who will then hold it upon the same trusts as those affecting the land for the beneficiaries of the settlement.[33]

Under the draconian terms of section 18(1)(a) of the Act, an unauthorised disposition of settled land is *void*[34]; there is, surprisingly, no exception in favour of a purchaser of a legal estate without notice that the land is settled. The unfortunate but inevitable result is that if a tenant for life fraudulently disposes of the land for his own benefit,

[28] *Re 90 Thornhill Road, Tolworth, Surrey* [1970] Ch. 261.

[29] A possible exception arises under SLA 1925, s.24 (see note 23).

[30] See *Cardigan v. Curzon-Howe* (1885) 30 Ch. D. 531.

[31] SLA 1925, s.18(1)(a).

[32] With respect to dispositions of a "principal mansion house" as defined by the Act (if the settlement expressly so requires), felling of timber (if he is impeachable for waste; see p. 22), and sale of settled chattels (which requires an order of the court). (SLA 1925, ss.65-67.)

[33] SLA 1925, s.18(1)(b).

[34] Except to the extent of passing the tenant for life's own beneficial interest; and of course the purchaser has a remedy against the tenant for life personally for breach of contract.

the purchaser acquires no title even though he acted in good faith and had no means of knowing that the land was subject to a settlement.[35]

Dealings between the tenant for life and the estate

If special provision had not been made by the Act, the fiduciary position of the tenant for life would have precluded any dealing between himself and the estate. For example, it would not have been possible for him to purchase or take a lease of the settled land for his own benefit.

Of course he already holds his life or other interest beneficially, and by virtue of this is entitled to occupy the settled land or receive the rents and profits during his life. However, it may be that he wishes to acquire a more permanent interest, such as the fee simple or a long lease for his own purposes. Equity resolves any possible conflict between duty and interest by generally prohibiting such dealings (even though shown not to be prejudicial),[36] but by section 68 of the Act they are permitted if a prescribed procedure is followed. The tenant for life must inform the trustees of the settlement of his wish, *e.g.* to purchase all or part of the settled land, and the trustees of the settlement then take over the powers of the tenant for life with regard to that transaction. They will decide whether the transaction should be permitted and, if they agree in principle, will negotiate the terms of the transaction with the tenant for life.

Overreaching

When the tenant for life sells the land, or any part of it, in exercise of his statutory power of sale, the purchaser must pay his purchase money to all the trustees of the settlement and ensure that they are at least two in number or a trust corporation (*i.e.* a corporation authorised by law to undertake trust business).[37] If he does so he will acquire the land free from the interests of the beneficiaries under the settlement, even though he knows of their existence.[38] Nevertheless, the beneficiaries are not prejudiced, because, as we have seen, the proceeds of sale are held by the trustees upon the same trusts as those

[35] *Weston v. Henshaw* [1950] Ch. 510, in which the tenant for life (for the purpose of mortgaging the property for his own benefit) suppressed the vesting instrument, and produced previous title deeds appearing to show that he was the beneficial owner, solely entitled in fee simple. This transaction was contrary to SLA 1925, s.18(1)(a) and (b), (see note 33 above). See note 42 for the conflict between this section and SLA 1925, s.110.

[36] *Fox v. Mackreth* (1791) 2 Cox Eq. 320.

[37] SLA 1925, s.18(1)(b) and (c). Capital money may alternatively be paid into court.

[38] *Ibid.* s.72; LPA 1925, s.2.

upon which the land was held by the tenant for life before the sale. The interests of the beneficiaries, are said to be overreached, therefore, because they are taken away from the land and attached instead to the proceeds of sale. Any other disposition which the tenant for life is authorised to make by the Act, such as a mortgage or lease, has a similar overreaching effect.

As an illustration, suppose that land has been settled upon A for life, with remainder to B in fee simple. A is the tenant for life and the legal fee simple will have been vested in him by the vesting instrument. Now suppose that in the exercise of his statutory power of sale A has sold half the settled land. The half that has not been sold remains vested in A and he holds it upon trust for himself for life, with remainder to B in fee simple. The proceeds of sale of the other half will have been paid to the trustees of the settlement, and the purchaser accordingly will take the land free from the interests of A and B. The trustees normally will invest the proceeds in authorised trustee securities.[39] These securities will be registered in the names of the trustees of the settlement, who will hold them upon trust for A for life, with remainder to B. A will be entitled to the income from the investments during his life, and after A's death B will be entitled absolutely, and may require the trustees to transfer the investments into his own name.

In addition to beneficial interests subsisting or capable of arising under the settlement, a disposition by the tenant for life overreaches certain financial charges, even if created before the settlement and even if registered under the Land Charges Act 1925 or 1972.[40]

The "curtain" principle

On a sale, lease, mortgage or other disposition of settled land, a purchaser dealing in good faith with the tenant for life is conclusively taken to have given the best price, consideration or rent that could reasonably be obtained, and to have complied with all the requisitions of the Act.[41] The purpose of this provision is to protect the purchaser, not the tenant for life. If, for example, the tenant for life sells at an undervalue, he will be liable for breach of trust to the other beneficiaries under the settlement, but the purchaser will be protected. On the other hand, a purchaser cannot rely on this provision unless he deals with the tenant for life *as such, i.e.* on the faith of the

[39] See SLA 1925, s.73, for other authorised modes of applying capital money. These include the purchase of other land (freehold or a leasehold having 60 years or more to run), which will be brought into the settlement and conveyed to the tenant for life by a subsidiary vesting deed.

[40] Annuities, limited owners' charges and general equitable charges, as defined by that Act: see p. 230.

[41] SLA 1925, s.110(1).

vesting instrument, and pays any capital money to the trustees of the settlement.[42]

The purchaser is neither bound nor even entitled to inspect the trust instrument[43] as this relates to interests which will be overreached by the conveyance to him and he is therefore in no way concerned with it. It is therefore said to be "behind the curtain" as regards the purchaser. On the other hand, he is very much concerned with the vesting instrument, which is designed to give him information that he requires, including the names of the trustees of the settlement, to whom he must pay his purchase money, and he is, in general, required to assume the accuracy of the statements in this instrument.[43] There are certain exceptions to these rules, of which the most important are subsisting settlements created before 1926 and imperfectly constituted post-1925 settlements.

Pre-1926 and imperfect settlements

Until 1926 a strict settlement could be created either by conveying the land to trustees on trust for the beneficiaries in succession, or by conveying it directly to the beneficiaries themselves, *e.g.* to A for life, with remainder to B in fee simple. Neither of these procedures is possible after 1925, and accordingly there are transitional provisions[44] which ensure that in all cases where a pre-1926 settlement was still in existence at the end of 1925 not only the powers of disposition but also the entire legal estate should be vested in the tenant for life, and that a vesting instrument should be executed in his favour. The detail of these elaborate provisions need not concern us although their broad effect is, first, that the legal estate was automatically vested in the tenant for life on January 1, 1926,[45] and, secondly, that the tenant

[42] See *Weston v. Henshaw,* (a decision based on SLA 1925, s.18), see note 34. This interpretation was criticised in *Re Morgan's Lease* [1972] Ch. 1, where Ungoed-Thomas J took the view that s.110 applies whether or not the purchaser knows that the other party to the transaction is a tenant for life. There is an apparent conflict between s.18 (see p. 48) and s.110 which is highlighted by these two first instance cases. The more recent case of *Bevan v. Johnston* [1990] 2 EGLR.33 fails to clarify the position; it applies s.18 and there is no mention of s.110. Perhaps these provisions may be reconciled by applying s.18 where a transaction is totally unauthorised under SLA 1925, for example where the tenant for life acts fraudulently (see *Weston v. Henshaw* where he purported to be sole beneficial owner); and using s.110 where there is an authorised transaction under the Act, so that the tenant for life exercises powers which belong to him but does not comply with all the necessary formalities. For example, where the tenant for life is authorised to grant an option (under SLA 1925, s.51) but may fail to comply with the provision that it should be at the best price reasonably obtainable (*Re Morgan's Lease*).

[43] SLA 1925, s.110.

[44] SLA 1925, Sched. 2; LPA 1925, Sched. 1.

[45] Except where the legal estate was vested in personal representatives immediately before that date, in which case they held it on trust to convey it to the tenant for life (subject to their powers of administration).

for life could require the trustees of the settlement to execute a vesting deed declaring that the legal estate was vested in him in accordance with the provisions of the Settled Land Act 1925. The old settlement remains in effect, but only as a trust instrument, and this is one of the cases in which the curtain principle does not operate. Accordingly a purchaser must examine the trust instrument in order to ensure that the land disposed of is comprised in the settlement and is vested in the appropriate person as tenant for life, and that the trustees are the properly constituted trustees of the settlement.[46]

If after 1925 a settlor attempts to create an *inter vivos* settlement otherwise than by the authorised method, the legal estate does not pass.[47] If, for example, the settlor employs one document only, purporting to deal with both the legal estate and the beneficial interests, or if he purports to convey the legal estate to trustees instead of to the tenant for life, the legal estate will remain with the settlor. The abortive settlement takes effect as a trust instrument only, and the tenant for life can require that the legal estate be vested in him. Although the legal estate is still with the settlor, the Act provides[48] that it is the trustees of the settlement who must execute the vesting deed in favour of the tenant for life; the effect of the deed is then to take the legal estate from the settlor and vest it in the tenant for life. This is another case, however, in which the curtain principle does not apply.[49]

Further section 13 of the Act (known as the paralysing section) provides that where a tenant for life is entitled to a vesting instrument, until that vesting instrument has been executed, any purported *inter vivos* disposition of settled land, by any person (other than a personal representative), shall not take effect to convey the legal estate. It shall operate only as a contract to carry out the transaction once the vesting instrument has been executed. (It should be noted that this section however, does not prevent the tenant for life from disposing of his equitable interest.) An exception to the section applies where the purchaser of the legal estate is without notice that the tenant for life is entitled to a vesting instrument. For example, a settlor settles Blackacre on A for life or until he marries, remainder to B for life, remainder to C absolutely. A vesting instrument is duly executed vesting the legal estate in A as the tenant for life; A subsequently marries, but before executing a vesting deed in favour of B (vesting in B the legal estate as the next tenant for life) he sells the legal estate to a purchaser, P. Prima facie, section 13 will apply so that the disposition operates as a contract to convey the legal estate to P, once a vesting instrument has been executed in B's favour. However,

46 SLA 1925, s.110.
47 *Ibid.* s.4.
48 *Ibid.* ss.4, 9.
49 See note 46.

P may come within the exception of a purchaser without notice as he would not have been aware that B was entitled to a vesting instrument, as the fact that A's beneficial interest was determinable will only be revealed in the trust instrument which is behind the curtain. Therefore, it may be argued that P is without notice, and that the paralysing section does not apply and so P acquires the legal estate.[50]

It should be noted also that the section does not prevent a disposition by personal representatives (where the settlement arises by will), nor does it apply where the settlement has come to an end before a vesting instrument has been executed,[51] or where land is settled only by reason of being subject to family charges.[52]

Duration of settlement

Once a settlement comes into operation the land remains settled land so long as any beneficial interest under the settlement subsists or is capable of arising, or so long as the beneficial owner is an infant.[53] Suppose, for example, that land is settled on A for life, with remainder to B in fee simple, but subject to a jointure rentcharge for A's widow (*i.e.* subject to a charge upon the land for payment of an annuity to A's widow during her widowhood). Upon the death of A, leaving a widow, the land remains settled land because it is still subject to the charge, and B is the tenant for life. If B, as tenant for life, sells the land under his statutory power of sale, the widow's rentcharge will be overreached. The widow will not be prejudiced, however, because the proceeds of sale will be paid to the trustees of the settlement, who will be responsible for paying the annuity to the widow out of the income from the proceeds. Alternatively, in this particular case, when the land is settled land by reason only that it is subject to such a charge for the payment of money, the Law of Property (Amendment) Act 1926 allows B to sell the land subject to the charge as if it were not settled land and himself receive the proceeds of sale.

The purpose of this curious provision is obsolete. Parliament, having in 1925 decided to include land subject to family charges in the definition of settled land and thus enable the overreaching machinery of the Settled Land Act 1925 to be used, seems only partly to have changed its mind in 1926 by empowering the beneficial owner (who is also "tenant for life" under the Act) to dispose of the land with the

50 Note that if all the correct documents have been executed so that there is a properly constituted settlement but there is subsequently an unauthorised dealing s.18 will apply (see p. 47), rather than s.13.

51 *Re Alefounder's W.T.* [1927] 1 Ch. 360.

52 See below.

53 SLA 1925, s.3.

charge still attached. It is difficult to understand how nowadays that could be of advantage to anyone—whether the vendor, the purchaser or the annuitant. The most that could be said in its favour is that it avoids the necessity of a vesting instrument and other formalities under the Settled Land Act 1925 although of course, paradoxically, the land in the purchaser's hands is still nominally settled land, and he is the "tenant for life" (with the same power to dispose of it either under the Settled Land Act 1925, or under the 1926 Act). If on the other hand the object of proceeding under the 1926 Act is merely to enable the vendor (as beneficial owner, rather than as tenant for life) to receive the proceeds of sale himself, this could in any event be achieved more effectively by arranging with the annuitant to release her annuity in return for an appropriate share of the proceeds, or by making a payment into court under section 50 of the Law of Property Act 1925, whereupon the rentcharge would be discharged (and the land, in whoever's hands it might be, would cease to be settled land).

Death of tenant for life

If on the death of a tenant for life the land remains settled land, the trustees of the settlement are entitled to a grant of probate (if the tenant for life died testate) or letters of administration, limited to only the settled land. They then become his special personal representatives with regard to the settled land,[54] and must vest the settled land in the next tenant for life.[55] On the other hand, if when a tenant for life dies the land ceases to be settled land, the land will devolve upon his general (*i.e.* ordinary) personal representatives,[56] who will vest it in the person or persons entitled to it. For example, if land is settled on A for life, with remainder to B for life, with remainder to C in fee simple, then on the death of A the settled land will devolve upon A's special personal representatives. They will vest the land in B, the next tenant for life, by means of a vesting assent.[57] But when B dies the land will cease to be settled land as C is now entitled absolutely. It will therefore devolve upon B's general personal representatives and they will vest it in C by a simple written assent. (A vesting assent will not be appropriate as the land will have ceased to be settled land).

Determination of tenant for life's interest

If the tenant for life has a determinable interest, *e.g.* if land is settled on A for life or until he marries, or until he ceases to reside on

[54] AEA 1925, s.22.
[55] SLA 1925, s.7.
[56] *Re Bridgett and Hayes' Contract* [1928] Ch. 163.
[57] SLA 1925, s.8.

the land, with remainders over, the legal estate and statutory powers of disposition will be vested in him. If his interest later determines (on his marriage or on his ceasing to reside, as the case may be) he ceases to be tenant for life and no longer has the statutory powers. However, the legal estate remains with him as there is no statutory divesting. He holds the legal estate as a bare trustee, and is bound to convey it to the person next entitled. If the remainderman is entitled absolutely an ordinary conveyance will be appropriate; if not, *i.e.* if the settlement continues and the remainderman is tenant for life, A should convey the legal estate to him by vesting deed.[58]

Say that land is settled on A for life or until he marries, with remainder on B in fee simple. A difficult question would arise if A, having married, in good faith but mistakenly purports as tenant for life to exercise the statutory powers and to dispose of the land, after his interest has determined. Such a disposition would clearly be in breach of trust, but the question is whether a purchaser from A would acquire good title as against the persons entitled under the settlement. The position appears to be that the Settled Land Act 1925 does not apply and cannot be relied on, as on A's marriage the land is no longer settled (B now being entitled absolutely). The purchaser will acquire, therefore, the legal estate as it was still vested in A at the time of the disposition but he is not protected by the provisions of the Act and the usual rules regarding overreaching, even though he paid the purchase money to the trustees of the settlement believing that he was able to overreach. (This is because A holds the legal estate on bare trust for B, *i.e.* on a simple trust for the sole absolute owner, and such a trust cannot be overreached, unless B consents.)[59] However, in the case of unregistered land, it is questionable whether the purchaser acquires the land subject to B's interest; the beneficial interests under the settlement bind him only if he had notice of them under the old doctrine of notice. He necessarily had notice that there was a trust, but it was a trust which he assumed he was overreaching, and which he assumed under section 110 of the Settled Land Act 1925 he was precluded from investigating. It may be doubted whether in these unlikely circumstances equity would regard him as bound by the particular interests of those entitled under the settlement, and it seems probable that the purchaser would take free from these interests and that the beneficiaries' rights would be confined to their respective interests in the proceeds held by the trustees.[60]

[58] *Ibid.* ss.7, 8.

[59] Note para. 7.1 of Law Commission Report No. 181 (1989) on the failure of the 1925 legislation to deal with bare trusts, and the recommendation in Law Commission Report No. 188 (1989), para. 4.27 that the statutory provisions of overreaching should apply to bare trusts.

[60] But a contrary view is expressed in M & W pp. 335 *et seq.*

Deed of discharge

If a settlement comes to an end because the former tenant for life becomes absolutely entitled, the trustees of the settlement may be required to execute a deed of discharge, *i.e.* a deed declaring that they are discharged from the trusts of the settlement. The purpose of the deed is to ensure that a purchaser is aware of the change that has taken place. In the event of any difficulty the court may be asked to make an order of discharge which will have the same effect. Unless the deed or order of discharge states the contrary (*e.g.* indicates that the land is still settled land under a derivative settlement) a purchaser of the land will be entitled to assume that the land has ceased to be settled land and is not subject to a trust for sale.[61]

Thus, a deed of discharge would be required if the settlement came to an end by reason of some dealing with the beneficial interests, *e.g.* if the tenant for life had an entailed interest and barred the entail or if he purchased the remainderman's interest. In such a case the former tenant for life would now be entitled absolutely, and could call for a deed of discharge to enable him to make title as beneficial owner (rather than as trustee), and in particular to receive any proceeds of sale himself.

A deed of discharge is *not* necessary, however, if the settlement has come to an end because the remainderman is now absolutely entitled, on the death of the tenant for life or on the tenant for life's marriage (where he has a determinable interest). In that event, as we have seen, the legal estate will devolve upon the tenant for life's general personal representatives, and they will transfer it by simple assent or ordinary conveyance to the person or persons entitled. A subsequent purchaser upon investigating the title to the land will see that it has been disposed of by this means, and will be bound and entitled to assume that the land in question has ceased to be settled land,[62] and that he is no longer required to pay the purchase money to the trustees of the settlement or into court.

TRUSTS FOR SALE

Trusts for sale are not solely employed as an express method of creating settlements of land outside the provisions of the Settled Land Act. They are equally important in two quite different situations, where a trust for sale is imposed by statute, namely co-ownership[63]

[61] SLA 1925, s.17.
[62] *Ibid.*, s.110(5).
[63] See Chap 9 regarding co-ownership. The general discussion of trusts for sale in the present chapter should be taken as applying equally to statutory trusts for sale, as to express trusts for sale.

(under the Law of Property Act 1925, ss.34-36) and intestacy (under the Administration of Estates Act 1925, s.33), commonly referred to as statutory trusts for sale.

Technically a trust for sale of land is not a settlement of land, but of money, by reason of the equitable doctrine of conversion. This is based on the maxim "equity looks upon that as done which ought to be done."[64] As the trustees are under an obligation to sell the land, equity regards the land as having already been sold, and this is so even if the trustees have the usual power to postpone sale. Trustees for sale of land always have power to postpone the sale unless the trust instrument otherwise provides).[65] The interests of the beneficiaries under a trust for sale, therefore, are in *theory* converted into interests in money from the beginning. The doctrine creates problems of definition, and appears to serve no useful purpose today. Nevertheless, clearly it cannot of itself deprive a beneficiary under a trust for sale of the right to occupy the land, provided his interest is in possession, not in remainder or reversion.[66]

Procedure

To create a trust for sale *inter vivos* the settlor conveys the land to trustees upon trust to sell it and to hold the net rents and profits pending sale and the proceeds of sale after sale upon trust for certain beneficiaries, *e.g.* on trust for A for life, with remainder to B absolutely. The trustees then have the legal estate in the land (*i.e.* the legal fee simple or, if the property is leasehold, the legal term of years) and the beneficiaries have successive equitable interests in the land or (technically) in the proceeds of sale. Thus, in the example given, A has the right to occupy the land or to receive the net rents and profits of the land pending sale and the income from the investments of the proceeds of sale after sale, as he has the interest in possession. Upon the death of A, B is entitled absolutely and if the land has been sold B will be entitled to require the trustees to transfer to him the investments made with the proceeds of sale; if the land remains unsold the trustees must convey it to B: in either case the trust for sale is at an end.

Both the conveyance of the land to the trustees and the declaration of the trusts can be done in one document; there is no two-document rule as in the case of strict settlements. But, except in simple cases, it is good conveyancing practice to employ two documents, namely (i) a conveyance upon trust for sale and (ii) a separate trust instrument. If

[64] For another application of this maxim, see p. 27.
[65] LPA 1925, s.25.
[66] See p. 73.

this is done, the conveyance transfers the land and imposes the trust to sell it, but does not set out the beneficial interests: these are set out in the trust instrument. The "curtain" principle then operates, *i.e.* a purchaser of the land from the trustees is not concerned with the trust instrument.

When land is given by will upon trust for sale normally there are two documents. The testator's personal representatives will transfer the land to the trustees by a written assent upon trust for sale. This assent will then correspond to the conveyance upon trust for sale and will not declare the beneficial interests. The will itself operates as the trust instrument. It must be referred to in order to ascertain what the beneficial interests are, but so far as a purchaser is concerned it is "behind the curtain."[67]

Effect of dispositions

Under section 27 of the Law of Property Act 1925, a purchaser from trustees for sale is not concerned with the trusts affecting the land or the proceeds of sale, and this applies even though the trusts might be declared in the instrument which vested the legal estate in the trustees.[68] However, the proceeds must not be paid to fewer than two persons as trustees for sale, unless the trustee is a trust corporation.[69] The beneficial interests under the trust are then overreached, in accordance with section 2 of the Law of Property Act 1925, in much the same way as they are on a disposition by a tenant for life of settled land.[70] What the provisions of the Law of Property Act 1925 fail to indicate, however, is the effect of a disposition where capital money has not been paid as required by the Act, *e.g.* where the disposition is made by a sole individual trustee. An "unauthorised" disposition of settled land is rendered void by section 18 of the Settled Land Act 1925[71] but there is no equivalent provision in the Law of Property Act 1925 with respect to land held on trust for sale. The result appears to be that a purchaser from a sole individual trustee for sale acquires the legal estate (because the disposition to him is not void). However, with unregistered land he takes subject to the beneficial interests under the trust unless he has no notice of them. Of course, in the case of an express trust for sale he necessarily has notice of them, as the conveyance on sale to the trustees reveals the existence of a trust. It is only where a trust for sale arises by statute or by implication that the plea of purchaser without notice might avail

[67] AEA 1925, s.36.
[68] LPA 1925, s.27(1).
[69] *Ibid.* s.27(2).
[70] See p. 48.
[71] See note 35.

him.[72] Where the land is registered and there is a disposition by a sole individual trustee, there may be an entry on the register (called a restriction), warning the purchaser that he must ensure that a second trustee is appointed in order to overreach any beneficial interests under the trust. If there is no such entry the purchaser will still be bound by the interests of a beneficiary in actual occupation, who will have an overriding interest (but not otherwise).[73]

Consents to dispositions

Express trusts for sale are commonly made subject to a condition that the land shall not be sold without the consent of named persons.[74] The courts may infer also a condition that the consent of a beneficiary must be obtained where a settlor has directed that such a beneficiary may occupy the land for life.[75] If the trustees fail to obtain the requisite consents (or an order of the court) they will be in breach of trust, but a purchaser is protected if two such consents are obtained.[76]

Further, the Act provides[77] that trustees for sale shall so far as practicable give effect to the wishes of the persons of full age who are for the time being entitled in possession, so far as this is consistent with the general interest of the trust. In the event of dispute, the wishes of the beneficiaries with the majority interest in value should prevail. However, it is notable that this duty to consult does not mean that the trustees are bound to follow the wishes of the majority beneficiaries, if these are inconsistent with the general interest of the trust.

As we have seen, trustees for sale generally have power to postpone sale. However, since there is a trust for sale and therefore an obligation to sell the land, any trustee or any person beneficially entitled can in principle insist upon an immediate sale. If the co-trustees refuse to join in the sale, or if any requisite consents to sale cannot be obtained, application may be made to the court for an order of sale under section 30 of the Law of Property Act 1925. However, in deciding whether to order sale the courts will consider

[72] See p. 68.

[73] LRA 1925, s.70(1)(g). As to restrictions and overriding interests see pp. 223–226 and also p. 70 regarding co-ownership.

[74] Such a condition would generally be void in the case of strict settlements (see p. 45 note 24.

[75] *Re Herklots' W.T.* [1964] 1 W.L.R. 583, in which the consents of both the beneficiary in possession and the remainderman were held to be required in the special circumstances.

[76] LPA 1925, s.26(1).

[77] LPA 1925, s.26(3). The provision applies to all statutory trusts for sale but only to those created expressly if they indicate an intention that it shall apply. It is difficult to envisage circumstances where trustees could properly ignore the provision, but in any case a purchaser is not concerned to see that it is complied with.

the true purpose of the trust; this may often be something quite other than sale of the land, as where the settlor indicates an intention that the successive beneficiaries shall have the right to reside there.[78] In such circumstances it is unlikely that a sale would be ordered if this would defeat the manifest purpose of the trust. In a dispute between a beneficiary entitled in possession and a remainderman the wishes of the former are likely to prevail, but in some circumstances an order of sale might be refused if sale would unduly prejudice the interest of the remainderman. Also, if a person whose consent is expressly required has an interest contingent on the land remaining unsold, it may be doubted whether the court could properly dispense with his consent and order sale, since the effect of doing so would be to defeat his interest altogether.[79] Paradoxically, it thus appears that as a means of retaining land unsold the trust for sale may be more effective than the strict settlement, under which the tenant for life has virtually arbitrary powers of disposition, and a virtually unfettered discretion whether or not to exercise them. Moreover, the courts, under the jurisdiction conferred by section 30 of the Law of Property Act 1925, are able to exercise over trusts for sale a measure of control which is signally lacking in the case of settlements under the Settled Land Act 1925.[80]

Powers of trustees for sale

Section 28 of the Law of Property Act 1925, provides that trustees for sale shall, in relation to land and to the proceeds of sale, have all the powers of a tenant for life and the trustees of a settlement under the Settled Land Act 1925. Before exercising any such power, however, the trustees must obtain the same consents, if any, as would have been required on a sale of the land. The trustees, for example, will have the same powers of granting leases of the land as a tenant for life would have had, and the same powers of investment as the trustees of the settlement would have had, if the land had been settled land.

One of the consequences of this provision is that trustees for sale who have sold part of their land may use the proceeds of sale for the purchase of other land, being freehold or a leasehold having at least 60 years to run.[81] Any such land will be conveyed to the trustees and will be held by them upon trust for sale.[82] But it has been held that once trustees for sale have sold all their land they no longer possess this power, and therefore cannot buy land unless such a power is expressly conferred upon them by the terms of the trust.[83]

[78] See note 75.
[79] *Re Inns* [1947] Ch. 576. The effect may be to render the land unsaleable and even to cast doubt on the "binding" nature of the trust for sale (see p. 40 note 4).
[80] *Cf.* p. 47.
[81] See *Re Wellsted's W.T.* [1949] Ch. 296, C.A.
[82] LPA 1925, s.28.
[83] *Re Wakeman* [1945] Ch. 177: this is logic carried to excess.

Another consequence of the provision is that capital money held by trustees for sale may be applied to payment for improvements to land still held by them in the same way that capital money under the Settled Land Act 1925 may be used to pay for improvements. Trustees for sale always have power to pay for the cost of repairs out of income. It will sometimes happen that a particular repair is also an improvement within the Settled Land Act 1925, or some other improvement of a permanent nature,[84] in which case the trustees will have a discretion as to whether that repair shall be paid for out of income or out of capital. Subject to this, income from the land, *e.g.* where it is let to tenants, will of course be paid to the person beneficially entitled in possession under the trust.

Trustees for sale may by writing revocably delegate from time to time their powers of leasing, accepting surrenders of leases, and management to any person of full age (not being merely an annuitant) for the time being beneficially entitled in possession to the net rents and profits of the land during his life or for any less period.[85]

SPECIAL (OR AD HOC) TRUSTS FOR SALE AND AD HOC SETTLEMENTS

If the trustees of a trust for sale are either (i) two or more persons approved or appointed by the court, or their successors in office, or (ii) a trust corporation, a conveyance by them to a purchaser has a somewhat wider overreaching effect than would otherwise be the case. Certain equitable interests having priority to the trust for sale can be overreached which could not have been overreached if the trust for sale had not been in this special category.[86] A trust for sale may be specially set up in order that a contemplated sale of the land shall have this wider overreaching effect, in which case the trust for sale is called an *ad hoc trust for sale.*

Very similarly, an estate owner may set up an *ad hoc settlement* under the Settled Land Act 1925, for the express purpose of overreaching equitable interests which could not otherwise have been overreached. The trustees of the settlement must then be two or more persons approved or appointed by the court or a trust corporation.[87]

These provisions of the Law of Property Act 1925 and the Settled Land Act 1925 are little used and are relatively unimportant.[88]

[84] *Re Smith* [1930] 1 Ch. 88.
[85] LPA 1925, s.29.
[86] *Ibid.* s.2(2).
[87] SLA 1925, s.21.
[88] See M. & W. pp. 405–410.

9. Co-ownership

Co-ownership subsists when two or more persons have concurrent (not successive) interests in the same property. For example, if land is granted to A and B in fee simple, A and B are co-owners, but if land is settled on A for life with remainder to B in fee simple, A and B are not co-owners.

The main forms of co-ownership are joint tenancy and tenancy in common.[1] The principal difference between the two is that the right of survivorship (or *jus accrescendi*) applies to joint tenancy, but not to tenancy in common. Thus, if A, B and C are joint tenants in fee simple and A dies, A's interest survives (or passes) to B and C, who become owners of the whole. If B then dies his interest likewise survives to C, who becomes sole owner of the land; co-ownership is then at an end. It follows that a joint tenant has nothing that he can leave by his will or that will pass to his statutory next of kin if he dies intestate. The *jus accrescendi* is itself a result of the notion that joint tenants are one person holding the whole interest in the property indivisibly. A joint tenant is said to hold *per mie et per tout* (potentially both the least and yet the whole), in the sense that if he predeceases the other joint tenants his ownership dwindles to nothing, whereas if he survives the others he emerges as sole and absolute owner.

If A, B and C are tenants in common in fee simple and A dies, his interest does not survive to the others, but devolves upon his personal representatives, forms part of his estate and ultimately passes under his will or intestacy to his heirs or statutory next of kin. Tenants in common have a right to a distinct share in the property, although not yet divided; they are said therefore to hold a "tenancy in undivided shares" to which the doctrine of survivorship does not apply. As will be seen later in this chapter, it is possible for a beneficial joint tenancy to be converted into a tenancy in common by the process called *severance*.

STATUTORY TRUST FOR SALE

After 1925, with one exception, whenever a disposition of land (by deed or by will) creates beneficial co-ownership in possession,

[1] "Tenancy" in this context means simply ownership, whether freehold or leasehold, and should not be confused with the relationship between landlord and tenant under a lease.

whether it be joint tenancy or tenancy in common, the land is held, under statute, upon trust for sale.[2] The trustees are then said to hold the land upon "statutory trusts," *i.e.* upon trust to sell it and to hold the net rents and profits pending sale, and the proceeds of sale after sale, upon trust for those entitled in equity, *i.e.* the beneficial co-owners according to their interests. It will be observed that the statutory trust for sale does not apply to the land unless the co-owners are entitled in possession. If, therefore, land is settled on A for life, with remainder to B and C in fee simple, the land will be settled land under the Settled Land Act 1925, so long as A is alive. Upon the death of A, however, B and C will be entitled in possession and a statutory trust for sale will then apply to the land, as there is now an immediate trust for sale.

The one exception to this general rule is that if land is settled on two or more *joint* tenants for life (and no express trust for sale is imposed) the land will be settled land under the Settled Land Act 1925, and the joint tenants for life will together constitute the "tenant for life" for the purposes of that Act.[3] If, on the other hand, they are entitled as tenants in common the general rule applies, and the land will be held on statutory trust for sale.[4]

THE TRUSTEES

As has been seen, where a trust for sale arises a distinction must be made between the position of the trustees, who hold the legal estate subject to the statutory trusts, and the beneficiaries who hold the beneficial (or equitable) interests under those trusts.[5]

The trustees of the statutory trust for sale are normally the beneficial co-owners themselves (provided they are of full age) or, if there are more than four, the first four named. There is an exception, however, where co-ownership arises by will: in this case the testator's personal representatives will normally constitute the trustees for sale.[6]

Section 1(6) of the Law of Property Act 1925 expressly provides that after 1925 a legal estate cannot be held in undivided shares. Indeed, section 34 of the Act further provides that a conveyance of land to persons as tenants in common operates to vest the legal estate in them *jointly* on the statutory trusts on trust for themselves as beneficial tenants in common.

[2] The main provisions are in LPA 1925, ss.34-36.
[3] SLA 1925, s.19(2).
[4] *Ibid* s.36(1).
[5] See above and pp. 56–57.
[6] The exception is purely technical in that beneficiaries of full age and absolutely entitled can in any event require the legal estate to be vested in themselves (*Saunders v. Vautier* (1841) 4 Beav. 115).

Trustees always hold therefore as joint tenants. It follows that, even if the deed or will creates beneficial tenancy in common, the *legal estate* must be held jointly. The purpose of these provisions, as may be said generally of the 1925 legislation, is to simplify conveyancing. If, before 1926, a legal estate in land was held by A, B and C as tenants in common, it might be disposed of without difficulty so long as all of them were alive. If in turn each died leaving his share to his four children say, the land would now belong equally to twelve persons, all of whom would have to join in a conveyance to a purchaser if the land was to be sold. Such difficulties cannot now arise, since a legal estate can only be held *jointly*, by not more than four trustees, and remains vested in the surviving trustees upon the death of any of them. A sale by the trustees will overreach[7] the beneficial interests subsisting under the trust, whether they are held jointly or in common, and however diverse they may be.

Some examples will show how these provisions operate in practice.

(i) Land is conveyed to A, B and C as tenants in common in fee simple. The legal estate vests in A, B and C as joint tenants in fee simple, as trustees, upon the statutory trusts for the benefit of themselves as tenants in common in equity (*i.e.* as beneficiaries under the trust for sale). If A then dies, the right of survivorship will operate with regard to the joint tenancy of the legal estate and the legal fee simple will remain vested in B and C, the surviving trustees of the trust for sale. However, A's beneficial (or equitable) interest as tenant in common will pass to his personal representatives and will form part of his estate.

(ii) If land is conveyed to A, B and C as joint tenants in fee simple, and A and B are of full age, but C is an infant, the legal estate will vest in A and B as joint tenants, as trustees, upon the statutory trusts for the benefit of themselves and C as joint tenants in equity (*i.e.* as beneficiaries under the trust for sale). If A then dies, B will remain the sole surviving trustee (and a further trustee should be appointed to act with him before a sale of the land is made, so that overreaching can take place).

(iii) If land is conveyed by deed to A and B as joint tenants in fee simple, the legal estate will vest in A and B as joint tenants as trustees upon the statutory trusts for the benefit of themselves as joint tenants in equity. If A dies, B will remain the sole owner at law and in equity. The trust for sale will then be at an end and B as sole owner, will be entitled to sell the land without the necessity of appointing an additional trustee to act with him.[8]

[7] See pp. 30 and 70.

[8] See pp. 73–75.

JOINT TENANCY OR TENANCY IN COMMON

Since 1925, as we have seen, a legal estate cannot be held in undivided shares; the equitable interest of the beneficial co-owners under the trust for sale, on the other hand, may be held either jointly or in common. Which it is will usually be indicated by the terms of the grant. A conveyance on sale or transfer is drafted by the purchaser, not the vendor, and it is for co-purchasers to decide whether they wish to hold jointly, or to have shares, and to word the conveyance or transfer accordingly. The normal practice is to include in the conveyance or transfer an express declaration of trust as to how the beneficial interest is to be held, and this will be conclusive in any subsequent dispute between the parties.[9] Thus, if land is conveyed to A and B "jointly at law and in equity,"[10] both the legal estate and the beneficial interest will be held by A and B as joint tenants. Conversely, if land is conveyed to A and B as tenants in common, or if *words* are used, such as "equally" or "in equal shares" (called *words of severance*),[11] or if the grant otherwise shows an intention that each co-owner shall have a distinct share, then A and B will hold the beneficial interest as tenants in common (although of course the legal estate will be held jointly).

It is only where the terms of the grant are silent or ambiguous on the point that it becomes necessary to invoke certain rules in order to determine the nature of the beneficial interest of co-owners. Here the general rule is that a grant to two or more persons without words of severance creates a beneficial joint tenancy. Thus, if land is conveyed simply to A and B, they will be entitled jointly both at law and in equity. But this rule is subject to two qualifications.

First, there are certain circumstances in which equity may presume that a tenancy in common was intended, unless there is an express indication to the contrary namely:

(i) When the co-owners have purchased the property and put up the purchase money in unequal proportions: the presumption then is that they intend to have shares in the property proportionate to their contributions.[12]

[9] *Barton v. Morris* [1985] 1 W.L.R. 1257, *Goodman v. Gallant* [1986] Fam. 106. *C.f. Huntingford v. Hobbs* (1992) 24 H.L.R. 652, where the clause in a registered transfer that the survivor of co-owners can give a valid receipt for capital monies (which is normally used where the doctrine of survivorship is intended to apply) was not sufficient to constitute an express declaration of trust, to hold as joint tenants. Note that an express declaration of trust will not preclude a resulting trust in favour of a *third party* in the circumstances discussed below, see pp. 68–70.

[10] "Jointly," on its own, might refer only to the legal estate (although in that sense it is redundant).

[11] As to severance see p. 66.

[12] But this is conclusively rebuttable by an express declaration of trust: see *Barton v. Morris,* note 9 (property was conveyed to A and B jointly, though B contributed only £900 of £40,000 purchase price: B was held solely entitled on A's death).

(ii) When the co-owners are mortgagees, having taken the property as security for a loan which they have made: in this case it is immaterial whether they have advanced the loan money equally or unequally.

(iii) When the co-owners are partners and hold the property as part of their partnership assets.

The second qualification to the general rule concerning beneficial co-ownership is sometimes expressed by saying that joint tenancy cannot exist without the presence of the *four unities*. These are the unities of possession, interest, title and time. Unity of *possession* means that each co-owner has possession of the whole, and none can lay claim to separate ownership of any particular part of the property. This is essential to any form of co-ownership, not merely to joint tenancy. Unity of *interest* means that each co-owner has the same interest both in quantum and in duration. Thus, if one co-owner has a three-quarters interest and the other a one-quarter interest, or if one has a life interest and the other a fee simple concurrently, this unity is lacking and they hold as tenants in common. Unity of *time* means that the interest of each co-owner has vested at the same time, so that if property is given to all the children of A who attain 21, this unity will usually be lacking. Unity of *title* means that each co-owner derives title from the same instrument. It follows that if a joint owner assigns his beneficial interest the assignee becomes tenant in common since he holds, not under the original grant, but under the assignment.

As a touchstone for joint tenancy the four unities appear to add nothing to the basic criteria outlined above. The first unity (possession) is irrelevant, since it applies to all forms of co-ownership. The second (interest) is self-evident — co-owners who have distinct shares or interests, whether equal or unequal, are by definition tenants in common. (Joint owners are notionally one person owning the whole property and so individual ownership of a share or interest necessarily precludes joint tenancy).[13] The third unity (time) is misleading, since there is nothing to prevent co-owners in whom a beneficial interest vests at different times from holding jointly if the grant so indicates.[14] Finally, the fourth unity (title) is redundant as assignment by a joint owner creates a tenancy in common, not because unity of title is lacking between the assignee and the other joint owners (a purely formalistic concept), but because in substance the law recognises assignment as a means of severance, *i.e.* converting joint tenancy into tenancy in common.[15] Thus, the question of joint tenancy or tenancy in common can be answered quite satisfactorily without recourse to the four unities doctrine.

[13] See p. 61.
[14] See M. & W. pp. 421–422.
[15] See below.

SEVERANCE

Severance is a process by which joint tenancy is converted into tenancy in common, thereby eliminating the *jus accrescendis* or right of survivorship. Of course, after 1925 severance is only possible with respect to the beneficial interest under the statutory trust for sale, because the legal estate cannot be held in undivided shares.

The *jus accrescendi* precludes severance of a joint tenancy on death (whether by will or by intestate succession), but there is nothing to prevent joint beneficial owners from effecting a severance during their lifetimes (*inter vivos*). In principle an absolute owner can do what he wishes with his own property, and it follows that joint owners can, simply by agreement among themselves, convert their beneficial joint tenancy into tenancy in common.[16] Equally, a course of conduct indicating such an agreement may suffice to sever the beneficial interest.[17] Failing such agreement, any joint tenant can since 1925 sever his interest by giving written notice to the others.[18] The other means by which severance can be affected are by assignment or by acquiring a different estate in the same land or by homicide.[19]

As examples, A, B and C are joint owners at law and in equity, and subsequently agree to hold the beneficial interest as tenants in common, the result is (i) that they still hold the legal estate jointly on trust for sale, but (ii) that the beneficial interest is now held in equal shares (as severance always takes place in equal proportions irrespective of the amount of any initial contributions). When A and B later die, C will remain sole trustee of the legal estate, holding it on trust for himself (one-third share) and for those entitled under the will or intestacy of A (one-third share) and of B (one-third share). Suppose, however, that A and B would not agree to sever, but that C served a notice of severance on them. The result would be (i) that A, B and C would remain joint trustees of the legal estate, but (ii) that they would now hold it on trust for A and B (two-thirds) as joint tenants, and C (one-third) as tenant in common. On A's death the *jus accrescendi* would operate with respect both to the legal estate and to his beneficial interest. B and C could then be the joint trustees of the legal estate and in equity B would be solely entitled to two-thirds and C to one-third.

Severance also occurs where a joint tenant assigns his beneficial interest *e.g.* by sale, gift, mortgage or bankruptcy, although, once again, this cannot affect the legal estate. Thus if A, B and C are jointly entitled to the beneficial interest and A assigns his interest to

[16] *Williams v. Hensman* (1861) 1 J & H 546.

[17] *Burgess v. Rawnsley* [1975] Ch. 429.

[18] LPA 1925, s.36(2) proviso. No severance of the legal estate is permitted.

[19] The unlawful killing of one joint tenant by another automatically severs the beneficial joint tenancy—as the killer should not benefit from his actions.

X, X will become tenant in common as between himself and the others, who will remain joint tenants between themselves.

Again, if A, B and C are joint tenants for life and A acquires a different estate from that held as joint tenant *e.g.* the fee simple in remainder or in reversion, severance will take place. A's life interest will merge in the fee simple and he will become a beneficial tenant in common as between himself and B and C. It must, however, be noticed that if one of several joint tenants acquires the interest of another, so that his interest becomes greater merely in quantum than that of the others, severance occurs with regard only to the interest so acquired. For example, if A, B and C are joint tenants in fee simple of the beneficial interest and A acquires the interest of B, A will become tenant in common as between himself and C with regard only to the one-third interest which he has acquired from B. He will remain joint tenant with C in relation to the remaining two-thirds interest.

Where land is unregistered, whatever method of severance of joint tenancy is used, notice of severance should be written on the deed by which the property was originally conveyed to the joint tenants. This procedure is commonly called 'endorsing a memorandum of severance on the conveyance'. In the absence of such a memorandum, the beneficial interests of tenants in common, arising from severance, would be overridden on a sale by a *sole* surviving joint owner, provided that he conveys as "beneficial owner".[20] For example, suppose A and B purchase property as beneficial joint tenants and subsequently A serves a written notice of severance on B, but fails to note the severance on the original conveyance to A and B. On A's death B might purport to sell the property as sole "beneficial owner". In these circumstances, as there is no memorandum of severance on the original conveyance, warning the purchaser that the beneficial joint tenancy has been converted into a tenancy in common (and thus that A's estate is now entitled to A's equitable share), the purchaser is entitled to assume that B sells as sole beneficial owner *i.e.* as the absolute owner, under the doctrine of survivorship and that he purchases free from any beneficial interests.[21]

In the case of registered land, when co-owners purchase property as beneficial joint tenants they are registered as the joint proprietors of the property. On severance of the joint tenancy they, of course, remain joint registered proprietors of the legal estate, as this cannot be severed. Nevertheless, the beneficial interests held as tenants in common, should be protected by the entry of a restriction on the

[20] And complies with the other provisions of the Law of Property (Joint Tenants) Act 1964. See pp. 73–75 below.

[21] Again, so long as the conditions laid down in the Law of Property (Joint Tenants) Act 1964 are met, see pp. 73–75. But it may be doubted whether a purchaser who, by some other means, had actual notice of severance would be permitted to rely on that Act.

register.[22] This warns a purchaser that no disposition of the land can be made by a sole surviving proprietor (unless by order of the Registrar or the court) and so on sale a second trustee must be appointed in order to overreach the beneficial interests. If no such restriction is entered the purchaser will still be bound by the interest of a beneficiary in actual occupation, who will have an overriding interest.[23]

IMPLIED CO-OWNERSHIP

The position has been considered where dispositions are made *expressly* in favour of beneficial co-owners. However, co-ownership may also arise by implication, *e.g.* where land has been conveyed into the name of one person (A) alone, but another (X) has paid a substantial contribution to the purchase price. In such cases, unless it appears that X's intention was to make a gift (or a loan) to A, a *resulting trust* may arise in favour of X to the extent of his contribution.[24] This means that the property returns to benefit X and so the land will be held by A, on trust for himself and X, as beneficial tenants in common. This principle has acquired particular importance in recent years, mainly in cases concerning the matrimonial or quasi-matrimonial home.

It appears from these cases,[25] that, for a resulting trust to arise, where contributions have been made, there must be a common intention between the parties that they should hold as co-owners. It has long been accepted that a common intention will be inferred from a party making a direct contribution to the purchase price of the property *e.g.* by paying the mortgage instalments or the deposit for the property. However, it now seems clear that minor contributions to maintaining the property will not be sufficient to imply a resulting trust *e.g.* painting and decorating the property or contributing to the household expenses.

If there is insufficient contribution to infer a resulting trust but there is an agreement or understanding between the parties, that they will hold as beneficial co-owners and a party, relying on that agreement acts

[22] As they are minor interests, see pp. 225–226. No restriction need be registered where co-owners hold as joint tenants in law and equity as the doctrine of survivorship applies and the sole survivor can give a valid receipt for the purchase monies.

[23] Under LRA 1925, s.70(1)(g), see pp. 223–224.

[24] *Dyer v. Dyer* (1788) 2 Cox. Eq. 92, *Gissing v. Gissing* [1971] A.C. 886 and *Lloyd's Bank Plc v. Rosset* [1991] A.C. 107. *Cf.* the situation where a constructive trust arises (note 26 below) or proprietary estoppel, discussed at pp. 161–162 and see *Grant v. Edwards* [1986] Ch. 638. As to improvements to matrimonial property, see Matrimonial Proceedings and Property Act 1970, s.37.

[25] See in particular *Gissing v. Gissing* and *Lloyds Bank Plc v. Rosset,* note 24 above.

to his detriment, by making contributions to the property in the belief that he has an interest, the courts may impose a constructive trust and thus enforce the claim to an interest in the property.[26]

If implied co-ownership between A and X is established the following rules apply:

(i) The legal estate in the land is held by A as trustee on trust for sale.[27]

(ii) As beneficial co-owner in equity X is entitled equally with A to possession of the land, and is entitled to be consulted before any disposition of the land is made.[28]

(iii) As sole trustee, A is unable to pass a good title, *i.e.* on a sale, mortgage or other disposition of the land he cannot overreach X's beneficial interest. Nevertheless a third party acquiring a legal estate from A will not be bound by X's interest (which of course is merely equitable) if X has consented expressly or impliedly to the disposition,[29] or if the third party had no notice of X's interest (in the case of unregistered land) or if the interest is *not* overriding nor a protected minor interest (where land is registered).[30]

In the case of unregistered land what constitutes notice for this purpose is problematical. It is necessary to distinguish between two different questions, namely (a) whether a purchaser has notice that some person other than (or as well as) the vendor is in occupation, and (b) whether the fact that such person is in occupation is of itself notice that he has, or may have, a beneficial interest. Since a purchaser investigating his vendor's title is bound to make proper enquiries and inspections, he will almost inevitably have constructive notice of the fact of occupation.[31] The question remains whether this necessarily points to the conclusion that the occupier has a beneficial interest in the land. Occupation which is inconsistent with the vendor's title will usually amount to constructive notice of the occupier's interest: thus if A is purporting to sell with vacant possession, occupation by a tenant will be constructive notice of his rights under the lease.[32]

[26] See *Eves v. Eves* [1975] 1 W.L.R. 1338. and pp. 161–162. Alternatively, the circumstances may give rise to proprietary estoppel, see note 24 above.

[27] By a somewhat strained interpretation of SLA 1925, s.36(4). See *Bull v. Bull* [1955] 1 Q.B. 234, *Williams & Glyn's Bank Ltd v. Boland* [1981] 1 A.C. 487.

[28] *Bull v. Bull*; *Williams & Glyn's Bank Ltd v. Boland*, see n. 27 and pp. 58, 59 and 71–73.

[29] In any event, where it is deemed to be the common intention of the parties that the mortgage takes priority, X's interest cannot have priority over a mortgage entered into at the time when A and X acquired the land, see *Bristol & West Building Society v. Henning* [1985] 1 W.L.R. 778 (unregistered land) and *Paddington Building Society v. Mendelsohn* (1985) 50 P. & C.R. 244 (registered land).

[30] See p. 57 and pp. 223–226.

[31] See p. 30 note 14.

[32] *Hunt v. Luck* [1902] 1 Ch. 428.

Joint occupation by a member of A's family or household, however, seems not to be inconsistent with A's title. Nevertheless, a purchaser should still be put on enquiry as to whether the family members hold any beneficial interests in the property; if full enquiries are not made, it is likely that a purchaser will have constructive notice of any beneficial interests they may have.[33] Where land is registered, the fact that the registered proprietor is in occupation does not exclude possession or occupation by others, be they a spouse or family members. If such other person has a beneficial interest under a trust for sale, it is capable of being protected on the register, by entering a restriction, as it is a minor interest. Even if this has not been done, if the beneficiary is also in actual occupation of the land he will have an overriding interest, which will bind a purchaser, unless overreached.[34]

In view of this it has become the invariable practice to make full enquiries, not only as to who is occupying the property, but also as to who, apart from the vendor, has or may have a beneficial interest. It is on the latter point that serious doubts may arise. The question whether someone whose name does not appear on the legal title has acquired a beneficial interest under a resulting trust is a difficult one of mixed fact and law, which may require a decision of the court. In practice, therefore, persons who are occupying the property, and who *might* be held to have a beneficial interest, are usually asked for their formal consent to the transaction, or for an undertaking to release their interest.

One final point needs to be made. As has already been seen,[35] where land is held on trust for sale, and a dispute arises as to sale, any person interested may apply to the court, under section 30 of the Law of Property Act 1925, and in most cases an order for sale and a division of the proceeds between those beneficially entitled will be the almost inevitable result. It follows that any protection afforded to an occupier who has a beneficial interest in the land is unlikely to prevent the land being sold if an application is made under this section.

OVERREACHING

If in the example discussed above the land had originally been conveyed into the names of A *and* B as joint owners and trustees for

[33] See *Kingsnorth Finance Co Ltd v. Tizard* [1986] 1 W.L.R. 783 (an unregistered land case where the purchaser was held to have imputed notice, through an agent, of a separated wife's equitable interest in the property, as the couple's children still lived in the property). *Cf. Caunce v. Caunce* [1969] (unregistered land, where joint occupation of a wife was held not to constitute notice of her interest). The decision in *Caunce v. Caunce* was criticised in *Williams & Glyn's Bank Ltd v. Boland* (a case concerning registered land): see note 27.

[34] *Williams & Glyn's Bank Ltd v. Boland* (see note 27). As to minor interests, overriding interests and actual occupation, see pp. 223–226.

[35] See p. 58 and see also pp. 71–73 below.

sale of the legal estate, but A, B and X had all contributed to the purchase, a conveyance on sale or a mortgage by A and B would comply with the statutory requirement as to payment of capital money,[36] and accordingly would overreach all beneficial interests under the trust, including that of X. At this point it is necessary to consider more fully what is meant by "overreach."

The expression is not defined by statute, nor does it occur in the specific provisions protecting purchasers (including lessees and mortgagees) from either a tenant for life of settled land or trustees for sale.[37] However, section 2 of the Law of Property Act 1925 refers to "conveyances overreaching certain equitable interests," and in this context the term has generally been equated with *detaching* beneficial interests from the land in the hands of the purchaser and *attaching* them to the proceeds in the hands of the trustees.

If the land is sold, the notion that the purchaser's estate is unencumbered with any beneficial interests under a trust affecting the land, and that those beneficial interests themselves attach to the proceeds of sale, is intelligible. But if the land is merely mortgaged to secure a loan representing only a fraction of the land's value, it makes little sense to regard the interests of the beneficiaries as attaching only to the sum loaned. For this reason it might be more apt to define overreaching simply as "gaining priority over." Alternatively, the effect of overreaching in the case of a mortgage can be expressed in terms of detaching the beneficial interests from the land (as security in the hands of the mortgagee) and attaching them (a) to the sum loaned, and (b) to the equity of redemption, *i.e.* the mortgagor's interest in the land subject to the mortgage.[38] As concerns either a purchaser or a mortgagee the result is the same; he gains priority over the beneficial interests. His estate or mortgage accordingly is not subject to them, and the beneficiaries under the trust, whether or not they were in actual occupation of the land at the date of the disposition,[38] are relegated to their rights against the trustees personally.

RIGHTS OF BENEFICIAL OWNERS UNDER TRUSTS FOR SALE

The trust for sale imposed by statute whenever beneficial co-ownership in possession arises is evidently intended to achieve two

[36] "proceeds of sale or other capital money shall not be paid to . . . fewer than two persons as trustees for sale, except where the trustee is a corporation . . ." (LPA 1925, ss.2(1)(ii), 27(2)).

[37] SLA 1925, s.72 (see pp. 48–49; LPA 1925, s.27(1) (see pp. 57–58).

[38] *City of London B.S. v. Flegg* [1988] A.C. 54, reversing a decision of the Court of Appeal which had raised serious doubts as to the efficacy of the whole overreaching process.

purposes: first, to simplify conveyancing[39] and secondly, to establish a procedure for resolving disputes between co-owners.[40] In connection with the latter purpose, a distinction should be drawn between three quite different situations in which a trust for sale may operate. First, where it is employed merely as a means of avoiding the application of the Settled Land Act 1925 in the case of settlements. Secondly, where it is employed with the positive intention that the property should in fact be sold at once, and that the beneficiaries should be entitled only to their respective shares or interests in the proceeds of sale, not to the land itself. Thirdly, where it is imposed by statute, regardless of the parties' intention, in the case of beneficial co-ownership in possession.

Of these three situations, the third is by far the most important today, applying as it does to most private houses as well as to very many commercial partnership properties. It has little in common with the other two situations, which in turn differ totally from one another. Nevertheless, the same statutory provisions, in respect of the trust for sale machinery, apply in principle to all three; and, in particular, all three are governed alike by section 30 of the Law of Property Act 1925. Under this section if trustees for sale refuse to sell or to exercise their powers, or if any requisite consent cannot be obtained, any person interested may apply to the court for an order giving effect to the proposed transaction, and the court may make such order as it thinks fit.

In the first situation, where a settlement is made by way of express trust for sale, it has already been noted that an order for sale is likely to be refused if the court holds that sale would defeat the underlying purpose of the trust.[41] In the second situation, however, where the terms of a disposition make it clear that the beneficiaries are intended to take the proceeds, not the land itself, an order for sale will be virtually mandatory if a dispute arises between them.[42]

It is in the third situation, where beneficial co-owners are entitled in possession, that most disputes occur, particularly with respect to the matrimonial[43] or quasi-matrimonial home, when the relationship between the co-owners breaks up. Little purpose would be served by attempting to review here the vast body of case law on this vexed and important topic. However, what should be remembered is that the inherent problems of co-ownership, if the parties cannot agree either to continue living together, or to dispose of the property and divide

[39] By overreaching.
[40] Under LPA 1925, s.30.
[41] See pp. 58–59.
[42] See *Barclay v. Barclay* [1970] 2 Q.B. 677.
[43] In disputes between husband and wife the courts should proceed under their matrimonial rather than their property jurisdiction (*Williams v. Williams* [1976] Ch. 278).

the proceeds, can in the last resort be resolved only by applying to the court, and the court may then have little choice but to order a sale of the property. Indeed it is of the essence of a trust for sale, at least in principle, that the property must be sold, unless all the owners agree in postponing sale, or unless it appears that sale would defeat the true purpose of the trust.[44] Manifestly if the parties are in dispute there is no such concurrence, nor does the original purpose of the trust continue, if that purpose was joint occupation.

What is not clear, however, is that the equitable doctrine of conversion (by which, in theory, an interest in land held on trust for sale is regarded from the outset as an interest in money)[45] is of no relevance in deciding questions of substance. Beneficial co-owners under the statutory trust for sale have an interest in land, and are entitled to possession of the land.[46] If a dispute arises, and the court is constrained to order sale, this is not because it regards the parties as interested in the proceeds only, but because sale may be the only fair or practicable solution. On the other hand, the doctrine may govern questions of definition: thus, the expression "personalty" used in a will, for instance,[47] has been held to include a trust for sale in land.

DETERMINATION OF CO-OWNERSHIP

Co-ownership may come to an end by union or by partition.

1. By union

One co-owner may become solely entitled to the whole beneficial interest, *e.g.* by operation of the *jus accrescendi.* In that event the beneficial co-ownership will be at an end. The statutory trust for sale will cease to apply,[48] and by the Law of Property (Amendment) Act 1926 nothing in the Law of Property Act 1925 affects the right of a survivor of joint tenants, who is solely and beneficially interested, to deal with his legal estate as if it were not held on trust for sale.

[44] *Re Mayo* [1943] Ch. 302, *Jones v. Challenger* [1961] 1 Q.B. 176; distinguish *Re Buchanan-Wollaston* [1939] Ch. 738. See also *Jones v. Jones* [1977] 1 W.L.R. 438 (a co-owner out of occupation was not entitled to rent from another in occupation); distinguish the situation in *Dennis v. McDonald* [1982] Fam. 63 (where a co-owner was wrongfully excluded by another and was entitled to occupation rent).

[45] See p. 56.

[46] *Bull v. Bull; Williams & Glyn's Bank Ltd v. Boland.* (see note 27). The absurd implications of the contrary view need hardly be stated.

[47] *Re Kempthorne* [1930] 1 Ch. 268, *Irani Finance Ltd. v. Singh* [1971] Ch. 59 (regarding charging orders). *Cf. Cooper v. Critchley* [1955] Ch. 431.

[48] *Re Cook* [1948] Ch. 212.

Nonetheless, a purchaser might still be concerned to ensure that there has been no previous severance of the beneficial interests preventing the doctrine of survivorship from applying. If there had been severance the trust for sale would continue, and the appointment of another trustee would be necessary if the beneficial interests were to be overreached. In order to simplify proof of title, where land is unregistered, the Law of Property (Joint Tenants) Act 1964 provides that the survivor of joint tenants[49] shall, in favour of a purchaser of the legal estate, be *deemed* to be solely and beneficially interested if the conveyance contains a statement that he is so interested.[50] Say, for instance, A and B originally co-owned property as beneficial joint tenants, but on A's death, B, as sole surviving owner of the property purports to sell to a purchaser. To rely on the Act the purchaser must satisfy himself that:

- (i) in the original conveyance A and B bought as beneficial joint tenants,
- (ii) there is a death certificate providing evidence of A's death,
- (iii) in the conveyance to the purchaser, B states that he is solely and beneficially interested in the property,
- (iv) there is no memorandum (or note) of severance on the conveyance[51] to A and B (which would be evidence that their joint tenancy had been severed after they bought),
- (v) a bankruptcy search for A and B is clear (as the bankruptcy of either would have automatically severed the joint tenancy).

If any of these conditions is not satisfied the purchaser should insist that a second trustee is appointed to overreach any beneficial interests which may exist.

Where land is registered the Act does not apply. As has been seen, where the land is originally purchased as beneficial joint tenants both the co-owners will be registered as joint proprietors of the property. If one of two joint tenants dies, on the production of the death certificate, the survivor can apply to have the deceased's name deleted from the register. Again a purchaser may be concerned that the co-ownership has not in fact terminated because severance has taken place previously or another person has a beneficial interest in the

[49] This must mean joint *beneficial* owners in equity, thus the Act would not apply if, although the conveyance to the joint tenants contained no words of severance, the case was one in which there was an unrebutted equitable presumption of tenancy in common (see pp. 64–65). Nor does it protect a purchaser against interests held by a tenant in common under a resulting trust (see p. 68).

[50] S.1(1) as amended by the Law of Property (Miscellaneous Provisions) Act 1994, Sched. 1, para. 3, due to come into force on July 1, 1995.

[51] See p. 67.

property under implied co-ownership. A purchaser can be satisfied that there has been no severance (and also that he is not bound by the interests of a beneficiary under implied co-ownership), if he sees i) that there is no restriction on the register, warning a purchaser that he must overreach and ii) that there is no beneficiary in actual occupation of the premises, with an overriding interest.[52]

2. By partition

Partition is a physical division of the land amongst the beneficial co-owners. This can be effected by the trustees, with the consent of the beneficiaries, and the court may on application order partition if it thinks fit.[53]

[52] See pp. 223–226.
[53] LPA 1925, ss.28, and 30. Or alternatively sale of the property, which may be more convenient.

10. The perpetuity rule

COMMON LAW RULE

The courts have always striven to prevent property owners, and in particular land owners, from tying up their property by means of settlements for an excessive length of time. To a considerable extent this is now governed by legislation, such as the Settled Land Act 1925, which as we have seen greatly simplifies dispositions of the legal estate in land that is subject to a settlement. Equally, however, it is the policy of the law to limit the extent to which equitable or beneficial interests in land or its proceeds or income may be tied up. Two weapons which the judges invented for this purpose were known as the old and the modern perpetuity rules, both of which existed until 1926. The Law of Property Act 1925 abolished the old rule, leaving us with only the modern rule to consider. It is called the modern rule in order to distinguish it from the other rule, but in fact it is a rule of some antiquity.[1]

The operation of the modern rule (hereafter referred to as the "common law rule") has been substantially modified by the Perpetuities and Accumulations Act 1964, but it is necessary to consider it first without reference to the Act. As is explained below, the Act does not replace the common law rule, and if a disposition complies with that rule the Act does not apply.

The first point to notice about the common law rule is that it applies only to *contingent* interests in property.[2] An interest is contingent for this purpose so long as the identity of the beneficiary in question is unknown or so long as any condition which has been

[1] In its present form the rule was finally settled in *Cadell v. Palmer* (1833) 1 Cl. & Fin. 372.

[2] Including both realty and personalty. The rule does not apply to a vested interest *i.e.* an interest where no conditions need be fulfilled and the beneficiaries are ascertainable. The existence of a prior interest does not mean that a gift is contingent *e.g.* where there is a gift to A for life, remainder to B for life, B has a vested interest, although the interest is not vested in possession until A dies.

attached to the grant of his interest remains unfulfilled. Thus, if property is given to the first son of A, and when the gift comes into operation A has no son, the interest given to the son is contingent; the identity of the first son is unknown, and of course A might never have a son. Again, if property is given to B if and when he attains the age of 21, and he has not already attained 21 when the gift comes into operation B's interest is contingent; a condition has been attached to his interest which has not yet been fulfilled, and which might never be fulfilled.

The law allows a certain period for the vesting of a contingent interest *i.e.* for the conditions to which the gift is subject to be fulfilled and for the beneficiaries to be ascertained. This period is known as the "perpetuity period." The perpetuity period is the period of the lives of any persons referred to (expressly or by implication) in the gift, who are living or conceived when the gift comes into operation, plus a further period of 21 years. The underlying principle is to treat as valid only those gifts which *cannot* vest beyond a period comprising the lives of the present generation plus a further 21 years (the rationale being to enable the next generation to attain its majority).[3] The lives of any persons may be relevant for determining the perpetuity period, provided that i) they are referred to expressly or by implication in the gift, ii) they are living or conceived when the gift comes into operation, and iii) they exclusively have some causal connection with the vesting of the interest. Only human lives can be the lives in being. The expression "lives in being" may conveniently be used to denote these lives that are *relevant* in defining the perpetuity period in a particular case.

Frequently the lives in being will be implied as there is no one expressly named in the grant as the life or lives in being. In such a case, the implied lives will be those persons whose lives have some obvious connection with the vesting of the gift. Therefore, the implied lives in being will be, often (but not always), the potential beneficiaries of the gift or the source of potential beneficiaries *e.g.* a parent or grandparent. However, it is not absolutely necessary to receive any benefit or to be a relative of the potential beneficiaries to be the implied life in being.

Under the perpetuity rule, *a contingent interest is void if it might possibly vest after the end of the perpetuity period.* In other words an interest is void unless, when the gift comes into operation, it is certain that the interest will vest, *i.e.* that the identity of the beneficiary will be known and any condition attached to the gift will be fulfilled, before the end of that period — if indeed the interest ever *does* vest. It is in the nature of any contingent interest that it might *never* vest,

[3] The Family Law Reform Act 1969 reduced the age of majority from 21 to 18 years, but the perpetuity period has remained unaltered.

(*e.g.* a gift to A when Harry becomes king and Harry may never become king), but for the purposes of the perpetuity rule that is irrelevant. The rule is designed merely to avoid late vesting, and to ensure that the destination of property cannot remain in doubt beyond the prescribed period. If an *inter vivos* gift does fail for perpetuity there will normally be a resulting trust to the donor, *i.e.* the property returns to the donor. In the case of a gift by will, the property will normally go to the beneficiaries entitled to the residue of the estate, (*i.e.* the residuary devisee or legatee) or to the person entitled on intestacy.

It is important to note that the rule is applied, and the perpetuity period starts to run, at the date when the gift comes into operation. There is no waiting to see whether the gift vests within the perpetuity period. A contingent interest is therefore to be judged valid or void *ab initio*,[4] (*i.e.* at the beginning when the gift comes into operation), in the light of the facts as they are at that date (and in particular with respect to lives *then* in being). The operative date is (a) the date on which the deed was executed, in the case of a gift *inter vivos,* (b) the date of the testator's death, in the case of a gift by will.

We may now consider some examples:

(i) Property is given to A for life with remainder absolutely to his first son to attain 21. Unless when the gift comes into operation a son of A has already attained 21, the remainder is contingent. The question therefore is whether this interest might possibly vest after the end of the perpetuity period. As the source of potential beneficiaries, A is the only relevant life in being, and since any son of his who attains 21 is bound to do so (if at all) within 21 years after A's death, the interest is valid.[5] Note that, unless A himself is already dead, the lives of any of his sons living when the gift comes into operation cannot be regarded as relevant in defining the perpetuity period. This is because it is possible that no such son might attain 21, but that A might have a further son (born after the gift came into operation, and therefore not a life in being), who might attain 21, and do so more than 21 years after his brothers' deaths (though not, of course, more than 21 years after his father A's death).

(ii) T by his will leaves property to his first grandson to attain 21. Unless at T's death a grandson has already attained 21 the gift is contingent. If any of T's children survive him, they (as the source of potential beneficiaries and being alive at the date of T's death) will constitute the relevant lives in being. The gift is clearly valid since no grandchild of T can possibly attain 21 years more than 21 years after

[4] It is here that the 1964 Act makes the most important of its changes: see pp. 84–85.

[5] If an interest is conditional on attaining an age *greater* than 21, and would be void for that reason alone, the age of 21 is substituted (LPA 1925, s.163, a provision now repealed for instruments taking effect after July 15, 1964, to which the 1964 Act applies), but note the different rules for special powers of appointment, see p. 84.

the death of the survivor of T's children. The gift would be even more obviously valid if no child of T survived him, since any grandchildren living at T's death would themselves be the relevant lives in being, as their lives effect the vesting of the gift.

The same gift would be void, however, if made *inter vivos.* Whether or not children or grandchildren of T were living at the date of the gift, T himself (as the ultimate source of potential beneficiaries) would be the only relevant life in being. He might subsequently have a child[6] (who of course would not be a life in being as he was born after the date of the gift), who in turn might have a child, who might be the first grandson of T to attain 21. This might happen more than 21 years after T's death.

(iii) In the above examples, the lives in being, by reference to which the perpetuity period was defined, were not specified by the donor, but were to be inferred from their connection with the vesting of the gift. Exceptionally, the gift itself may define the period within which it is to vest, by specifying the relevant lives in being. In one case,[7] a testator directed that property should be divided amongst such of his descendants as should be living 20 years after the death of the survivor of the descendants of Queen Victoria living at the testator's death. Clearly the gift did not infringe the perpetuity rule, since it was expressly limited to vest within the perpetuity period. Nevertheless such a gift would fail[8] if the specified lives in being were so numerous or so obscure as to be untraceable.

(iv) The converse of the above example occurs where an interest is made contingent on the happening of some event unconnected with the life of any particular person. Thus if property is given "to A in fee simple when the House of Lords is abolished," the identity of the sole beneficiary is known (as it was not in the previous examples), but the interest is contingent upon an event that may or may not happen. Unless it is certain that the event will happen (if it ever does) within the perpetuity period the interest is void *ab initio.* In this case the perpetuity period is a bare 21 years: although the beneficiary A is alive, his life has no causal connection with the contingency specified, and the interest might therefore vest (in his personal representatives) after his death.[9] The result would of course be different if the property were given "to A in fee simple if the House of Lords is abolished during his life."

(v) Similarly, an interest limited to vest at the expiry of a stated interval after the date of the gift will generally be void if the interval exceeds 21 years, *e.g.* where a testator leaves property to all his

[6] At common law no evidence is admissible to prove that a person is beyond the age of child bearing or begetting (but see p. 84).

[7] *Re Villar* [1929] 1 Ch. 243.

[8] For uncertainty, not for perpetuity: see *Re Moore* [1901] 1 Ch. 936.

[9] See *Re Engels* [1943] 1 All E.R. 506.

descendants (born whether before or after his death) who shall be living 30 years after his death.[10] Such an interest would, however, be valid if it were confined to living and identified beneficiaries, such as the testator's children. Here the interest would be conditional merely on survival to the vesting date (rather than on having been born by that date), and for this purpose the children themselves are, of course, relevant lives in being.

CLASS GIFTS

A class gift is a gift to a class of persons within a certain description, the amount of any one person's share being dependant on the number of members in the class.[11] For example, a gift of "£5000 to be divided between my grandchildren" is a class gift; whilst a gift of "£5000 to each of my grandchildren" is not.

For the purposes of the perpetuity rule a class gift is wholly contingent until the identity of *every* possible member of the class is known. Such a gift, therefore, is *wholly void* if when the gift comes into operation there is any possibility that the identity of every possible member of the class might not be known within the permitted period.[12] For example, if a testator gives property to be divided amongst all A's grandchildren (whether living at the testator's death or born thereafter), and A is alive when the will comes into operation, the gift is wholly void. This is because there is a possibility that A might have a child, who in turn has a child (A's grandchild) more than 21 years after A's death, thus outside the perpetuity period. Even grandchildren of A who are living at the date of the testator's death will take nothing as, under the perpetuity rule, a class gift is either wholly valid or wholly void.[13]

[10] As to whether such a gift would now be valid *ab initio* under the 1964 Act, see p. 84, note 18.

[11] *e.g. Re Villar* (note 7).

[12] *Pearks v. Moseley* (1880) 5 App. Cas 714 (but see p. 85).

[13] However, in some circumstances the rule of construction for class gifts, known as the rule in *Andrews v. Partington* (1791) 3 Bro. C.C. 401, may prevent infringement of the perpetuity rule. Under this rule, once one beneficiary has satisfied the condition in possession, the class closes to include all the potential beneficiaries then alive. For instance, suppose there was a devise in T's will to "his grandchildren to reach 21." If one beneficiary has satisfied the condition when the gift comes into operation, at the testator's death *e.g.* B, a grandchild is 21 at T's death, the class will close at that time to include all the grandchildren alive or conceived at the testator's death—any grandchildren conceived and born later being excluded from the class. The lives in being will then be the grandchildren alive at the testator's death—their lives have an exclusive connection with the vesting of the gift, as no grandchildren conceived and born after T's death can enter the class. Thus, the gift will be valid for perpetuities as it must vest in the grandchildren in the class, if at all, within the perpetuity period. Note however, that the rule will not assist where no potential beneficiary satisfies the relevant condition when the gift comes into operation. Further it does not apply if there is a contrary intention expressed *e.g.* a devise in a will "to my grandchildren *whenever born*" to reach 21.

SUBSEQUENT INTERESTS

If an interest infringes the perpetuity rule, a subsequent interest will not thereby be invalidated unless it is made dependent upon the same contingency. For example, if property is given for life to the first son of A to become a barrister, with remainder to B absolutely, the gift to the son is void unless either A is dead or a son of his has already become a barrister by the time that the gift comes into operation. There is no certainty that the identity of the first son to become a barrister will be known within the life of A plus a further period of 21 years. But the remainder to B is vested when the gift comes into operation (his identity is known and no condition has been attached to the gift) and it is valid. It will be observed that the perpetuity rule is in no way concerned with the question how long it may be before an interest falls into possession; it is solely concerned with the question how long it may be before a contingent interest ceases to be contingent and thus vests.

Had the gift been to the first son of A to become a barrister, but if no son of A becomes a barrister then to B, the gift to B would have been void. It would have been made dependent upon the same contingency which invalidated the prior gift.[14]

POWERS OF APPOINTMENT

The owner of property may transfer it to trustees directing them to hold it upon trust for such persons, or such members of a specified class of persons, as D may appoint. D is then said to have a power of appointment; he has the power to nominate the persons who are to take the property. D is called the donee of the power. A power of appointment is normally exercisable either by deed or by will, unless the instrument creating it otherwise indicates. If D is at liberty to appoint the property to anyone he pleases, including himself, the power is said to be a *general power* of appointment, but if D may appoint the property only amongst members of a specified class of persons, such as his own children, the power is said to be a *special power.*[15] The significance of the distinction is that property subject to a general power can virtually be treated by the donee as his own, whereas a special power has the effect of preventing him from so doing.

[14] See *Proctor v. Bishop of Bath and Wells* (1794) 2 Hy. Bl. 358.

[15] A power is also to be treated as a special power if exercisable only with the concurrence or consent of another person (1964 Act, s.7, confirming the common law rule: see *Re Earl of Coventry's Indentures* [1974] Ch.77).

For the purposes of the perpetuity rule the actual grant of a power of appointment itself is treated as the grant of an interest in property (as well as the interest arising from exercising the power). Therefore, the grant of the power is invalid unless when the grant comes into operation it is certain that the power will vest, if it vests at all, in an ascertainable person within the perpetuity period. Secondly, with one exception, the grant of a power is also void if any appointment under it could be made after the end of the perpetuity period. For example, if property is settled on A (a bachelor at the date of the grant) for life, with remainder to A's first son for life, with remainder to such of that son's children as he by deed or will may appoint, the power given to A's son is void. The perpetuity period in this case is the life of A together with a further period of 21 years, and A's son might make an appointment which came into operation after the end of this period. This second rule, however, has no application to a general power of appointment exercisable by the donee at any time without obtaining the consent of any other person.

Given the validity of the power, it may next become necessary to consider the validity of any appointment which the donee of the power makes in exercising it (unless, of course, the interest created by the appointment is itself vested). If the power is a general power, the appointment is treated in the same way as a gift of the donee's own property, and accordingly the perpetuity period for any contingent interest created by the appointment will start to run only when the appointment takes effect, *i.e.* when the power is *exercised.* If the power is a special power, however, the perpetuity period is regarded as having started to run when the power was *granted.* It follows that the lives in being with respect to appointments made under a special power are confined to those in being when the power was granted, whereas in the case of a general power they will include those in being when the power is exercised.

An example will illustrate the difference. Suppose that A holds a power of appointment over certain property, that he appoints by will to such of his children as may attain the age of 30, and that at his death he has two children, S aged 6 and D aged 3. The interest created by the appointment is contingent, and will remain so until both S and D attain 30 (or die previously). If the power were a *general* one, the perpetuity period would not start to run until the power was exercised, *i.e.* when the appointment took effect on A's death. S and D would themselves be the relevant lives in being, and the interest would be valid as it stands. If the power were a *special* one (*e.g.* to appoint amongst A's issue), however, the perpetuity period would be regarded as having started to run when the power was granted, at which time the only relevant life in being was A himself. It is evident that neither S nor D will attain 30 within the perpetuity period, *i.e.* within 21 years after A's death, and the interest would accordingly fail at common law, but by section 163 of the Law of Property Act 1925[16] it would be validated by substituting 21 for the stipulated age of 30.

THE PERPETUITIES AND ACCUMULATIONS ACT 1964

This Act makes important changes in the rule against perpetuities. It came into force on July 16, 1964, and (subject to minor exceptions) applies only to instruments taking effect on or after that date.[17] Its main provisions are of a *relieving* character, *i.e.* they are designed to try and save an interest from invalidity if it *infringes* the common law perpetuity rule. As the rule stands apart from the Act it must be applied first and the provisions of the Act have no application if the interest is valid without recourse to the Act. It it still necessary, therefore, to know the common law rule as it was before the Act.

There follows, in outline, some of the main provisions of the Act:

Section 1

A period of years not exceeding 80 may be specified by the grantor as the perpetuity period applicable to any disposition, instead of the normal period of lives in being plus 21 years.[18]

Section 2

For the purposes of the perpetuity rule, males under 14 years of age and females under 12 or over 55 years of age are presumed to be incapable of having children; but evidence is also admissible to show that a living person will or will not be able to have a child.[19]

Section 3

This, the most radical of the Act's provisions, abolishes the "no wait and see" rule.[20] It provides that an interest is not to be treated as void

[16] This section applies if the instrument creating the special power takes effect after 1925, but before July 16 1964; see note 5. Where the instrument creating the special power takes effect after July 15, 1964, the age reduction rules in s.4. of the 1964 Act apply; see note 17 and p. 85.

[17] With respect to appointments made under a special power of appointment, the Act applies only where the instrument creating the power takes effect on or after that date.

[18] It is doubtful whether this would apply to the gift mentioned at p. 81, note 10, unless the instrument expressly provided that the period stipulated should be the perpetuity period (see *Re Green's W.T.* [1985] 3 All E.R. 455).

[19] *C.f.* note 6. The possibility of adoption is also excluded by the presumption as to females over 55.

[20] See note 4.

on the ground merely that it *might* vest after the end of the perpetuity period. On the contrary it shall be treated as though it were not subject to the perpetuity rule until such time as it becomes established that it *will* vest after the end of the period.

Furthermore, for this purpose (*i.e.* for the purpose of "waiting and seeing" whether an interest does in fact vest within the period allowed) there is a statutory perpetuity period defined by reference to the lives of certain categories of persons specified in the section ("the statutory lives"). These include potential beneficiaries who are alive at the time of the grant and who under the stricter rule of common law, would often have been discounted.

Section 4

This section (a) repeals and replaces section 163 of the Law of Property Act 1925, and provides for age reduction, not to 21, but to the nearest age (of 21 or over) that will prevent infringement of the perpetuity rule[21]; (b) abolishes the rule that a class gift is either wholly valid or wholly void, by providing for exclusion of those members of the class whose inclusion would render the gift void.[22] It should be noted that these provisions only will be applied where the disposition has not already been validated either by section 2 (eliminating the possibility of a child being born) or by section 3 (allowing "wait and see" during the perpetuity period).

An example will illustrate the point; suppose T in his will leaves property to "the first child of his daughter A to reach 30" and at T's death A is alive. Initially, the common law rule must be applied to ascertain whether the gift is void for perpetuities. At common law A is the life in being (as she is the ultimate source of beneficiaries) and the perpetuity period is A's life plus 21 years. Thus the gift is void as A's first child may reach 30 more than 21 years after A's death. As the gift fails at common law the Act then must be applied. Section 2 will validate the gift if A is over 55 at the testator's death, as it is assumed that she can have no more children. Those children born (or conceived) at the testator's death, therefore, must be the lives in being and the first child must reach 30 (if at all) within their life times. This section will be of no assistance if A is still of child bearing years; in such a case the "wait and see" principle in section 3 will be applied. It is possible to "wait and see" for the statutory perpetuity period, which is the period of all the statutory lives plus 21 years. The statutory lives will include any potential donees (*e.g.* A's children alive at the time of T's death) and the parents and grandparents of any potential donees alive at the date the gift takes effect. If the first child does not reach

[21] S.4(1) and (2) and see note 5.
[22] S.4(3) and (4) and see p. 81.

30 by the end of the statutory perpetuity period, then the age reduction rules in section 4(1) apply. Suppose A's child B (who is not a statutory life in being as he was not born or conceived at T's death) will be aged 24 at the end of the statutory perpetuity period, under this provision, the age of 24 can be substituted as the vesting age; being the nearest age to 30 which will validate the gift.

If, on the other hand, this was a class gift to "all A's children who marry", the procedure would be slightly different. Let us assume that the same process has been followed by applying the common law rule and the relevant sections of the Act but that potentially the gift is invalid at the end of the statutory perpetuity period, as some of the children are married and some are not. Under section 4(4) the class will be split, so that the gift is valid in respect of those children who have fulfilled the condition at the end of the statutory perpetuity period and those who are not married will be excluded from the gift. On the other hand, if the gift was a class gift to "all A's children to marry and reach 30", if necessary, the age reduction rules under section 4(1) (as discussed previously) and then the class exclusion rules in section 4(3) may be combined to try and save as much of the gift as possible, by the end of the statutory perpetuity period.

Section 5

This validates, where necessary,[23] a gift limited to vest on the death of the survivor of a named person and any spouse of that person. Before the Act, a gift "to all the children of A who shall be living at the death of the survivor of A and any wife he may marry" was void, because A was the only relevant life in being, and any wife he married might survive him for more than 21 years, at which time the gift to the children would still not have vested. By section 5, however, such a gift is to be treated as if it were limited to vest (at the latest) immediately before the end of the perpetuity period. It follows that if a wife of A does survive him for 21 years, the gift to the children will vest in such of A's children as are living *at that time* (regardless of whether subsequently they survive A's wife).

Section 9

This section, subject to certain conditions, exempts from the common law perpetuity rule options granted to a lessee to purchase the reversion. It further provides that other options to acquire (for valuable consideration) any interest in land are subject to a perpetuity period of 21 years only.

[23] *i.e.* having "waited and seen" whether the gift in fact vests within the perpetuity period.

Section 10

By section 10, when a lifetime disposition creating any interest in land is void against a third party as it breaches the perpetuity rule, it is also void as regards the original parties to the contract. Thus, when an interest created *inter vivos* is void for perpetuity, no contractual remedy is available against the original grantor of the interest.[24]

EXCEPTIONS TO THE PERPETUITY RULE

1. Contractual obligations

Before the Act of 1964 the perpetuity rule did not apply to an action, whether for damages or for specific performance, to enforce a contractual obligation. For example, if a lease for 99 years conferred upon the tenant for the time being an option to purchase the reversion, and an action was brought against the original landlord upon his covenant to sell the reversion to the tenant, the perpetuity rule had no application, since the landlord's obligation, though contingent (in the sense that the option when granted might or might not be exercised), was merely contractual.[25] It was otherwise if an action was brought against a subsequent owner of the reversion. The perpetuity rule then applied because the action was based, not on a contractual obligation (as there was no privity of contract between the parties) but on the ground that the grant of the option created an immediate (but contingent) equitable interest in the reversion which would be enforceable by a decree of specific performance.[26] It followed that if the option might be exercised beyond the perpetuity period the contingent interest to which it gave rise was void and a subsequent owner of the reversion was not bound by it. However, an action for breach of contract would lie against the original grantor.[27] Similar principles applied to any other option to purchase land. The original grantor (or his estate) could always be sued, but the perpetuity rule applied to an action against a successor in title of the grantor (other than his personal representative) so it might fail. The Act of 1964 has made important changes in these rules which we have just considered[28] but it must be remembered that the Act applies only to instruments taking effect after its commencement *i.e.* after July 15, 1964.

[24] See note 25.
[25] *Hutton v. Watling* [1948] Ch. 26.
[26] In accordance with the principle discussed at pp. 27–28.
[27] *Woodall v. Clifton* [1905] 2 Ch. 257, *Worthing Corpn. v. Heather* [1906] 2 Ch. 532.
[28] ss.9 and 10. see p. 86.

2. Leases and mortgages

The perpetuity rule has no application to provisions in a lease, such as a covenant for renewal of the lease, which are designed to regulate the relationship of landlord and tenant, and are not concerned with merely ancillary matters. A similar exception applies to most provisions in mortgages.

3. Interests following a fee tail

The perpetuity rule does not apply to a remainder which is to take effect during the continuance of a fee tail or at the moment of its determination. For example, if Blackacre is settled on A in tail with a proviso that if at any time the tenant in tail of Blackacre should become entitled to Whiteacre in fee simple, Blackacre is to go over to B in tail, the remainder to B will be valid. This exception is somewhat misleading because the barring of the entail[29] at any time would defeat the remainder.

4. Charities

A gift over, upon a certain event, from one charity to another charity is valid even if that event might occur after the end of the permitted perpetuity period.

OTHER RULES

The perpetuity rule is one of several evolved originally by the courts, and later modified by statute, with the object of ensuring that property, including both capital (in the form of land, or a fund) and income (in the form of rents or interest or dividends), shall be freely disposable within a reasonable time by someone who is absolutely entitled. The perpetuity rule itself is primarily concerned with contingent interests arising out of settlements of capital. Certain other rules, which are outlined below, are concerned with directions as to the income of property. Their main application is to personal property such as trust funds and stocks and shares: accordingly they merit only brief mention in a book on real property.

The rule against perpetual trusts

If property is given to trustees on trust to apply the income to a certain purpose *e.g.* the maintenance of a tomb in a churchyard, the

[29] See p. 18.

interest created is already vested, and therefore no question arises on the perpetuity rule itself. Such dispositions nevertheless are objectionable on a number of grounds, of which the most relevant in the present context is that they tie up indefinitely the *corpus* or capital of the trust. Accordingly such trusts, commonly referred to as *purpose trusts,* are generally held void, although it seems they may be valid if expressly confined to the perpetuity period. This rule, which may be regarded as a particular aspect of the more general rule against inalienability,[30] is not established with the same clarity as the perpetuity rule itself. Its operation is not affected by the Perpetuities and Accumulations Act 1964.[31]

The rule is of little practical importance: it does not apply to charitable trusts, and private trusts on the other hand will usually be void, regardless of any question of perpetuity, if the objects are not ascertainable human beneficiaries.

The rule against accumulations

Property is sometimes given to trustees on trust to accumulate the income, *i.e.* to use it to purchase additional similar property,[32] for a stated period, and then hold the property and the accumulation on trust for specified beneficiaries.[33]

If the beneficiaries are of full age (*i.e.* 18 or over) and, apart from the direction to accumulate, absolutely entitled in possession to the property, they can set aside the direction and demand that the property itself be transferred to them by the trustees.[34] For example, if a testator leaves property on trust for A absolutely, but directs that until A reaches the age of 30 the income shall be accumulated, A can put an end to the accumulation at any time (provided he is of full age) and require the trustees to transfer the property to him. It follows in general that accumulation can effectively be directed only when beneficiaries of full age are *not* absolutely entitled in possession, *i.e.* when they have either a contingent interest only, or a future interest in the property. Thus, if in the above example the gift to A had been conditional on his attaining 30, A could require neither the property itself nor the income to be paid to him unless and until he attained 30.[35]

[30] See p. 17.
[31] See s.15(4).
[32] The instrument may also direct that the income from the additional property be similarly applied.
[33] Accumulations may also be directed for specific purposes, such as paying debts or raising portions. Such accumulations are in general exempt from the rule discussed here.
[34] Under the rule in *Saunders v. Vautier* (1841) 4 Beav. 115. The rule is equally applicable where the beneficiary is a charity.
[35] An express direction to accumulate excludes the operation of LPA 1925, s.175 (under which contingent gifts carry intermediate income).

Of course such a contingent interest would be valid if it complied with the perpetuity rule, and at common law any direction to accumulate that was confined to the perpetuity period would be valid. As a result of *Thellusson v. Woodford,*[36] however, Parliament resolved to subject accumulations to a more stringent rule, and accordingly passed the Accumulations Act 1800.

The rule today is to be found in the Law of Property Act 1925, ss.164-166, as amended by the Perpetuities and Accumulations Act 1964 (for instruments taking effect after the commencement of that Act). Today a direction to accumulate income if it is to be valid must be for one of the following periods:

(i) The life of the grantor or settlor.

(ii) 21 years from the death of the grantor, settlor or testator.

(iii) The minority or respective minorities of any person or persons living or conceived at the death of the grantor, settlor or testator.

(iv) The minority or respective minorities of any person or persons who under the terms of the instrument directing accumulation would, for the time being, if of full age, be entitled to the income directed to be accumulated.

To these the 1964 Act has added:

(v) 21 years from the date of the making of the disposition.

(vi) The minority or minorities of any person or persons living or conceived at that date.

In general a settlor may choose whichever of the periods he prefers, but where the direction is that income shall be wholly or partially accumulated for the purchase of land, only period (iv) may be chosen.

It will be observed that the only life period mentioned in the rule is the life of the settlor. It follows that a *testator* cannot validly direct accumulation of income during the lifetime of any person.

The term "minority", which is used in periods (iii), (iv) and (vi) refers to the infancy of a given person, *i.e.* the period from the moment when that person is born until he attains full age. If the settlor decides to make use of period (iii) or (vi) he must limit himself to the minorities of persons who are living or conceived at his death or the date of the settlement. But he may direct accumulation of income during the minorities of any such persons: those persons need not be beneficiaries. If the settlor decides to employ period (iv) he is not limited to the minorities of persons living or conceived at his own death or the date of the settlement. However, on the other hand, he can direct accumulation of income only during the minorities of certain beneficiaries, *i.e.* the beneficiaries who would, for the time being, be entitled to the income directed to be accumulated, if of full age. For example, property may be settled on A (a bachelor at the

[36] (1805) 11 Ves. 112.

date of the grant) for life, with remainder to such of A's children as are living at A's death, with a direction that if at A's death any such child is an infant the income from his share of the property shall be accumulated for him during his minority. This direction is valid under period (iv) although it does not fall within the terms of the period (iii) or (vi) as the direction is not to accumulate during the minorities of persons who are living or conceived at the death of the settlor or the date of the settlement.

Breach of the rule

If a direction to accumulate income is for a period exceeding that permitted by the perpetuity rule, the direction is wholly void.[37] If the direction does not infringe the perpetuity rule but infringes the accumulations rule, the direction is not wholly void. It is good for whichever of the permitted periods is most appropriate to the particular case, and is void only for the excess over that period. This means that the court will select whichever of the permitted periods it considers to be most appropriate in the particular case, and the direction to accumulate will then take effect for this period or for the period directed in the instrument, whichever turns out to be the shorter. For example, if a testator directs that the income of certain property shall be accumulated during the life of A and that the property with its accumulations shall then be divided equally among all A's children living at A's death, this direction does not infringe the perpetuity rule. However, it does infringe the accumulations rule. In this case the court will select the period of 21 years from the death of the testator as being the most appropriate period. Accumulation of income will then take place during this 21 year period or the period of the life of A, whichever turns out to be the shorter. If A is still living at the end of the 21 year period accumulation of income must then cease, but distribution of the property cannot take place until the death of A, as until A dies it cannot be ascertained who are the beneficiaries entitled to the property. The income accruing from the property between the end of the 21 year period and the death of A is to "go to and be received by the person or persons who would have been entitled thereto if such accumulation had not been directed"[38]; this will usually be the person or persons entitled to the testator's residuary estate.[39]

[37] It is doubtful whether the "wait and see" provisions of the 1964 Act, s.3 apply: see M. & W. pp. 304–306.

[38] LPA 1925, s.164(1).

[39] Or entitled on intestacy: see *Re Green's W.T.* [1985] 3 All E.R. 455.

11. Contracts for the disposition of land

The same substantive requirements apply to contracts to sell or otherwise dispose of land as to other contracts, *i.e.* all the conditions for the formation of a contract must be satisfied, such as offer and acceptance, intention to create legal relations and consideration. In addition, certain other rules apply to contracts for the disposition of land; these rules having been considerably altered following the enactment of the Law of Property (Miscellaneous Provisions) Act 1989, which generally applies to such contracts made *on or after* September 27, 1989. However, as disputes still may arise involving contracts entered into before this date it is necessary to consider the law prior to the Act, as well as the implications of the Act itself.

CONTRACTS PRE SEPTEMBER 27, 1989

Section 40(1) of the Law of Property Act 1925 applies to contracts created before September 27, 1989. This provides that "no action may be brought upon any contract for the sale or other disposition of land or any interest in land, unless the agreement upon which such action is brought, or some memorandum or note thereof, is in writing and signed by the party to be charged [*i.e.* the party sued] or by some other person thereunto by him lawfully authorised."

It is not necessary that the agreement itself should be in writing. All that is required is that before any action is brought to enforce it there shall be in existence some written document which is signed by the defendant and which sufficiently describes the subject-matter, identifies the parties, and states the consideration and other material terms of the agreement. No particular form is required, and it may be possible to spell out a sufficient memorandum from several documents (*e.g.* letters), one only of which is signed by the defendant, so long as on the face of them they are connected.[1] Even a document

[1] *Cf. Timmins v. Moreland Street Property Co. Ltd* [1958] Ch. 110, *Elias v. George Sahely & Co. (Barbados) Ltd* [1983] A.C. 646.

denying liability under the alleged contract will suffice, provided that it acknowledges that the contract exists. However, it seems that a document purporting to set out the terms of an agreement "subject to contract" (*i.e.* one which is not intended to be legally binding) cannot constitute a sufficient memorandum of an oral contract previously concluded in similar terms.[2]

If there is insufficient written evidence to satisfy the requirements of section 40(1), neither party can enforce the contract by an action for damages. The contract is not void, however, and may be relied on, *e.g.* as a *defence* to an action by a defaulting purchaser to recover his deposit.[3] More important, it may be enforced in equity by an action for specific performance, despite the lack of written evidence, provided that there are sufficient acts of part performance of the contract by the plaintiff. The equitable doctrine of part performance[4] is designed to prevent unfair advantage being taken of the absence of written evidence, where one party has allowed the other to act on the faith of an agreement between them. The conditions for its application include the following:

First, the parties must have made a definite binding contract: this condition is not satisfied if, for example, they have merely entered into an agreement "subject to contract," or into a family arrangement not intended to have legal effect.[5] Secondly, the contract must be specifically enforceable: the equitable remedy of specific performance is discretionary, and may be refused on a number of grounds, *e.g.* mistake, misrepresentation, undue delay, or breach of covenant.[6] Thirdly, the acts relied upon must be those of the plaintiff and must be referable to some contract of the kind alleged.[7] In most cases a change of possession is regarded as sufficient evidence of a contract of sale or of an agreement for a lease, *i.e.* entering into possession is generally a sufficient act of part performance by the purchaser or tenant, and giving up possession is generally sufficient on the part of the vendor or landlord. This third condition, however, has given rise to many difficulties and it seems now that the emphasis generally is on showing that the party seeking to enforce the contract has relied to his detriment on acts of part performance.[8]

[2] *Tiverton Estates Ltd v. Wearwell Ltd.* [1975] Ch. 146, not following *Law v. Jones* [1974] Ch. 112, and doubting *Griffiths v. Young* [1970] 1 Ch. 675.

[3] *Thomas v. Brown* (1876) 1 Q.B.D. 714.

[4] The doctrine is recognised in LPA 1925, s.40(2).

[5] *Re Gonin* [1979] Ch. 16 (which appears otherwise to be inconsistent with *Steadman v. Steadman* [1976] A.C. 536) may be regarded as having been decided on this ground. *Cf. Maddison v. Alderson* (1883) 8 App. Cas. 467, *Wakeham v. Mackenzie* [1968] 1 W.L.R. 1175.

[6] See, *e.g., Warmington v. Miller* [1973] Q.B. 877.

[7] *Kingswood Estate Co. Ltd v. Anderson* [1963] 2 Q.B. 169.

[8] *Steadman v. Steadman,* above, from which it also appears that a mere payment of money may in certain circumstances amount to part performance.

CONTRACTS MADE ON OR AFTER SEPTEMBER 27, 1989

Section 40(1) of the Law of Property Act 1925 and the doctrine of part performance generally do not apply to contracts relating to land entered into on or after September 27, 1989; instead the provisions of the Law of Property (Miscellaneous Provisions) Act 1989 are relevant. Under section 2(1) and (3) of this Act any contract for the sale or other disposition of an interest in land must i) be made in writing, ii) incorporate all the expressly agreed terms in one document (or where there is an exchange of contracts in each contract) and iii) the document must be signed by or on behalf of each party to the contract.

Considering each of these requirements in turn, it is clear that the first provision differs substantially from the old law, in that the contract itself *must be in writing* rather than just *evidenced* in writing. This means, for example, that a contract for the sale, lease or mortgage of land must be in writing, whether it is a contract to create a new estate or interest in the land or to dispose of an existing estate or interest. The result is that any oral agreement to dispose of land will be void and no contract exists. For example, to create a valid equitable charge by a deposit of the Land Certificate there must be a mortgage agreement, in writing, fulfilling the requirements of the 1989 Act.[9] Secondly, under section 2(2) of the Act, all the terms of the contract may be incorporated in a document either by being set out in that document or by reference to some other document. It appears to be a drastic repercussion of this second requirement that if one of the agreed terms is omitted from the document, however minor, the whole contract is void.[10] Finally, the third provision means that both parties must sign the contract, and not just the party wishing to sue under the contract (as in the case of the old law). It is usual conveyancing practice for the sale of land to involve two stages,[11] the first being the exchange of contracts for sale. Normally, identical contracts are prepared and each party signs his own copy of the contract, and the contracts are then exchanged. The 1989 Act caters for this procedure by providing that only one document, including all the terms, need be signed by each party;[12] there is no need for both parties to sign each contract, in order to satisfy the Act. Another potential problem area, concerning options to purchase land, now appears to be resolved. It seems that an agreement granting an option

[9] See *United Bank of Kuwait Plc v. Sahib,* [1995] 2 WLR 94 and pp. 184–185.

[10] Possibly rectification of the contract would be available if the omission is by mistake, making the contract effective. See *Joscelyne v. Nissen* [1970] 2. QB 86 and *Wright v. Robert Leonard (Developments)* [1994] NPC 49, C.A.

[11] See p. 28.

[12] LP(MP)A 1989, s.2(3).

to purchase land in the future must be signed by both parties for the option to comply with section 2, otherwise it is void. However, the subsequent notice exercising the option, given by the grantee of the option to the grantor, need not be signed by both parties, as it is the original grant of the option itself which creates an immediate equitable interest in the land and service of the notice is merely a unilateral act by the grantee exercising the right to purchase.[13]

There are certain transactions to which the Law of Property (Miscellaneous Provisions) Act 1989 does not apply. The most common of these is a contract for the grant of a short term lease not exceeding a term of three years, taking effect in possession and complying with section 54(2) of the Law of Property Act 1925.[14] Also, contracts made in the course of a public auction and contracts relating to investments in land under the Financial Services Act 1986 are excluded from the Act[15], as their own special procedures apply.

One initial concern regarding this new legislation is that the position of the parties to a contract, which does not comply with these rigid rules, may be prejudiced by the abolition of the more flexible doctrine of past performance. However, it seems that in severe cases equity may still intervene, enforcing the contract by means of the doctrine of proprietary estoppel.[16] Indeed, the Act also expressly states that its provisions do not affect the creation or operation of resulting, implied or constructive trusts,[17] so these still may be imposed by equity, if needs be, to save a contract.

THE EFFECT OF CONTRACTS FOR THE DISPOSITION OF LAND

As has already been seen, the effect of a contract for the disposition of land, provided that it complies with the appropriate provisions outlined above, is that not only can it be enforced by an action for damages or for specific performance, but also it is regarded in equity as at once giving rise to an equitable interest in the land.[18] The *legal* estate or interest does not vest in the transferee, however, until the formal conveyance or transfer, lease or other instrument has been executed.[19]

[13] See *Spiro v. Glencrown Properties Ltd* [1991] Ch. 537.
[14] LP(MP)A 1989, s.2(5)(a) and see pp. 99–101.
[15] LP(MP)A 1989, s.2(5)(b) and (c).
[16] See pp. 161–162.
[17] LP(MP)A 1989, s.2(5).
[18] See p. 27.
[19] And, in the case of registered land, the disposition has been registered as applicable. See Chap. 226–227.

12. Leases and tenancies

As we have already seen, the leasehold gained recognition as an estate in land at a relatively late stage in the development of land law.[1] Over the centuries its' importance has gradually increased, and now the term of years or leasehold estate is established, alongside the fee simple or freehold estate, as one of only two possible forms of legal ownership of land.[2] Nevertheless, it retains features which distinguish it from all other estates and interests.

The main distinguishing feature of the leasehold is that it constitutes both an estate in land, and a contract between the lessor (or landlord) and the lessee (or tenant), imposing numerous obligations which continue throughout the term of the lease. Although these obligations are enforceable, as we shall see,[3] not only between the original parties but also between their respective successors in title, the basis on which they are enforceable is that of a continuing relationship between landlord and tenant,[4] rather than on a purely proprietary basis. The law of landlord and tenant, which regulates the rights and obligations of the parties between themselves, can be regarded as ancillary to the law of property, which determines the rights of ownership (*i.e.* the estate) that each holds as against a third party.

Because of its social and economic importance the law of landlord and tenant, in the sense referred to above, is now subject to extensive statutory controls. These are aimed at securing a fair balance between the parties, and to that extent override the common law of contract. Insofar as they relate to security of tenure (the protection of the tenant's right to possession) and rent restriction, these provisions under the Rent Acts are dealt with in the next chapter.

It should also be mentioned that the term "lease" is often used not only to describe the leasehold estate itself but also the document which creates that estate. The alternative words (other than a term of

[1] See pp. 5–6, 7–8.

[2] LPA 1925, s.1(1) (see pp. 31–33).

[3] See Chap. 16.

[4] Analogous with but distinct from the historical relationship between feudal lord and tenant under the doctrine of tenure. See pp. 3–4.

years) which are frequently used to describe the leasehold estate are "leasehold interest" or "demise" or "tenancy," (although the term "tenancy" is usually reserved for short term leases).

ESSENTIALS OF A LEASE

Many different transactions may have as their object the occupation by one party of land belonging to another, but a transaction will create a lease, as distinct from something else, only if it has certain characteristics. The importance of the distinction between a lease on the one hand, and some other transaction such as a licence on the other, is twofold. First, a lease as an estate in land is capable of binding persons other than the original parties to the lease[5] (as a right *in rem*), whereas in principle a licence creates no estate or interest in the land and is binding, if at all, only between the original parties (a right *in personam*).[6] Secondly, a tenant under a lease may have the protection of extensive statutory provisions (see above) whereas in general an occupier under a mere licence has no such protection.

The essential requirements of a lease are as follows:

Exclusive possession

Unless the occupier is entitled to exclusive possession, *i.e.* unless he has the right to exclude all other persons from the premises, any agreement under which he occupies another's property is a mere licence, not a lease. Thus in the case of a lodging agreement, under which the householder normally remains in general control of the premises, and retains virtually unlimited rights of access for the purposes of providing board and other services, the lodger is a licensee, not a tenant.[7]

Estate in land

Even where there is a right to exclusive possession, the transaction will not create a lease unless it appears from the circumstances of the case that the intention or the effect of the agreement between the parties is to create the relationship of landlord and tenant, *i.e.* not merely to create legal relations (indicating a contract, and giving rise

[5] As to whether a lease will actually bind third parties, see Chap. 21 on registration.

[6] See Chap. 15.

[7] *Marchant v. Charters* [1977] 1 W.L.R. 1181. But see *Street v. Mountford* [1985] A.C. 809.

to personal rights and obligations), but to create an estate or interest in the land (giving rise to property rights enforceable by and against non-parties).[8] It follows that there will be no lease where the circumstances point merely to a family arrangement of some kind,[9] or where an employee occupies premises of his employer merely for the purposes of his employment.

The distinction between lease and licence is one of substance not form. However worded, an agreement will create a lease if *in fact* it gives the occupier exclusive possession and there is nothing in the circumstances of the case to negate the relationship of landlord and tenant.[10] Reviewing the considerable body of case law on the matter, the House of Lords, in *Street v. Mountford,*[11] has blocked attempts to disguise as a licence, the grant of a tenancy, by the use of devices by landlords, which are really shams, designed merely to avoid the provisions of the Rent Acts legislation. However clearly the parties may have expressed their intention, it is now the *effect* of the transaction that is decisive.

Certainty of term

Both the commencement date and the duration of the term must be certain: a lease which fails to satisfy this condition is void.[12] For example, an agreement under which land was let until it was needed for road widening was void for uncertainty of term.[13]

The duration of a periodic tenancy *i.e.* a lease where there is no fixed term but where a tenant is in possession and pays rent periodically, (*e.g.* from month to month or year to year) may appear indefinite as it is not certain initially how long the lease will last. Nevertheless, it may be regarded as sufficiently certain for this purpose, in that it can be determined by either party serving a notice terminating the tenancy, called a *notice to quit.*[14]

LEGAL AND EQUITABLE LEASES

In general, if a lease is to be a legal lease (*i.e.* if the lessee is to obtain a legal estate), it must be granted by deed. As an exception, a

[8] *Barnes v. Barratt* [1970] 2 Q.B. 657.

[9] *Errington v. Errington and Woods* [1952] 1 K.B. 290.

[10] *Addiscombe Garden Estates Ltd v. Crabbe* [1958] 1 Q.B. 583, *Facchini v. Bryson* [1952] 1 T.L.R. 1386; contrast *Shell-Mex B.P. Ltd v. Manchester Garages Ltd* [1971] 1 W.L.R. 612.

[11] See note 7.

[12] *Lace v. Chantler* [1944] K.B. 368, *Harvey v. Pratt* [1965] 1 W.L.R. 1025.

[13] *Prudential Assurance Co. Ltd v. London Residuary Body* [1992] 2 A.C. 386, but if the tenant is in possession paying rent a periodic tenancy may arise. See below and pp. 101–102.

[14] See pp. 101–102.

lease for three years or less taking effect in possession at the best rent reasonably obtainable, without taking a fine or a premium (being a lump sum paid in consideration for the grant of a lease) will be a valid legal lease however granted — even if it is granted merely by word of mouth.[15] This exception includes periodic tenancies, such as monthly or yearly tenancies, provided that the basic term does not exceed three years. A lease that is not within the exception given above and not granted by deed is void at law. However, where the tenant goes into possession with the landlord's consent a *tenancy at will* arises, which will become a legal periodic tenancy if the landlord accepts rent.[16]

An equitable lease will arise if the lessor has only an equitable estate from which he can grant a lease. Also, perhaps less obviously, an equitable lease will be created where there is an agreement[17] to grant a legal lease, *e.g.* where a freehold owner enters into a contract to grant to a lessee, a legal lease for a 10 year term but as yet the lease has not been executed and actually granted. Further, an equitable lease will occur where there is an informal lease, *i.e.* where the proper formalities required by law to create a legal lease have not been complied with. An example of such an informal lease is where a 10 year lease of a legal estate has been granted, but only in writing, whereas it should be by deed in order to create a legal lease. In equity, such an informal lease, which is void at law, may be treated as an agreement to grant a lease, provided that it is for value.[18] On the basis that equity looks upon that as done which ought to be done,[19] an agreement to grant a lease (arising by either of the two methods mentioned above), is therefore a valid equitable lease. As between landlord and tenant, an equitable lease has the same effect as a legal lease, *i.e.* all the obligations created by the agreement or by the informal lease can be enforced by the same means and to the same extent as if they were set out in a properly executed lease. In some respects, however, an equitable lease is not as good as a properly executed legal lease. In particular its' enforcement relies on the doctrine of specific performance, which is a discretionary remedy.[20] Also, an equitable lease requires registration in order to be enforce-

[15] LPA 1925, ss.52–54, and LP(MP)A 1989, s.2(5)(a).

[16] See p. 102.

[17] Which, if made on or after September 27, 1989, must be in writing and comply with the other provisions of the LP(MP)A 1989, s.2 (although note the exception in s.2(5)(a) of the Act), see pp. 95–96. As to the position pre September 27, 1989 see pp. 93–94.

[18] And complies with the LP(MP)A 1989, s.2, see note 17 above.

[19] This principle is discussed at pp. 27–28. In its application to leases it is known as the doctrine of *Walsh v. Lonsdale* (1882) 21 Ch.D. 9.

[20] See p. 27. In particular it is only available if the applicant comes to court with 'clean hands'. *E.g.* see *Warmington v. Miller* [1973] Q.B. 877 where an equitable lease was not enforced as it would be in breach of the terms of the head-lease.

able against a third party. Where land is unregistered it should be registered under the Land Charges Act 1972, failing which it will be void against a subsequent purchaser from the landlord. In the case of registered land it must be protected by an entry on the register, as a minor interest or it may be an overriding interest under section 70(1)(g) of the Land Registration Act 1925, if the tenant is in actual occupation or in receipt of rents; in such cases a purchaser from the landlord will take subject to the lease.[21]

DIFFERENT KINDS OF LEASES

1. Leases for a fixed term

An example of a lease for a fixed term would be a lease for a duration of 15 years. In general, such leases come to an end automatically at the end of the agreed term and no notice to quit is required. However, there are important statutory exceptions, which are considered in Chapter 13.

2. Yearly tenancies

A yearly tenancy is otherwise known as a tenancy from year to year: the tenancy continues from year to year until one side or the other brings it to an end by serving the requisite notice to quit. Such a tenancy may be created expressly or it may arise by implication of law. It arises by implication of law when the parties to a tenancy do not expressly agree what the nature of the tenancy shall be and the tenant tenders, and the landlord accepts, some payment of an annual rent. For example, if the parties have agreed on the payment of a yearly rent by four equal quarterly instalments, the payment of a quarter's rent will give rise to a yearly tenancy. A particular case in which a yearly tenancy may arise by implication of law occurs when a tenant under a lease for a fixed term holds over after the end of the term (*i.e.* remains in possession) and then makes some payment of an annual rent which the landlord accepts. In this case the terms of the old lease continue to apply to the new yearly tenancy so far as they are not inconsistent with the nature of such a tenancy.

At common law, in the absence of contrary agreement, in order to determine a yearly tenancy one party must give to the other at least half a year's previous notice expiring at the end of one of the years of the tenancy, *i.e.* expiring on an anniversary of its commencement. Half a year's notice means 182 days' notice unless the tenancy began

[21] See Chap. 21 regarding registered and unregistered land. For the further disadvantages of equitable leases, see pp. 112, 146.

on one of the customary quarter days (which are Lady Day (March 25), Midsummer (June 24), Michaelmas (September 29) or Christmas (December 25)), in which case it means the two previous quarters. However, the parties can make what bargain they like and vary the above rules, unless precluded from doing so by statute.

3. Other periodic tenancies

These too may be created expressly or may arise by implication of law, as in the case of yearly tenancies. For example, if the parties have not agreed upon the precise nature of the tenancy, but have agreed that a quarterly rent shall be paid, the payment of a quarter's rent will give rise to a quarterly tenancy. It is how the rent is measured which determines the period of the tenancy, *e.g.* a monthly rent of £500 payable weekly creates a monthly tenancy.

At common law, subject to contrary agreement, such a tenancy can be brought to an end only at the end of one of the periods of the tenancy, and the length of notice required is the same as that of the period upon which the tenancy is based. For example, if a monthly tenancy began on the 15th of a month it can be brought to an end on the 15th of any month, and for this purpose notice to quit must have been given at least one month before that date. Although in general the parties can vary the common law rule by special agreement, section 5 of the Protection from Eviction Act 1977 provides that where the letting is of a dwelling, notice[22] must be given at least four weeks before the date on which the tenancy is to determine, and this provision applies notwithstanding any contrary agreement. It should be understood that the Act does not *reduce* the length of notice required where, under the common law rule, a longer period of notice is necessary.

Any provision excluding the right of one or both parties to serve a notice to quit will be void[23] for, as we have already seen, it must be possible to serve such a notice for the lease to be of certain duration. Further, any provision only allowing notice to be served when a particular uncertain event occurs *e.g.* when the landlord requires the premises for occupation, will be ineffective for the same reason and the periodic lease can be ended by giving the common law period of notice.[24]

4. Tenancies at will and at sufferance

A tenancy at will arises whenever a person occupies as tenant the land of another with that other's consent, on terms that either party

[22] The notice must be in writing, and contain such information as may be prescribed by regulations made by statutory instrument.

[23] See *Centapoly Ltd v. Matlodge Ltd* [1974] Ch.1 and *Prudential Assurance Co. Ltd v. London Residuary Body,* see note 13 above.

[24] See the House of Lords decision in *Prudential Assurance Co. Ltd v. London Residuary Body,* (note 13 above); overruling the Court of Appeal in *Re Midland Railway Co's Agreement,* [1971] Ch. 725.

may determine the tenancy at any time. It may be created expressly or by implication, as where a tenant whose lease has expired holds over with the landlord's consent, or where a tenant takes possession under an agreement for a lease. The relationship between the parties to a tenancy at will is essentially personal,[25] and accordingly terminates if either party dies, or if either party assigns his interest in the land.[26] The tenant is liable to pay any rent that has been agreed; otherwise, unless the parties have agreed that no rent is payable, the tenant must pay a reasonable sum for use and occupation of the land. Once the tenant has tendered and the landlord has accepted a periodic rent, the tenancy will be converted into a periodic tenancy, on the basis discussed above.

A tenancy at sufferance (which is not perhaps a true tenancy) arises when a tenant without the landlord's consent holds over after a previous tenancy has come to an end. A tenant at sufferance is bound to pay compensation to the landlord for his occupation of the land. Moreover tenants who hold over after notice to quit has been given are liable to certain statutory penalties which are payable to the landlord.[27]

5. Leases for lives, etc.

A lease for a life or lives, or for a term of years determinable with a life or lives, or on the marriage of the lessee (*e.g.* a lease for 50 years which, the lease provides, shall come to an end automatically on the death of a specified person or on the lessee's marriage) is converted by section 149 of the Law of Property Act 1925 into a lease for 90 years. After the end of the life or lives, or the marriage of the lessee, either party may determine this lease by giving at least one month's notice expiring on any quarter day which is applicable to the tenancy or, if there is no such quarter day, any customary quarter day. This provision applies only to leases at a rent or in consideration of a fine. If no rent is payable the result may be to create a settlement, the lessee being tenant for life. It follows that in order to avoid this consequence a nominal rent must be imposed.[28]

6. Perpetually renewable leases

Another curious provision, this time in the Law of Property Act 1922, applies to perpetually renewable leases, *i.e.* leases which give to the tenant a perpetual right of renewal. For example, a lease for seven years may provide that the tenant shall have the right, not less than

[25] *Wheeler v. Mercer* [1957] A.C. 416.
[26] Or if the tenant commits voluntary waste. (As to waste generally, see p. 23).
[27] Landlord and Tenant Act 1730, Distress for Rent Act 1737.
[28] See *Griffiths v. Williams* (1977) 248 E.G. 947 (p. 159 below).

one month before the end of the term, to require the landlord to grant a new lease for seven years upon the same terms as the original lease including the provision for renewal. The Act converts such leases into terms of 2,000 years, determinable by the *lessee* by the giving of at least 10 days' notice expiring on any date on which, but for the Act, the lease would have come to an end if it had not been renewed, *i.e.* in the example given above, the end of any seven-year term. If the lease provides for payment of a fine on renewal, then (a) if the lease was granted before 1926, the fine is commuted into additional rent, but (b) if the lease was granted after 1925, the provision for payment of the fine is void.

The 1922 Act also renders void any contract to renew an existing lease for a term of more than 60 years from the termination of the current lease.

7. Reversionary leases

The Law of Property Act 1925, s.149, renders void the grant after 1925 of a lease which is to take effect more than 21 years after the date of the grant.[29] The same section invalidates a contract to grant such a lease, *i.e.* a lease the term of which is to commence more than 21 years from the *grant* of the lease; but this does not invalidate a contract to grant a lease, the term of which is to start more than 21 years from the date of the *contract.*[30] For example, if a contract is entered into in 1995 to grant a lease in 2035, the term of which is to commence immediately on the grant, then the contract is valid.

TERMINATION OF LEASES

We have already seen that a lease may come to an end by effluxion of time, in the case of a fixed term lease, or may be determined by the service of notice to quit in other cases. We must now consider some other ways in which a lease may come to an end.

Forfeiture

A landlord is said to forfeit a lease when he prematurely brings the lease to an end because of the tenant's breach of some obligation under the lease. Forfeiture is therefore important to the landlord of a fixed term lease, as it provides him with the security of being able to recover possession of the premises in the event of a breach of

[29] See p. 33.
[30] *Re Strand and Savoy Properties Ltd* [1960] Ch. 582.

covenant by the tenant, rather than just relying on a personal action claiming damages. In general, if a landlord wishes to have this right of forfeiture it must be expressly provided for in the lease; the law does not imply such a right, even if the tenant fails to pay the rent. The landlord may provide for the right either by stating in the lease that the tenant's performance of his obligations is a condition of the lease, or by inserting into the lease an express right of re-entry, *i.e.* a provision that the landlord may re-enter and determine the lease upon breach by the tenant of his obligations. A right of re-entry may in general be exercised either by peaceably re-entering the premises or by bringing court proceedings. Peaceable re-entry is affected by physically entering the land and changing the locks, but if in so doing the landlord uses force where he knows there is someone opposed to re-entry he may be guilty of a criminal offence.[31] It is for this reason that forfeiture is normally enforced by a court action for possession. Indeed, this is the *only* lawful method where premises are let as a dwelling and any person is lawfully residing there[32]. Commencing a court action by serving a writ (in the case of the High Court) or summons (in the county court) operates in law as a re-entry, but the lease is not extinguished until the landlord obtains judgment for possession. Until then the tenant is accountable to the landlord for mesne profits[33] during the period of his continued occupation and the lease still subsists.

Waiver

A landlord may lose his right of forfeiture in respect of a particular breach of the tenant's obligations by waiving the right. Waiver may be express or implied. There is usually an implied waiver if the landlord with knowledge of a breach does any act showing that he has elected to treat the lease as still in existence, *e.g.* by claiming rent accruing due after the breach,[34] or by distraining for rent accruing due whether before or after the breach. The remedy of distraint consists of seizing and selling the tenant's goods for the purpose of recovering arrears of rent. The act of distraining shows an election to treat the lease as still in existence, because the remedy of distress can be used by a landlord only as long as the relationship of landlord and tenant subsists. But a landlord's claim for possession on the ground of breaches of covenant is not inconsistent with an alternative claim for an injunction restraining further breaches, and the two may properly be joined in the same action.[35] Furthermore, if the landlord assigns the reversion, *i.e.*

[31] Criminal Law Act 1977, ss.6 and 7, replacing the Forcible Entry Acts 1381–1623.
[32] Protection from Eviction Act 1977, s.2.
[33] *I.e.* compensation paid for wrongful possession of the land.
[34] See *Central Estates (Belgravia) Ltd v. Woolgar (No. 2)* [1972] 1 W.L.R. 1048.
[35] *Calabar Properties Ltd v. Seagull Autos Ltd* [1969] 1 Ch. 451.

conveys his estate expressly subject to the lease, this does not of itself constitute a waiver of previous breaches by the tenant, and the assignee accordingly acquires the assignor's (*i.e.* the previous landlord's) right to forfeit the lease[36].

Restrictions on right of forfeiture

Even where a landlord has expressly reserved a right of forfeiture for breach of a tenant's obligation, and has not waived the right, the law imposes certain restrictions as to when and how it can be exercised.

1. Forfeiture for non-payment of rent

At common law a landlord cannot exercise a right of re-entry for non-payment of rent unless he has made a formal demand for the rent upon the premises before sunset on the last day on which the rent has to be paid. However, nowadays the term of the lease may, and usually will, exempt the landlord from the need to make this formal demand. Also even if there is no such express provision, section 210 of the Common Law Procedure Act 1852 will exempt the landlord from doing so if half a year's rent is in arrears and unpaid *and* there are not sufficient goods on the premises to enable him to recover the rent by distress.

Where a formal demand is made, or the landlord is exempted, and the arrears of rent remain unpaid, the landlord can proceed to re-enter the premises by peaceable re-entry or by servicing court proceedings. If the landlord serves court proceedings for possession and the rent is at least six months in arrears, the tenant has a statutory right under section 212 of the Common Law Procedure Act 1852, to have the proceedings stayed, if he pays the arrears and costs before trial and he is then entitled to possession under his old lease. Otherwise, even after the landlord has re-entered for non-payment of rent, the tenant may ask the court for relief against forfeiture *i.e.* he may ask that his lease be restored to him. The court has a discretionary power to grant such relief; the power is equitable in origin, but it is regulated in some cases by section 210 of the Common Law Procedure Act 1852. Under this Act, where the landlord has been exempted from making a formal demand and has obtained possession through a court action, the tenant can make an application for relief within six months of the judgment being executed, *i.e.* the landlord actually obtaining possession. It seems that this provision does not apply where forfeiture is enforced by peaceable re-entry, rather than

[36] *London & County (A. & D.) Ltd v. Wilfred Sportsman Ltd* [1971] Ch. 764.

court proceedings[37] and so in those circumstances, in theory, the tenant can apply at any time for relief under the court's equitable jurisdiction (which is discussed below).

The power to grant relief is based on the principle that the landlord's right of re-entry is merely a security for performance of the tenant's obligations. Accordingly the court may relieve the tenant from forfeiture of the lease if he is now prepared to discharge his obligations, *i.e.* to pay the rent together with any costs incurred by the landlord, provided always that the court is satisfied that it would be just and equitable to grant relief.

2. Forfeiture for breach of other obligations

Section 146 of the Law of Property Act 1925 contains certain general provisions which apply to forfeiture for breach of a tenant's obligations other than to pay rent and certain other obligations, which are specially mentioned below. Under these provisions the landlord is required to serve a statutory notice upon the tenant (commonly referred to as a "section 146 notice") and, if applicable, to give him a reasonable time within which to comply with it. If the tenant does comply he avoids forfeiture. If he does not, and the landlord seeks to obtain possession by commencing court proceedings or by peaceably re-entering the premises, under the same section, the court still may grant relief against forfeiture, as shall be seen later.

The section 146 notice must:

(a) specify the particular breach complained of, and
(b) require the tenant to remedy it, if it is capable of remedy, and
(c) require the tenant to make compensation in money (if the landlord so requires).

A notice which does not comply with the above provisions is invalid and any subsequent forfeiture proceedings based on a defective notice will also be invalid.

It should be noted that a notice dealing with a breach which is incapable of being remedied need only specify the breach and any compensation sought. Therefore, it is important to determine whether or not the breach complained of is capable of remedy. The traditional approach to this problem is to distinguish between the breach of a negative covenant *i.e.* a promise *not* to do something (*e.g.* not to sell food and drink); and the breach of a positive covenant *i.e.* a promise to do something (*e.g.* to keep premises in repair). According to this approach negative covenants are irremediable; the rationale being that once a prohibited act has been committed it is incapable of remedy as the very obligation is *not* to commit the act. So where

[37] *Thatcher v. C.H. Pearce & Sons (Contractors) Ltd* [1968] 1 W.L.R. 748.

premises were used for immoral purposes in breach of a negative covenant, the breach was held not to be capable of remedy, even though the immoral user had ceased.[38] Another example of a breach of a negative covenant, which has been held to be irremediable, is where a tenant has assigned or sublet premises when a covenant provides that he should not do so.[39] On the other hand, under this traditional view, a breach of a positive covenant is usually capable of being remedied, as under the covenant the tenant is obliged to take some action and although he has not done so yet, he may do so later. This distinction seems rather artificial, especially where, in the case of the breach of a negative covenant, the prohibited act has ceased and no lasting stigma has attached to the property nor is there any reduction in its value as a result. In view of this, the more modern, practical approach which has been adopted is to look at the effect of the breach, in deciding whether it is remediable. The test is whether, in reality, the landlord has been prejudiced by the breach; on the facts of the case, can the harm caused be remedied by making good the breach?[40]

The tenant must be given a *reasonable* time, after service of the section 146 notice, to remedy the breach, if it is capable of remedy. No express time limits are laid down by statute and what will constitute a reasonable period will vary depending on the facts. If the breach is of a positive covenant a reasonable time period will depend on the amount of work involved in complying with the covenant, for example, normally three months will be sufficient where repair work is necessary. However, only a brief period is usually needed to end a breach of a negative covenant. If the breach is irremediable, according to case law, the landlord should still give the tenant a short time, such as 14 days, to review his position, before the landlord proceeds with re-entry.[41]

It has been seen that whether the breach of covenant is capable of remedy affects the drafting of the section 146 notice and the period of time the landlord must wait before re-entering the premises. However, the nature of the breach does not affect the right of the tenant to apply for relief from forfeiture.[42] If the landlord re-enters the premises following non-compliance with the section 146 notice but the tenant subsequently applies for relief against forfeiture, whether or not the breach is capable of remedy, relief may be granted

[38] *Rugby School (Governors) v. Tannahill* [1935] 1 K.B. 87.

[39] *Scala House and District Property Co. Ltd v. Forbes* [1974] Q.B. 575.

[40] See *Expert Clothing Service & Sales v. Hillgate House,* [1986] Ch. 340 concerning a positive covenant and *Glass v. Kencakes Ltd* [1966] 1 Q.B. 611, regarding a negative covenant, where swift action was taken by the tenant to end the immoral user, of which he had no previous knowledge.

[41] *Scala House and District Property Co. Ltd v. Forbes* (see note 39).

[42] *Ibid.*

or refused as the court thinks fit, "having regard to the proceedings and conduct of the parties . . . and to all the other circumstances)."[43] Where the landlord sues for possession the tenant may apply for relief in the landlord's action. However, once a final judgment for possession has been obtained and executed then no application by the tenant will be entertained. In contrast, where the landlord has forfeited by peaceable re-entry, an application for relief can be made by the tenant either before or after the landlord has peaceably re-entered.[44] In this situation, there is no strict time limit within which the application for relief must be made, although delay in applying may mean that this discretionary, equitable remedy is not available to the tenant. There is therefore an incentive for the landlord to pursue the court action route because, once possession is obtained under a final judgment (or six months has expired after executing such a judgment in the case of a breach of covenant for non-payment of rent), he can then relet the premises certain in the knowledge that relief cannot be granted to the previous tenant.[45]

Finally, there are special provisions concerning the forfeiture procedure to be followed where the tenant is in breach of a repairing covenant. In particular, by the Leasehold Property (Repairs) Act 1938, if a lease is for seven years or more, of which at least three remain unexpired, the section 146 notice must inform the tenant of his right to serve a counter notice under the Act. If the tenant does this within 28 days the landlord cannot proceed further in a claim either for possession or for damages without the leave of the court. One of the grounds on which the landlord may obtain leave to bring forfeiture proceedings is that otherwise he will suffer or has suffered a substantial reduction in the value of his reversionary interest.[46]

3. Forfeiture for breach of inspection covenant in a mining lease

The rent payable under a mining lease is usually in the form of a royalty which varies with the amount of the mineral obtained by the tenant under the lease. The lease generally contains detailed provisions requiring the tenant to keep proper accounts and giving to the landlord a right of inspection of the accounts and of the working of the mine. Parliament has recognised the vital importance of such provisions to the landlord by enacting that section 146 of the Law of

[43] LPA 1925, s.146(2).

[44] The House of Lords clarified this point in *Billson v. Residential Apartments Ltd* [1992] 1 A.C. 494.

[45] See Law Com. No. 142 (1985) and Law Com. No. 221 (1994), to which is annexed the Termination of Tenancies Bill, which makes radical proposals to replace the entire regime of re-entry, waiver, notice and relief and to implement a termination order scheme.

[46] Leasehold Property (Repairs) Act 1938, s.1(5)(a).

Property Act 1925, shall have no application to a breach by the tenant of such inspection covenants. In the event of a breach by the tenant of such provisions, therefore, the landlord may forfeit the lease without serving the usual s.146 notice, and the court has no power to grant relief to the tenant.

4. Forfeiture on the bankruptcy of the tenant

The lease may contain provisions which allow the landlord to re-enter if the tenant becomes bankrupt or suffers the lease to be taken in execution. The latter occurs if the lease is a valuable asset and a creditor of the tenant obtains judgment against the tenant and by means of the appropriate procedure sells the tenant's interest in the lease, in order to repay what is due to him.

Section 146 provides that in the case of certain types of property of importance to the landlord he can forfeit the lease on the above grounds without having served a section 146 notice, and the tenant cannot be granted relief. These cases are where the lease is of (i) agricultural or pastoral land, (ii) mines or minerals, (iii) a public-house, (iv) a furnished house, or (v) property with respect to which the personal qualifications of the tenant are of special importance to the landlord. In any other case the provisions concerning the service of a section 146 notice and applying for relief apply for one year after the bankruptcy or taking in execution, and they apply indefinitely after the end of that year if during the year the lease has been sold by the tenant's trustee in bankruptcy or execution creditor.

5. Relief for sub-lessees

A lessee may grant a lease for a lesser term, called a *sub-lease.* The leasehold estate out of which the sub-lease is granted is called the *head-lease.* If a head-lease is forfeited any sub-lease automatically falls with it. However, the Law of Property Act 1925, s.146(4), as amended by the Law of Property (Amendment) Act 1929, gives to a sub-lessee the right to apply to the court for relief against the forfeiture of the head-lease.

Under this section a mortgagee has a similar right to apply for relief against forfeiture, in order to preserve his security.[47] The right to seek relief applies whatever the ground on which the head-lease has been forfeited (*i.e.* even if the head-lessee himself could not have applied for relief against the forfeiture). If relief is granted, the court will make an order vesting in the sub-lessee the property comprised in the head-lease for a term not longer than the residue of the sub-lease,

[47] *Grand Junction Co. v. Bates* [1954] 2 Q.B. 160, or under s.146(2): see *Escalus Properties Ltd v. Robinson, The Times,* April 21, 1995, C.A.

and on such conditions as the court thinks fit. In general, relief will only be granted to a sub-lessee if he complies with the tenant's obligations under the head-lease, and makes good any subsisting breaches. It follows that he may have to pay arrears of rent due under the head-lease.[48]

When a head-lease is forfeited for non-payment of rent a sub-lessee has a separate right to apply for relief against forfeiture under the Common Law Procedure Act 1852.

Other modes of determination

A lease will also come to an end if the tenant surrenders it to his landlord and the landlord accepts the surrender. Surrender may be express, in which case it should be by deed, or it may be implied by law, *e.g.* if the tenant gives up possession of the premises to the landlord and the landlord accepts that possession. If a lessee who has granted a sub-lease surrenders his lease to his landlord, the sub-lease will not be extinguished and the superior landlord will take subject to it.

A lease may also come to an end by merger. Merger occurs when the owner of the lease acquires the reversion, in which case the lease is said to merge in the reversion, and the lease ceases to exist.

Finally, it may be mentioned that section 153 of the Law of Property Act 1925 allows a lessee to execute a deed of enlargement enlarging his lease into the fee simple. The principal conditions are that the lease should have been granted for a) at least 300 years, of which 200 years or more remain unexpired, b) that no rent of any money value should be payable, and c) that no trust or right of redemption, for example, under a mortgage, should exist in favour of the reversioner.[49]

ASSIGNMENTS AND SUB-LEASES

Assignment of a lease

A lessee has an estate in land which, like any other estate or interest, he can dispose of by assignment, or which on his death will devolve under his will or intestacy. On assignment the lessee disposes of the whole of the remaining term of the lease and he retains no estate in the land. The lessee disposing of the lease is called the

[48] He would have a right of indemnity against the head-lessee, which of course would be worthless if the head-lessee is insolvent or has disappeared.

[49] For the possible implications of this provision, see M. & W. pp. 687–688.

assignor and person to whom the lease is assigned is called the *assignee*. If it is a legal term of years (including, it will be recalled, various forms of periodic tenancy which may be validly created even orally),[50] any assignment must be made by deed if it is to be capable of being effective at law.[51] However, an informal assignment or a specifically enforceable agreement[52] to assign may be treated in equity as transferring to the assignee the beneficial or equitable interest in the lease.

If the lessee holds only an equitable lease, he can assign[53] his rights thereunder, including his right to claim specific performance against the lessor, but in other respects the position of an assignee of an equitable lease against the lessor is less clear.[54]

Two further aspects of the assignment of a lease will be discussed later: first, the effect of an express provision in the lease prohibiting or restricting assignment[55]; secondly, the basis on which covenants in a lease are enforceable between the original parties and between their assigns.[56]

Sub-lease

A lessee who does not wish to part with his whole interest in the land may, instead of assigning the lease, create a sub-lease (or under-lease). This must be for a term at least one day less than the head-lease, otherwise the transaction will constitute an assignment, not a sub-lease. The *sub-lessor* grants the sub-lease to the *sub-lessee* and the sub-lessee will hold a legal term of years.[57] The same rights and obligations under the landlord-tenant relationship will attach to the sub-lease as attach to the head-lease, subject, of course, to any variations in their express terms. A further under-lease for a lesser term may be created by the sub-lessee, and so on.

RIGHTS AND OBLIGATIONS UNDER A LEASE

The rights and obligations of a landlord and tenant under a lease commonly fall into three categories:

[50] See pp. 99–100 and *Crago v. Julian* [1992] 1 W.L.R. 372.
[51] LPA 1925, s.52.
[52] Provided it complies with the same requirements as for the creation of an equitable lease, see pp 100–101 and Chap. 11.
[53] By written instrument (LPA 1925, s.53).
[54] As to the enforceability of covenants in an equitable lease on assignment see *Purchase v. Lichfield Brewery Co.* [1915] 1 K.B. 184, *Boyer v. Warbey* [1953] 1 Q.B. 234.
[55] p. 117.
[56] p. 165 *et seq.*
[57] Provided that the sub-lease complies with LPA 1925, ss.52–54; if not, it may be valid as an equitable sub-lease (see pp. 100–101).

i) implied obligations;
ii) usual covenants; and
iii) express covenants.

Each will be considered in turn.

Implied obligations of landlord and tenant

Certain obligations are imposed upon the landlord or the tenant by implication of law. In general, these implied obligations may be varied by express provisions in the lease, but in some instances variation is prohibited by statute.

Landlord's obligations

1. Implied covenant for quiet enjoyment

The landlord impliedly covenants (or promises) that the tenant shall have quiet enjoyment of the premises free from any interference by the landlord himself, or by anyone lawfully deriving title from the landlord.[58] It will be observed that the covenant is in a restricted form. Suppose, for example, the lease in question is a sub-lease which has been granted by A, the sub-lessor to B, the sub-lessee. If A, the sub-lessor loses his own lease by L, the superior landlord, exercising his right of re-entry, B, the sub-lessee will not be able to sue A (his own landlord), for damages for breach of A's implied covenant for quiet enjoyment. The sub-lessee, B, has not been disturbed in his possession of the premises by any act of his landlord or anyone deriving title from his landlord. The superior landlord does not claim title through his own tenant, A, but has a superior title which is called a *title paramount*. (As we have seen,[59] the sub-lessee's remedy in this case is to apply to the court for relief against forfeiture of the head-lease.)

Breach of the covenant will usually consist of some act of physical interference with the tenant's possession of the land,[60] but persistent threats intended to drive him out have also been held to constitute a breach.[61]

2. Derogation from grant

Like any other grantor, a landlord is not at liberty to *derogate from his grant, i.e.* to detract from the estate he has granted. Accordingly he

[58] *Cf. Celsteel Ltd v. Alton House Holdings Ltd (No. 2)* [1987] 1 W.L.R. 291.

[59] p. 110.

[60] *Markham v. Paget* [1908] 1 Ch. 697 (undermining) *Owen v. Gadd* [1956] 2 Q.B. 99 (scaffolding obstructing access); contrast *Browne v. Flower* [1911] 1 Ch. 219 (mere intrusion of privacy).

[61] *Kenny v. Preen* [1963] 1 Q.B. 499. It is a criminal offence unlawfully to evict or harass the occupier of residential premises (Protection from Eviction Act 1977, s.1).

must not do, or suffer to be done, anything which would render the premises unfit for the purposes for which they have been let. For example, a landlord can be restrained from using adjoining land in such a way as to prejudice the tenant's use of the demised premises.[62]

3. Condition of the premises

In general no obligation is implied on the landlord's part that the premises are fit for occupation, or that he will maintain them in repair.[63] There are, however, some exceptions:

(i) *Furnished houses.* On the letting of a furnished house there is (unless otherwise agreed) an implied condition that the premises are reasonably fit for human habitation at the commencement of the lease (but the landlord does not undertake to keep them so). This common law rule is known as the rule in *Smith v. Marrable.*[64]

(ii) *Landlord and Tenant Act 1985, s.8.* When a house is let at a rent which does not exceed £80 a year in London or £52 a year elsewhere (or half these amounts if the tenancy was granted before July 6, 1957)[65] there is an implied condition that the premises are fit for human habitation at the commencement of the tenancy, and the landlord impliedly agrees to keep them so. The parties cannot generally contract out of these provisions. Quite a small defect may amount to a breach of the landlord's obligation if as a result, the premises are dangerous.[66] But a landlord incurs no liability in respect of a defect unless he had notice of it. This rule applies even where the defect was concealed so that the tenant could not have notified the landlord of it (and the same rule applies when a landlord expressly covenants to keep the premises in repair).[67]

(iii) *Landlord and Tenant Act 1985, s.11.* If a lease of a dwelling house is granted after October 24, 1961, for less than seven years (or the landlord can determine the lease within seven years) there is an implied covenant by the landlord to keep the structure and exterior of the premises, including the drains and gutters, in repair, and to maintain any installa-

[62] *Harmer v. Jumbil (Nigeria) Tin Areas Ltd* [1921] 1 Ch. 200.

[63] As to the landlord's implied obligations with respect to premises retained by him, where these constitute the tenant's only means of access, see *Liverpool City Council v. Irwin* [1977] A.C. 239.

[64] (1843) 11 M. & W. 5 (bug-ridden premises).

[65] These limits are so low that the provisions rarely apply to modern lettings.

[66] *Summers v. Salford Corporation* [1943] A.C. 283 (a broken sash cord).

[67] *McCarrick v. Liverpool Corporation* [1947] A.C. 219.

tions. These include installations for the supply of gas, water, and electricity, for sanitation and for heating. When this provision applies any liability in respect of these matters which would otherwise be the tenant's is excluded. The parties cannot contract out of these provisions without the leave of the county court.

It should also be noted that local authorities have wide statutory powers[68] under which they may compel the owner of a house to maintain it in reasonable condition. This means that a tenant, by complaining to the local authority, may sometimes be able to compel his landlord to do work which, as between himself and the tenant, he is not contractually bound to do.

Tenant's obligations

A tenant is bound to pay the rent, to pay tenants' rates and taxes *i.e.* all ordinary rates and taxes (*e.g.* the council tax) and, if the landlord is liable to repair the premises, to allow the landlord to enter and view the state of repair.

Tenants generally are impeachable for voluntary waste, *i.e.* liable to pay damages to the reversioner if such waste is committed.[69] A tenant for a fixed term is also impeachable for permissive waste, so that he is under a general obligation to maintain the premises in repair. Periodic tenants are not impeachable for permissive waste, but are bound to use the premises in a tenant-like manner (*e.g.* to keep the drain pipes clear) and a yearly tenant may perhaps be bound to keep the premises weather-proof.[70]

The "usual covenants"

As has been seen, the grant of a lease is sometimes preceded by an agreement to grant the lease. Such an agreement may expressly provide that the lease shall contain the usual covenants, and if the agreement is silent as to what covenants the lease shall contain, these usual covenants will be implied terms of the agreement. What covenants are usual is then a matter of evidence and depends upon the practice of conveyancers in the locality, but the following covenants are usual by the general custom of conveyancers[71]:

[68] Now contained in the Housing Act 1985, Parts VI and IX as amended.

[69] See p. 23 and pp. 20–22 as to the different types of waste.

[70] See *Wedd v. Porter* [1916] 2 K.B. 91, doubted in *Warren v. Keen* [1954] 1 Q.B. 15, C.A.

[71] *Hampshire v. Wickens* (1878) 7 Ch.D. 555; *Hodgkinson v. Crowe* (1875) 10 Ch. App. 622.

(i) By the landlord, a covenant for quiet enjoyment, restricted to the acts of the landlord and those lawfully deriving title from him.

(ii) By the tenant, covenants to pay the rent and to pay tenant's rates and taxes, to keep the premises in repair, and to permit the landlord to enter and view the state of repair.

(iii) A condition[72] of re-entry, in favour of the landlord, for non-payment of rent by the tenant (but not for the breach of other covenants).

If the parties have expressly or impliedly agreed that the lease shall contain the usual covenants, then when the lease comes to be drawn up either party may insist upon the inclusion of the usual covenants and may prevent the insertion of any other covenant.

Express covenants

Mention may be made here of two covenants that are most commonly expressly included in leases.

1. Covenant to repair

The main principle which applies to the interpretation of such a covenant is that it is a covenant to repair, not to re-build, the premises. The covenantor is bound to maintain the premises in as good a condition as possible, regard being had to the age and condition of the premises at the commencement of the tenancy. Nevertheless, he is not bound to rebuild main parts of the structure which have become beyond ordinary repair. The covenant may, however, extend to the replacement of subsidiary parts of the premises, such as a wall, if they are beyond ordinary repair.[73]

Sometimes in addition to the word "repair", expressions such as "tenantable" or "good and substantial" repair may be used, which seem to have little, if any, effect.

On the other hand, often a covenant to repair is qualified by the addition of words such as "fair wear and tear excepted." Such words are restrictively construed by the courts, and although they will exempt the tenant from liability for the immediate consequences of the excepted cause, they will not exclude liability for consequential damage. For example, if a slate blows off the roof, the tenant is not immediately liable to replace it, but if he does not prevent the rain

[72] The breach of a condition automatically brings the lease to an end. *C.f.* a right of forfeiture for breaches of covenant which allows the landlord to forfeit if he wishes. See pp. 104–105.

[73] *Lurcott v. Wakely* [1911] 1 K.B. 905.

from entering and this causes the roof timbers to rot, he will be liable for the damage to the timbers.[74]

By the Landlord and Tenant Act 1927, s.18, the damages recoverable by a landlord, in these circumstances, may not exceed the reduction in value of his reversion, due to the breach of the covenant. Hence if at the end of the tenancy the landlord intends to pull down the premises he can recover nothing.[75]

2. Covenant against assigning, etc.

The lessee often covenants not to assign or under-let the premises. If the covenant is in this simple form, only an *inter vivos* disposition of the *whole* of the premises will amount to a breach; an under-letting of part of the premises, therefore, will not be a breach. However, it is rare to find a covenant in this simple form. Usually it requires the tenant not to assign or under-let or part with possession of the premises or *any part* thereof.

If the covenant is qualified, *i.e.* if it prohibits assignment or subletting *without the landlord's consent*, three statutory provisions come into operation.[76] First, by section 144 of the Law of Property Act 1925, subject to contrary agreement, the landlord may not demand payment for his consent.[77] Secondly, by section 19 of the Landlord and Tenant Act 1927, in spite of any contrary agreement, the landlord may not unreasonably withhold his consent.[78] Further, in the case of building leases for more than 40 years, of which more than seven remain unexpired, the landlord's consent is not required for an assignment or sub-letting.[79]

Thirdly, the Landlord and Tenant Act 1988 applies to qualified covenants and is designed to prevent delay by landlords in dealing with applications for consent. It provides that where a written application for consent to assign, sublet, charge or part with possession is received the landlord is under a duty to give his consent (and to do so within a reasonable time), unless it is reasonable not to give consent.[80] If consent is refused or conditions are imposed on giving consent, the landlord must set out in writing, within a reasonable

[74] *Regis Property Co. Ltd v. Dudley* [1959] A.C. 370.

[75] For a further restriction on the landlord's rights, see the Leasehold Property (Repairs) Act 1938 (p. 109).

[76] Note that these provisions do not apply to an absolute prohibition on assignment or subletting *i.e.* one with no provision for obtaining the landlord's consent.

[77] Other than a reasonable sum for legal or other expenses.

[78] It is proposed in the Landlord and Tenant (Covenants) Bill; H.L. Bill 1994–1995 (70) that this section should no longer apply to commercial leases and that instead the terms of assignment will be negotiated between the parties, See also p. 165.

[79] As long as written notice of the transction is served on the landlord within 6 months after the transaction is effected, see the Landlord and Tenant Act 1927, s.19(1).

[80] Landlord and Tenant Act 1988, s.1.

time, his reasons for this. The burden is on the landlord to show that his refusal or the conditions were reasonable or to show that consent was given within a reasonable period. If these provisions are breached the tenant may have a civil claim in tort against the landlord, for breach of statutory duty.[81]

There is no hard and fast rule as to the matters which a landlord may properly consider in deciding whether or not to grant his consent, but the personality of the proposed tenant and the nature of the proposed user of the premises are clearly relevant considerations.[82] As a general rule the landlord need consider only his own relevant interests, but there may be circumstances in which it would be unreasonable to withhold consent if the resulting detriment to the tenant far outweighed any benefit to the landlord.[83]

If consent is requested, and is unreasonably refused, the tenant will incur no liability by assigning without consent; but he will be in breach if he assigns without having sought consent, even though the assignment is one to which consent could not reasonably have been refused. An assignment made in breach of covenant is not void, and accordingly the assignee acquires the lease.[84] However, if the lease contains a condition of re-entry, the landlord will be able to forfeit the lease in the hands of the assignee: relief against forfeiture might be granted in the case of breach of a qualified covenant, if the assignment was not one to which the landlord could reasonably have objected, though presumably not if the covenant was absolute.

[81] Landlord and Tenant Act 1988, s.4.

[82] *Houlder Bros & Co. Ltd v. Gibbs* [1925] Ch. 198. However, it is generally unlawful to withhold consent on grounds of sex (Sex Discrimination Act 1975, s.31) or race (Race Relations Act 1976, s.24).

[83] *International Drilling Fluids Ltd v. Louisville Investments (Uxbridge) Ltd* [1986] Ch. 513.

[84] *Old Grovesbury Manor Farm Ltd v. W. Seymour Plant Sales & Hire Ltd (No. 2)* [1979] 1 W.L.R. 1397.

13. Security of tenure and rent restriction

In Chapter 12, the nature of a lease or tenancy was considered purely in terms of contract and property, but note was taken that this is pre-eminently a field in which for social, economic and political reasons the legislature has intervened to increasing effect in recent years. Legislation of this kind has two main objects, first to give security of tenure to the tenant, *i.e.* the right to remain in possession after the contractual term of the tenancy has expired; secondly to restrict the amount of rent that the landlord may lawfully charge. Statutory protection has been extended separately to residential, business and agricultural tenancies.

DWELLINGS

Protection has for many years been given to tenants of residential property by a long series of statutes, commonly known as the Rent Acts, beginning with an Act passed in 1915. Since then varying social, political and economic conditions have given rise to different systems and degrees of control. The principal statutes presently in force in respect of lettings by private landlords are the Rent Act 1977, as amended, which normally covers tenancies created prior to January 15, 1989, and the Housing Act 1988, which applies to tenancies granted on or after that date. It will be necessary, even in the short account which follows, to deal with both these basic systems, and with the rules relating to lettings by public sector landlords under the Housing Act 1985.

This area of land law is of undeniable practical importance, and cannot be neglected even in an introductory book; what is to be regretted is that the statutory provisions in question are excessively elaborate, and subject to continual change.

Regulated tenancies: Rent Act 1977

The main provisions of this Act apply to any tenancy entered into before January 15, 1989 (or which is created pursuant to a contract made before that date) under which a dwelling-house (which may be part of a house) is let as a separate dwelling. This is provided that (in most cases) the dwelling-house has a rateable value not exceeding £1,500 in London or £750 elsewhere.[1]

The Act does not apply where premises have been let solely for business purposes.[2] Furthermore the majority of mixed business-residential lettings, *e.g.* a small shop with rooms above, also fall outside the Act.[3] The requirement that the dwelling should be separate prima facie excludes shared accommodation, but a distinction is drawn between the tenant obliged to share with his landlord and the tenant obliged to share with others. The former has the more limited protection afforded to restricted contracts,[4] whereas the latter enjoys the main benefits of the Act with only minor modifications.

Amongst the lettings excluded from the Act are those:

(a) where no rent is payable or where the rent is less than two-thirds of the rateable value of the property[5];

(b) where the rent genuinely includes payments in respect of board or attendance *e.g.* cleaning (provided that the amount of the rent fairly attributable to attendance forms a substantial portion of the whole rent);

(c) in general where the tenancy is created by a "resident landlord," *i.e.* a landlord who resides in part of the same building (other than a purpose-built block of flats)[6];

(d) where the tenancy is a holiday letting or a letting to students by specified educational institutions;

(e) in general where the tenancy relates to an agricultural holding or a public house.

In cases (b) and (c), however, the tenant may have the limited protection afforded by the restricted contract provisions, which are discussed below.

[1] Lower rateable values apply where the dwelling was first rated before April 1, 1973. In the unusual circumstances where the Rent Act 1977 applies to tenancies created on or after April 1, 1990 there is a limit based on rental rather than rateable values, as the domestic rating system was abolished from that date onwards.

[2] Nor where the purpose is to provide more than one dwelling (*Horford Investments Ltd v. Lambers* [1976] Ch.39).

[3] *Wolfe v. Hogan* [1949] 2 K.B. 194.

[4] See p. 123.

[5] Again there is a low rental limit instead if the tenancy is entered into on or after the abolition of the domestic rating system, see note 1 above.

[6] Except for limited periods following sale or death, the landlord or his successor must *continue* to reside in the same building.

The Act is also excluded where the landlord is the Crown or a government department or a local authority, housing trust or similar body.

For the purpose of security of tenure, regulated tenancies under the Act are classified as two types, either *protected tenancies* or *statutory tenancies*. As long as the ordinary contractual tenancy continues it is a protected tenancy and as such the tenant is protected by the provisions of the Act with respect to rent. His security of tenure, *i.e.* his protection against eviction, is governed by the general law, not by the Act. However, once that contractual, protected tenancy comes to an end, the tenant must rely on the provisions of the Act for his security, and it is then that a statutory tenancy arises.

A statutory tenancy is based on the tenant's statutory right to remain in possession (despite termination of his contractual tenancy by notice, effluxion of time, forfeiture or otherwise), unless and until the court makes an order against him on specified grounds. Such a tenancy is subject to all the terms of the contractual tenancy, in so far as they are not inconsistent with the Act.

This statutory tenancy is a legal anomaly because the right to remain in possession is personal to the tenant, and he cannot dispose of it *inter vivos* or by his will (although there is provision whereby the tenant has a limited power with the landlord's consent to substitute another tenant in his place).

On the tenant's death, however, the right is transmitted to the spouse residing with the tenant at his or her death, or to the person living with the tenant, at the tenant's death, as his or her wife or husband. If there is no such person so residing then the right passes to some other member of the tenant's family, if such member had resided with the tenant for two years before the tenant's death.[7] In certain circumstances, a second transmission is also possible to a member of the original tenant's family, who is also a member of the first successor's family.[8]

Once the tenant has become a statutory tenant, there are certain grounds under which the landlord may obtain an order for possession by applying to court. These grounds fall into two categories, either discretionary or mandatory grounds. The discretionary grounds are either that suitable alternative accommodation is available or that one of the specified cases arise in Schedule 15, Part 1 of the Act.

These cases include, for example, where:

a) the tenant has breached certain of his obligations;

[7] These rules apply to deaths on or after January 15, 1989 under the Housing Act 1988, s.39. For deaths prior to this see the Rent Act 1977, s.2 and Sched. 1, Pt. 1.

[8] Under the Housing Act 1988, s.39 and Sched. 4, amending the Rent Act 1977, Sched. 1, a family member who is entitled on the death of the original statutory tenant obtains an assured periodic tenancy rather than a statutory tenancy, as does any type of second successor. As to assured tenancies see p. 123.

b) the tenancy was a service tenancy (*i.e.* the premises were let to the tenant as a result of his former employment by the landlord) and the premises are reasonably required as a residence for another employee of the landlord;

c) where the landlord[9] reasonably requires the premises as a residence for himself, his son or daughter over 18, or his father-in-law or mother-in-law (unless the tenant is able to satisfy the court that in the circumstances greater hardship would be caused by the making of the order for possession than refusing it).

In general the court must be satisfied that in all the circumstances it is reasonable to make an order for possession under one of the discretionary grounds.

There are also certain cases in which the court is bound to make an order for possession without the landlord having to establish reasonableness. An example of these mandatory grounds[10] includes where a former owner-occupier wishes to resume occupation or any member of his family who resided with the owner when he last occupied the dwelling as a residence. Another such ground is that a landlord requires the premises for occupation following his retirement.[11]

The provisions of the Act with respect to rent apply to all regulated tenancies, whether protected or statutory. The maximum rent recoverable is that *registered* for the dwelling-house in accordance with the provisions of the Act or, if no such rent is registered, the rent payable under the present tenancy. Applications for registration of a rent may be made to the rent officer by the landlord or by the tenant or jointly by both. There is nothing to prevent a tenant from agreeing to a rent on one day and applying to the rent officer on the next. The rent officer registers the rent if he thinks it fair; if not, he determines and registers a *fair rent*.[12] If either party objects, the matter is referred to a rent assessment committee. In determining a fair rent, regard must be had to all the circumstances (other than personal circumstances) and in particular to the age, character and locality of the dwelling-house and to its state of repair. Registered rents tend to be substantially lower than free market rents, because rent officers are required to exclude from consideration the scarcity of accommodation.

[9] Other than by a landlord who purchased the property after certain dates laid down in the legislation.

[10] See the Rent Act 1977, Sched. 15, Pt. II. (Case 11) and Pt. V.

[11] See the Rent Act 1977, Sched. 15, Case 12, as amended by the Housing Act 1980, s.66. However, to rely on this ground and Case 11, prior notice must usually be given and before commencement of the tenancy, stating that possession may be obtained in the future under these grounds.

[12] Subject to certain exceptions, no further application to register a different rent may be made within two years, the Rent Act 1977, s.67.

Restricted contracts

As we have seen, a tenancy to which the "resident landlord" exception applies, or under which the rent includes any payment for board or a substantial payment for attendance, or under which the tenant shares living accommodation with the landlord, is not a protected tenancy within the main provisions of the 1977 Act. In these cases, however, such tenancies are given limited protection as restricted contracts, by Parts V and VII of the Act.[13]

These provisions apply only to dwellings of which the rateable value is within the limits set by the Act, and they are excluded if any substantial payment is made for board, or if occupation is for the purposes of a holiday. Subject to these limitations, protection is given not only to a tenant under a lease, but also to a lodger or paying guest provided he has exclusive occupation[14] of some part of the premises.

The protection given is twofold. First, the contract of tenancy may be referred (by either party) to the local rent tribunal to determine a reasonable rent. The tribunal may confirm, reduce or increase the rent to the amount that it considers reasonable. Rents so determined are registered, and the landlord may not afterwards charge any greater rent than the registered rent unless the rent tribunal authorises an increase on the ground of a subsequent change of circumstances.[15] Secondly, although even such limited security of tenure as was afforded by the 1977 Act has been abolished for contracts made after November 27, 1980, a court making an order for possession against an occupier with a restricted contract now has power to stay or suspend the order, or postpone the date for possession, for up to three months, subject to terms as to payment for occupation.[16]

Assured tenancies: Housing Act 1988

This Act applies to tenancies in the private sector created on or after January 15, 1989, the policy being to gradually phase out regulated tenancies and restricted contracts,[17] subject to a few exceptions. The philosophy behind the legislation is that private lettings should be more open to market forces, thus encouraging landlords to

[13] As amended by the Housing Act 1980, s.69. Generally no tenancy or other contract made on or after January 15, 1989 can be a restricted contract, see the Housing Act 1988, s.36.

[14] Not "exclusive possession" in the technical sense (*Luganda v. Service Hotels Ltd* [1969] 2 Ch. 209).

[15] Also a review is possible if both parties consent to an application or if two years have elapsed since the last review, see the Rent Act 1977, s.80.

[16] Rent Act 1977, s.106A.

[17] See p. 120 and above.

let property, with the result that more private rental accommodation is available to alleviate housing problems. There are two fundamental changes made by the Housing Act 1988 (which generally favours the landlord more than the provisions of the Rent Act 1977): i) it broadens the grounds under which a landlord can obtain possession and therefore lessens a tenant's security of tenure and ii) it abolishes the fair rent system.[18] Nevertheless, for the present, many regulated tenancies created before January 15, 1989, under the Rent Act 1977, still exist and will continue to do so for some years to come, alongside assured tenancies governed by the 1988 Act.

An assured tenancy under the 1988 Act arises if, and so long as, a dwelling house is let as a separate dwelling to an individual tenant and it is the tenant's only or principal home.[19] Assured tenancies therefore differ from regulated tenancies, under the 1977 Act, in that the tenant must be an individual and it must be his only or principal house. An assured tenancy cannot be granted to a tenant who already holds under a regulated tenancy immediately prior to the new tenancy being granted,[20] so that device cannot be used to overcome the greater protection afforded to tenants by the 1977 Act.

Certain categories of tenancies are excluded from being an assured tenancy under Schedule 1 of the Housing Act 1988 and these are broadly similar to the exclusions under the 1977 Act. For example, high value properties, lettings by resident landlords (with some variations in the rules), holiday lettings and business tenancies cannot be assured tenancies. Nonetheless, unlike in the case of a protected tenancy, the provision of board and attendance does not prevent an assured tenancy from arising.

An assured tenancy may be a fixed term or periodic tenancy (any tenancy other than a periodic tenancy is a fixed term tenancy). (It is also possible to create an assured shorthold tenancy, the provisions concerning which are discussed later.) In addition to the express contractual terms of an assured tenancy, certain terms are implied by statute. It is an implied term of all assured tenancies that the tenant will give the landlord access to the dwelling house and to all reasonable facilities, so that the landlord may carry out repairs which he is entitled to undertake.[21] Further, it is implied into an assured periodic tenancy that no assignment or subletting shall occur without the landlord's consent.[22]

On expiry of the fixed term, an assured fixed term tenancy is automatically converted into a statutory periodic tenancy,[23] under

[18] See p. 122.
[19] Housing Act 1988, s.1 (1).
[20] Housing Act 1988, s.34 (1)(b).
[21] Housing Act 1988, s.16.
[22] Housing Act 1988, s.15 (1), although there are some exceptions to this under s.15(3).
[23] Housing Act 1988, s.5 (2).

which the tenant is entitled to remain in possession of the dwelling. In the case of an assured periodic tenancy, even after service of a landlord's notice to quit, the periodic tenancy still continues *i.e.* the service of the notice is ineffective. If the landlord seeks to obtain possession, in either case, he must obtain a court order unless the tenant terminates the tenancy *e.g.* by surrendering the tenancy or, in the case of a periodic tenancy, by serving his own notice to quit. An assured fixed term tenancy can be inherited by will or on intestacy. In respect of an assured periodic tenancy (including a statutory periodic tenancy[24] arising on expiry of an assured fixed term tenancy), the Housing Act 1988 includes statutory succession provisions. These are more restrictive than the provisions of the 1977 Act and the principal differences are that only one succession is permissible by a sole tenant and the tenancy cannot pass to members of a tenant's family. There can be one succession to the tenant's spouse (or a person who was living with the tenant as his or her wife or husband) and who immediately before the tenant's death was residing in the dwelling house, as his or her only or principal home. Where the statutory succession rules are relevant any disposition in a will is ineffective and the usual intestacy rules will not apply.[25]

To obtain a court order for possession of a dwelling let under an assured tenancy, the landlord must prove one of the grounds laid down in Schedule 2 of the Housing Act 1988. Further, before starting a possession action a notice of intention to commence possession proceeding must be served, in prescribed form, under section 8 of the Act.[26] The notice must state the grounds under which possession is sought, that proceedings will not be commenced until two weeks or two months have elapsed from service of the notice (depending on the ground relied on for possession), nor commenced later than 12 months after service of the notice.

There are certain discretionary and mandatory grounds under which possession can be obtained. Although these are in many cases similar to the grounds under the 1977 Act, they are often more generous. The discretionary grounds under which the court may order possession, if it is reasonable to do so, include:

(a) where alternative accommodation is available for the tenant (although if possession is obtained the landlord must pay the tenant's reasonable removal expenses);

[24] This is an interest in land. *Cf.* a statutory tenancy under the Rent Act 1977, see p. 121.

[25] Housing Act 1988, s.17. If there is no successor the tenancy can pass under the deceased tenant's will or intestacy, but the landlord may obtain possession under the mandatory ground in the Housing Act 1988, Sched. 2, Ground 7, providing that proceedings are normally commenced within 12 months of the former tenant's death. Further, the succession rules do not apply on the death of a tenant of a fixed term tenancy.

[26] The court can dispense with these requirements in most cases if it is deemed just and equitable to do so, see the Housing Act 1988, s.8(1)(b).

(b) where there has been persistent delay in paying rent, even though it is not in arrears at the time of the application;
(c) where the premises were let to an employee whose employment has ceased.[27]

The mandatory grounds fall into two categories: i) those requiring written notice to be given before commencement of the tenancy stating that possession may be obtained, in the future, under the grounds specified in the notice, and ii) those which do not.[28] The grounds under which prior notice must be served include:-

(a) that the landlord wishes to resume occupation of his only or principal house which he previously occupied at some time before the tenancy;
(b) that a mortgagee needs possession in order to sell the property with vacant possession, under his power of sale contained in a mortgage, granted before the tenancy commenced;
(c) that the landlord intends to demolish or reconstruct the whole or a substantial part of the dwelling house;
(d) where there are substantial arrears.

There is no provision for the registration of a fair rent, as such, in respect of an assured tenancy. At the outset the rent payable will be that agreed between the parties and, in the case of an assured fixed term tenancy, this will remain the case. However, under an assured periodic tenancy (including a statutory periodic assured tenancy) the landlord does have the statutory power to serve a notice of increase of rent in certain circumstances.[29] In such a case the tenant can challenge the new rent (if he does not it will be binding on him) and he may refer the matter to a rent assessment committee. The committee will assess the rent, based on the rent at which the dwelling house might reasonably be expected to be let, in the open market, by a willing landlord under an assured tenancy.[30] Therefore, unlike the fair rent system, this assessment will not result in a lower than market rent.

Assured shorthold tenancies

An assured shorthold tenancy is a tenancy which complies with all the normal requirements of an assured tenancy, but it must be for a

[27] Unlike under the Rent Act 1977 it is not necessary to show that the property is required for another employee, see p. 122.
[28] This notice is separate from the notice which must be served under the Housing Act 1988, s.8, see above and note 26.
[29] Also under the Housing Act 1988, s.13 the tenancy may include its own contractual provisions for rent reviews.
[30] Housing Act 1988, s.14(1) and (2), disregarding, for instance, the fact that there is a sitting tenant and that the tenant may have failed to comply with the terms of the tenancy.

fixed term of not less than six months[31] and a notice must be served, in a prescribed form, prior to the commencement of the tenancy, stating that it is an assured shorthold tenancy.[32] An assured shorthold tenancy can be granted for any length of term, subject to the minimum initial six month period. The same implied terms apply to an assured shorthold tenancy, as in the case of an assured periodic tenancy, prohibiting assignment without consent and allowing access to do repairs. Also, on the expiry of the fixed term a statutory periodic tenancy arises. This type of tenancy is of advantage to the landlord in that there is a simpler procedure available for obtaining possession. However, from a tenant's point of view, there are rent restrictions which prevent a landlord from charging more than market rent.

Any attempt to grant an assured shorthold tenancy to a tenant who immediately before, held an assured tenancy will be ineffective and presumably will result in a further assured tenancy being granted.[33] On the other hand, if the dwelling was previously let to the tenant on an assured shorthold tenancy and subsequently is relet to him on an assured tenancy, it is deemed that an assured shorthold tenancy is created, despite no prescribed notice having been served nor there being any minimum six month term.[34]

In addition to the usual statutory grounds which apply to an assured tenancy, there is a further mandatory ground for possession of a dwelling let under an assured shorthold tenancy, providing that certain conditions are fulfilled.[35] Broadly, under this ground, the court must make an order for possession if the original assured fixed term shorthold tenancy has come to an end and no further assured tenancy exists, apart from a statutory or assured periodic shorthold tenancy.[36] Also, the landlord must have served not less than two months' notice on the tenant stating that he requires possession.[37]

A tenant under an assured shorthold tenancy has a further opportunity to refer the rent payable under the tenancy to a rent assessment committee. The tenant can make one application to the committee, at any time after the grant of the tenancy, but not after the fixed term of

[31] With no term permitting the landlord to terminate the tenancy within the first 6 months, although the usual forfeiture clause is allowed, in the event of breach of covenant.

[32] Housing Act 1988, s.20. Assured shorthold tenancies are the successors to protected shorthold tenancies under the Rent Act 1977, which were short fixed term tenancies of not less than one year nor more than 5 years, which have now mostly been replaced by assured shorthold tenancies.

[33] Housing Act 1988, s.20(3).

[34] An exception to this is where the landlord serves a notice to the contrary, see the Housing Act 1988, s.20(5).

[35] Housing Act 1988, s.21.

[36] Housing Act 1988, s.21(1).

[37] The notice procedure varies depending on whether notice is served prior to or on the date the fixed term expires, or is served after expiry of the fixed term, when a statutory periodic tenancy has arisen. See the Housing Act 1988, s.21(1) to (4).

the tenancy has expired.[38] The committee will only review the rent if there are a sufficient number of similar dwelling houses in the locality let on assured tenancies (including assured shorthold tenancies) and the rent payable under the particular tenancy is significantly higher than the rent which the landlord might reasonably be expected to obtain, having regard to the rent payable under the other assured tenancies in the locality.[39] If the committee conducts a review, it will determine the rent which the landlord can reasonably expect to obtain under the assured shorthold tenancy. This provision is of use, therefore, if the landlord is charging an exorbitant rent, above the market rent. If revised, the new rent will last for the remainder of the fixed term and the contractual rent will no longer apply.

Secure tenancies

The Rent Act 1977 and the Housing Act 1988 do not apply when the landlord is a public body such as a local authority.[40] The Housing Act 1980, recognising (in provisions now replaced by the Housing Act 1985) the substantial increase in public housing in recent times and the need to protect occupiers of such housing, created a new form of secure tenancy. A secure tenancy arises[41] where a dwelling-house is let[42] as a separate dwelling by a local authority, a new town corporation, an urban development corporation, a housing action trust or a similar body to an individual who occupies it as his only or principal house.

A secure tenancy can be terminated only by an order of the court on one of the grounds specified in the Act, and the landlord must first have served a notice in prescribed form.[43] Some of the grounds for possession are similar to those applying to regulated and assured tenancies. However, in general the court cannot make an order unless it considers it reasonable to do so, and in some cases suitable alternative accommodation must be available.[44] There is provision for one succession to a secure tenancy on the death of the tenant.

Perhaps the most important of the rights conferred on secure tenants by the 1985 Act, as amended by the Leasehold Reform, Housing and Urban Development Act 1993, is the right to buy at a

[38] The usual rent control provisions relating to all statutory periodic assured tenancies will then apply, see p. 126.
[39] Housing Act 1988, s.22(3).
[40] See p. 119.
[41] Subject to exceptions, most of which correspond with the Rent Act 1977 and the Housing Act 1988 exceptions, but also include lettings to homeless persons.
[42] These provisions apply also to a licence.
[43] Housing Act 1985, s.83.
[44] For the grounds see the Housing Act 1985, Sched. 2.

discounted price the freehold or a long lease of the dwelling, and to acquire the dwelling on rent to mortgage terms.[45]

Dwellings occupied by farm workers

The Rent Acts have never applied to most so-called *tied cottages, i.e.* residential accommodation supplied to farm workers under their terms of employment. Two main reasons explain why the Acts do not apply. First, the arrangements under which the accommodation is provided are usually such as to create a mere licence,[46] rather than a lease. Secondly, in most cases either no rent is payable, or the rent is too low to bring the accommodation within the Rent Acts. This gap is bridged by the Rent (Agriculture) Act 1976, for tenancies commencing before January 15, 1989, and the Housing Act 1988, Part I, for tenancies commencing on or after that date, which will each be considered in turn.

The Rent (Agricultural) Act 1976 confers security of tenure (either as a protected occupier or, where his initial licence or lease is determined, as a statutory tenant) on a qualifying worker who under a relevant licence or tenancy occupies a dwelling-house which is in qualifying ownership.

In broad terms, a worker "qualifies" for this purpose if he has been employed in agriculture for not less than 91 out of the past 104 weeks. The licence or tenancy is "relevant" notwithstanding that it is a mere licence, or that little or no rent is payable, provided that it gives exclusive occupation of a separate dwelling. Subject to this, however, much the same limitations apply as have already been mentioned in relation to the Rent Act 1977. For example, farm workers employed and housed by resident landlords or by government departments fall outside the 1976 Act. A dwelling house will be in qualifying ownership if the agricultural worker's employer owns it or has an arrangement whereby it can be used for occupation by the agricultural worker.

A statutory tenancy arising under the 1976 Act is similar in most respects to its counterpart under the Rent Act 1977, but only one transmission can take place in favour of the tenant's family.[47] The grounds on which a landlord may be entitled to recover possession are

[45] *I.e.* the right to buy an interest in the dwelling initially at a price which means that interest is paid on the mortgage at a rate no greater than the rent previously paid. The landlord retains a share in the property, in respect of the balance of the purchase price, which is a charge on the property and which must be paid off eventually, usually on sale. See the Housing Act 1985, s.143, as substituted by the Leasehold Reform, Housing and Urban Development Act 1993, s.108.

[46] See Chap. 15.

[47] If the original tenant dies on or after January 15, 1989 and the transmission is to a family member, rather than a spouse, the successor will acquire an assured agricultural occupancy under the Housing Act 1988, Sched. 4, Pt. II, see below.

also similar, but with one important variation. If possession is sought solely on the ground that the house is needed for another worker, the landlord must apply to the local housing authority for suitable alternative accommodation for the statutory tenant. If satisfied that vacant possession of the house is required for the other worker and his family, that the landlord himself cannot reasonably provide suitable accommodation, and that the interests of efficient agriculture require it, the authority must then use its best endeavours to provide the alternative accommodation.

There is provision for the registration of rents for statutory tenancies in accordance with a procedure similar to that set out in the Rent Act 1977.

Generally, a tenancy or licence granted to an agricultural worker on or after January 15, 1989 will fall under the provisions of the Housing Act 1988, as an assured agricultural occupancy. To qualify as an assured agricultural occupancy, the tenancy must be an assured tenancy and not an assured shorthold tenancy (or only be excluded from being an assured tenancy because the rent is low or it is a letting of an agricultural holding). Alternatively, if it is a licence it must confer exclusive possession. In either case, the occupier of the dwelling must satisfy the agricultural worker condition[48] *i.e.* the dwelling must be in qualifying ownership and be occupied by a qualifying worker, as defined by the 1976 Act. The same provisions which govern an assured tenancy under the 1988 Act generally apply to an assured agricultural occupancy, including the rules relating to security of tenure and the role of the rent assessment committee. Nevertheless, there are some differences, for example, a possession order cannot be obtained on the grounds that the employment has terminated[49] and the provisions of the 1976 Act allowing possession on the basis of alternative accommodation provided by a local authority also apply to an assured agricultural occupancy.

Long tenancies of dwelling-houses

Limited security of tenure is provided to long leasehold residential tenants by Part I of the Landlord and Tenant Act 1954. This applies to a long tenancy for a term exceeding 21 years, at a low rent[50] granted before April 1, 1990 or created pursuant to a contract made before that date. (The position regarding those tenancies created on or after that date is dealt with further below.)

Such a tenancy is subject to the 1954 Act provided that the tenancy fulfils certain qualifying conditions which are broadly that the *only*

48 Housing Act 1988, s.24 and Sched. 3.

49 Housing Act 1988, s.25 and s.26.

50 *I.e.* for a tenancy granted before April 1, 1990, a rent less than two thirds of the rateable value of the property.

reason why the Rent Act 1977 does not apply is the low rent. Under the 1954 Act, the long tenancy is automatically continued after the end of the term if the tenant so desires, and the landlord may terminate it by notice in only two ways. Under the first, after service of notice, he may apply to the court for possession on grounds similar to those under the Rent Act 1977. Secondly, he may serve a notice proposing a statutory tenancy, in which case the terms of the tenancy will be settled by agreement between the parties or by the court. After commencement of the statutory tenancy, the rent will be governed by the provisions of the Rent Act 1977.

A long residential tenancy created on or after April 1, 1990 at a low rent[51] which otherwise would be an assured tenancy under the Housing Act 1988, is governed by the Local Government and Housing Act 1989. Further, from January 15, 1999 onwards, the 1989 Act will also cover all those long tenancies created before April 1, 1990 whose term has not expired on January 15, 1999. The provisions of the 1989 Act allow the tenant to remain in possession of the premises on the expiry of the fixed term, under a continuation of the long residential term, and thus the rules are similar to those under the 1954 Act, but with some differences as to the mode of termination by the landlord. First, the grounds for possession are the same as the discretionary grounds for possession for assured tenancies under the Housing Act 1988, with three additions. Secondly, if the landlord has no grounds for obtaining possession he may serve a notice, proposing an assured monthly periodic tenancy, with any dispute as to the rent or terms being decided by the rent assessment committee.

Nowadays, the security of tenure provisions discussed above are less important, because of the extensive rights given to long leasehold tenants of dwelling-houses and flats enabling them to acquire the freehold (commonly referred to as *enfranchisement*) or a further long lease, under the Leasehold Reform Act 1967 and the Leasehold Reform, Housing and Urban Development Act 1993, respectively.

Leasehold enfranchisement

Leases for a very long term such as 99 years or more are frequently granted at a low rent, or *ground rent*, so called because it was originally paid, in the case of building leases, in consideration of the tenant having the right to build on the land. Alternatively, where there was already a building on the land, the tenant would pay a *fine* or *premium* (*i.e.* a lump sum) for the property to the builder who erected the building and ground rent to the owner for use of the land.

[51] *I.e.* for tenancies entered into on or after April 1, 1990, rent of not more than £1,000 p.a. in Greater London and £250 p.a. elsewhere.

The tenant (and his successors in title) at the end of such a lease had no security of tenure, because the tenancy, being at a low rent, was excluded from the operation of the Rent Acts. The Leasehold Reform Act 1967[52] meets this, by giving to the tenant of a *leasehold house*[53] held for a term exceeding 21 years (at a rent less than two-thirds of the rateable value or for a tenancy entered into on or after April 1, 1990, at a rent within low rental limits),[54] a right to acquire on fair terms the freehold or an extended lease (of 50 years). This is provided that when he seeks to exercise the right the tenant has occupied the house, or some part of it,[55] as his only or main residence for the last three years or for periods amounting to three years in the last ten years.[56]

If the tenant elects to purchase the freehold, the method of calculating the purchase price is complex and varies depending on the rateable value of the house on March 31, 1990 or, for a house constructed after that date (when the domestic rating system was abolished), it depends on the amount of the premium paid when the lease was granted. The price payable is based broadly[57] on the market value of the house, but on the assumption that i) in the case of low value houses (determined by using the above test), the lease has been extended for 50 years under the Act, but that there is no right to enfranchisement or ii) in the case of higher value property, that there is no extension of the lease, but that the tenant has the right to remain in possession under Part 1 of the Landlord and Tenant Act 1954 or Schedule 10 of the Local Government and Housing Act 1989.[58] The second method of valuation therefore takes into account the marriage value when determining the open market price, *i.e.* the increase in the value which arises when the tenant's leasehold interest and the freehold interest of the landlord are merged; the landlord and tenant usually each being entitled to half. Enfranchisement under the 1967 Act has now been extended to a larger number of long leasehold

[52] As to the dubious principle of "equity" on which the Act was said to be based, see M. & W., pp. 1127–1128.

[53] For this purpose a flat is not a house. The Landlord and Tenant Act 1987, Part I, contains detailed provisions under which "qualifying" tenants of flats have the right of first refusal if a landlord intends to sell his reversion. Under the Leasehold Reform, Housing and Urban Development Act 1993, tenants of flats, in some circumstances, have a collective right to purchase the freehold of the premises, see below.

[54] See note 51 above. If still under these provisions a tenancy is excluded from the Act, an alternative test can be used based on the rent payable in the first year of the tenancy, to ensure that long residential leases at currently higher rents are now covered by the 1967 Act, see the Leasehold Reform, Housing and Urban Development Act 1993, s.63(2) and s.65.

[55] See *Harris v. Swick Securities Ltd* [1969] 1 W.L.R. 1604.

[56] See *Poland v. Earl Cadogan* [1980] 3 All E.R. 544.

[57] The detailed provisions are outside the scope of this book.

[58] See the Leasehold Reform Act 1967, s.9(1) and (1A).

houses by the Leasehold Reform, Housing and Urban Development Act 1993.[59] The price payable for such freeholds is calculated by a third method, which leads to a higher valuation than in the previous cases. It is based on the second method but it assumes, for instance, that the tenant's share of the marriage value cannot, by statute, exceed half and that the tenant is not entitled to remain in possession under the 1954 or 1989 Act.[60]

If the tenant claims a new lease, the rent is to be the current letting value of the site without the buildings, and may be revised after 25 years. In default of agreement as to price or rent, terms will be settled by the Leasehold Valuation Tribunal or, on appeal, by the Lands Tribunal. The county court also has general jurisdiction over claims.

In certain cases the landlord may oppose the tenant's claim (*e.g.* if the landlord proposes to demolish or reconstruct the house, or if he reasonably requires the house as a residence for himself or a member of his family), but only at the cost of compensating the tenant for the loss of his rights under the Act.

The right to apply for enfranchisement has now been extended to long leasehold tenants of *flats* by Part 1, Chapter 1 of the Leasehold Reform, Housing and Urban Development Act 1993, thereby enabling such tenants, to have more control over the management and upkeep of the structure and common parts of the property in which their flats are situated. The Act provides for *collective* enfranchisement, giving the tenants the right to buy together the freehold of the *whole premises* containing the flats, rather than an individual tenant the right to buy the freehold of his particular flat. Qualifying tenants of long leasehold flats are entitled to purchase the freehold of the premises, through a nominee purchaser, who buys on behalf of the other purchasing tenants *e.g.* through a managing company created for this purpose. The freehold premises must be owned by one person for the Act to apply. Further, in order for the right to arise, the premises must be a self contained building or a self contained part of a building and include at least two or more flats owned by qualifying tenants and the qualifying tenants must hold at least two-thirds of the total flats in the premises. This two-thirds rule means that the tenants may still have the right to buy the whole premises where part of the premises are held under business lettings or short term residential lettings. The Act provides for the leasing back to the landlord of certain parts in some circumstances *e.g.* a flat which is subject to a secure tenancy. Certain premises are excluded from being purchased, for example, where a certain proportion of the property is used for non-residential use or in some circumstances where there is a residential landlord.

[59] See note 54 above. It also now applies to some tenancies which were previously excluded because they were terminable on death or remarriage.

[60] See Leasehold Reform Act 1967, s.9(1C).

To be a qualifying tenant, the tenant must hold a long lease of a flat, initially granted for a term exceeding 21 years, and a low rent must be payable in the first year of the term.[61] In order to exercise the right to purchase the freehold collectively, a notice must be served on the freeholder stating, amongst other matters, those qualifying tenants who wish to buy (not all the qualifying tenants in the premises have to do so) and the proposed purchase price. The notice will only be valid if a) the qualifying tenants who serve the notice are not less than two-thirds of all the qualifying tenants and are tenants of not less than half of the flats in the premises, and b) at least half of the qualifying tenants who serve the notice satisfy a residence condition. The residence condition is that the tenant must have occupied the flat as his only or principal home for the last 12 months or for periods totalling 3 years in the last 10 years. The landlord then serves a counter-notice stating whether he accepts the tenant's right to buy the landlord's freehold and, if so, whether he accepts the tenant's proposals including as to price (if he does not, counter-proposals must be given). There are provisions whereby a landlord can object to the purchase of the freehold in limited circumstances. These include where two-thirds of all the long leaseholders of the premises have an unexpired term of 5 years or less and the landlord requires the premises for redevelopment.[62]

Schedule 6 of the 1993 Act sets out the mechanism for calculating the price to be paid for the freehold, which is based on the general presumption of a sale at market value, disregarding the right to enfranchise. Generally speaking, the landlord must be paid the combined total of i) the value of his freehold interest in the premises, plus ii) his share of the marriage value[63] and iii) he must be compensated for any loss or damage to his other property resulting from the purchase *e.g.* the inability to redevelop such property due to enfranchisement. In addition, the tenant must pay the landlord's reasonable costs in respect of the purchase. In the event of dispute, the price will be decided by the Leasehold Valuation Tribunal.

The 1993 Act also provides individual long leaseholders with the right to be granted a new extended lease, for the remainder of the term of their current lease plus a further 90 years, at a nominal rent, on the payment of a premium. The qualifying criteria for the right to arise are similar to those for collective enfranchisement, but they are slightly less stringent in some respects, as it is an individual right.

[61] For leases granted on or after April 1, 1990 the rent must not exceed £1,000 in Greater London or £250 outside; for leases granted pre April 1, 1990, but on or after April 1, 1963, the rent must not exceed two-thirds the rateable value of the property on the date the lease was granted; and for leases granted pre April 1, 1963 the rent must not exceed two-thirds the letting value when the lease was granted.

[62] Leasehold Reform, Housing and Urban Development Act 1993, s.23.

[63] See p. 132.

Again, the right is available to a qualifying tenant with a long lease of a flat, granted for a term exceeding 21 years, initially at a low rent. However, the tenant must satisfy a longer residence condition of 3 years rather than the 12 month condition described above.[64] The individual right to purchase an extended lease is in addition to collective enfranchisement, but the right cannot be exercised at the same time as enfranchisement. Broadly, the premium payable by the tenant will be the sum total of i) the reduction in value of the landlord's interest following the grant of the new lease, ii) the landlord's proportion of the marriage value (*i.e.* at its simplest the difference between the combined value of the existing lease and landlord's reversion and the combined value of the new lease and landlord's reversion subject to that lease) and iii) compensation for any loss or damage suffered to the landlord's other property as a result of the new lease. The tenant must pay also the landlord's reasonable costs.

BUSINESS PREMISES

Most tenancies of business premises (including mixed business-residential premises)[65] are protected by Part II of the Landlord and Tenant Act 1954. The broad effect of the Act is to continue the existing tenancy indefinitely unless and until terminated in accordance with the provisions of the Act. These require service by the landlord of a statutory notice to terminate the tenancy, which in turn gives the tenant the right to claim a new lease provided that he has served a counter-notice stating that he is not prepared to give up possession.[66]

In default of agreement between the parties, where such notices are served, a tenant will have to apply to the court for a new tenancy. Unless the landlord can establish one of certain statutory grounds set out in his notice, the court is bound to grant a new tenancy for a period not exceeding 14 years on such terms as it thinks fit, having regard to certain matters specified in the Act. The rent is fixed in accordance with current market values. In respect of other terms, the burden is on the party who seeks to depart from those of the existing tenancy to prove that the terms should be changed.[67] In principle there is no limit to the number of renewals.

The grounds on which a landlord may oppose a new tenancy include:

[64] The landlord can oppose the grant of a new lease on the same ground as in the case of enfranchisement, see above.

[65] See p. 120.

[66] Landlord and Tenant Act 1954, s.25. Alternatively, the tenant may initiate matters by serving a notice requesting a new tenancy, in response to which the landlord may serve a counter-notice opposing the grant of a new tenancy, see s.26 of the Act.

[67] *O'May v. City of London Real Property Co. Ltd* [1983] 2 A.C. 726.

(a) breach by the tenant of certain of his obligations;
(b) that the landlord intends to demolish or reconstruct the premises;
(c) that the landlord intends to occupy the premises himself (provided that the landlord's interest has not been purchased or created less than five years before the termination of the tenancy).

If a new tenancy is refused on certain of these grounds, notably the last two, the tenant is entitled to compensation from the landlord. This compensation will be the rateable value of the premises, unless the tenant and his predecessors have occupied the premises for business purposes for the last 14 years, in which case the amount is twice the rateable value.[68]

There are certain tenancies excluded from the Act, *e.g.* agricultural holdings, and tenancies for a certain term not exceeding six months.

Finally, under the Landlord and Tenant Act 1927, a tenant who leaves may recover compensation from his landlord for improvements which he has made to business premises if these have increased their letting value.

AGRICULTURAL HOLDINGS

Agricultural tenancies have since 1875 been regulated by a series of statutes, conferring on agricultural tenants (*i.e.* tenant farmers rather than agricultural workers) rights to compensation for improvements or disturbance. More recently and more importantly these provisions have included rights with respect to security of tenure and the control of rent.

The main provisions for security of tenure are now contained in the Agricultural Holdings Act 1986.[69] Under these provisions security of tenure is given to tenancies from year to year. Subject to certain exceptions, any letting, for value, for an interest less than a yearly tenancy is deemed to take effect as a yearly tenancy and so the security of tenure rules will apply. Further, a fixed term tenancy for two years or more does not determine automatically at the end of the term, but will continue as a yearly tenancy unless, either party serves a notice to quit not less than one year, nor more than two years, before

[68] This applies where notice terminating the tenancy is served on or after April 1, 1990, but alternative transitional provisions apply where the tenancy was entered into pre April 1, 1990 and notice is served before April 1, 2000. See the Landlord and Tenant Act 1954, s.37 and the Landlord and Tenant Act 1954 (Appropriate Multiplier) Order 1990.

[69] But under the provisions of the Agricultural Tenancies Act 1995 (which is not yet in force), security of tenure generally will be abolished for certain tenancies created after the legislation comes into force, see p. 138 and note 77.

the end of the original tenancy.[70] Nevertheless, there is a loophole as a tenancy of more than a year, but less than two years, does not fall under the security of tenure provisions, as this is not within the definition of a yearly tenancy.

To determine a yearly tenancy, under the general rules governing a tenancy of an agricultural holding, a full twelve months' notice is required, expiring at the end of the tenancy.[71] Under the Act, a tenant who receives such a notice to quit usually has the right to serve a counter-notice on the landlord, claiming the benefit of the Act. In such a case, the notice to quit will become inoperative unless the Agricultural Land Tribunal consents to it taking effect. It can do so only in six specified cases (*e.g.* in order to enable the landlord to carry out some purpose which is desirable in the interests of better farming) and it must be fair and reasonable for the landlord to insist on possession. However, the tenant has no right to serve a counter-notice where the landlord's notice has relied on one of eight grounds set out in the Act, *e.g.* where the landlord's interest in the holding has been materially prejudiced by an irreparable breach by the tenant of a term of the tenancy.[72] Any question as to whether the tenant has a right to serve a counter-notice is settled by arbitration.

Although the death of the tenant is one of the cases in which there is no right to serve a counter-notice, the Act provides, in relation to tenancies granted before July 12, 1984, that on the death of the tenant any member of his near family who has recently derived his livelihood from the holding for five years can apply to the Agricultural Land Tribunal for a tenancy. Such an application will be granted if the Tribunal is satisfied as to the applicant's suitability. If these succession rights apply, the Act also provides that a tenant who wishes to retire may nominate an eligible successor.[73]

A tenant who is required by his landlord to quit the land is (with some exceptions) entitled to compensation for disturbance. The basic amount of the compensation is not less than one year's and not more than two years' rent and in certain circumstances additional compensation will be payable.[74] A tenant who quits his holding may also be entitled to compensation for certain improvements carried out by him. The amount of the compensation is generally the increase in the value of the holding, but where the improvement is of a short term character the amount is the value of the improvement to a new tenant.[75]

[70] Agricultural Holdings Act 1986, ss.2 and 3.

[71] Agricultural Holdings Act 1986, s.25. This overrides the common law rule that 6 months' notice is required to determine a yearly tenancy.

[72] Agricultural Holdings Act 1986, Sched. 3.

[73] Agricultural Holdings Act 1986, Part IV.

[74] Agricultural Holdings Act 1986, s.60.

[75] Agricultural Holdings Act 1986, s.66 and Sched. 7 and 8.

Finally, there are provisions under the Act whereby, at intervals of not less than three years, either party may require the amount of the rent to be settled by arbitration.[76]

The Agricultural Tenancies Act 1995[77] when it comes into force will provide for the deregulation of agricultural tenancies by the creation of farm business tenancies, if certain conditions are fulfilled. The Agricultural Holdings Act 1986 will generally still apply to tenancies granted prior to the new legislation coming into force. The main aims of the Act are i) to abolish security of tenure for farm business tenancies and ii) to reduce the circumstances in which compensation is payable to a tenant on quitting the land. It also contains rent review provisions.

[76] Agricultural Holdings Act 1986, s.12 and 13.
[77] See note 69. This is likely to come into force on September 1, 1995.

14. Easements and profits

EASEMENTS

An easement gives the right to use the land of another in a particular way (a positive easement), or the right to prevent another from using his own land in a particular way (a negative easement). An example of a positive easement is a right of way over another's land; an illustration of a negative easement is a right of light, which prevents a neighbour from building on his land in such a way as to obstruct unduly the flow of natural light to the windows of a house or other building on adjacent land. In either case the land which benefits from the easement is called the *dominant tenement,* and the land over which the easement is exercisable is called the *servient tenement.* An easement is a right *in rem. i.e.* a right in land, which is capable in certain circumstances of binding successive owners of the servient tenement and benefiting successive owners of the dominant tenement.

An easement is defined in section 1(2) of the Law of Property Act 1925 as one of the interests in land which (since 1925) are capable of being legal, providing certain conditions are complied with. Otherwise, an easement may be equitable.[1]

The conditions of an easement

No right can be an easement unless it satisfies the following conditions:

(i) There must be a dominant tenement and a servient tenement *i.e.* one tenement to which the right is attached and another tenement which has the burden of the right.

(ii) The dominant and the servient tenements must be in different hands, or more precisely the two tenements must not be both owned and occupied by the same person in the

[1] As to the conditions which must be fulfilled for an easement to be legal or equitable and binding on successors in title, see pp. 143–144.

same capacity (or right). For example, if one tenement is owned beneficially and the other as trustee, the two tenements are not owned in the same right.

(iii) The right must *accommodate* the dominant tenement, *i.e.* in some way benefit the land.

(iv) The right must lie in grant, *i.e.* it must be one which could have been granted by deed. This means that there must be a capable grantor and grantee. So where, for example, the purported grantor is a statutory body with no power to grant easements, there can be no grant. In addition, the right must be sufficiently definite and so fall within the general category of rights which are capable of being easements.

A right which does not satisfy these conditions will not be an easement. It does not, however, necessarily follow that the law will not recognise the right at all. It may be a perfectly valid right such as a contractual licence,[2] but it will not be an easement.

As an easement is a right against the land of another it is clear that the land over which it is exercisable must be a servient tenement. Identifying a dominant tenement is more difficult. For there to be a dominant tenement the benefit of an easement must attach to a definite plot of land, so that only the occupiers of that plot have the benefit of the right. Further the dominant tenement must exist before the time of the grant.[3] An easement cannot, therefore, be created in favour of a grantee personally, *i.e.* independently of the ownership or occupation by him of adjacent land. This means, in technical language, that an easement cannot exist *in gross*.

The requirement that the easement must "accommodate" the dominant land, will only rarely fail to be satisfied. In *Hill v. Tupper*[4], however, a right to hire out boats on a canal (the supposed servient tenement) was held not to constitute an easement, although the boats were stored on land adjoining the canal (the supposed dominant tenement). The right was a mere commercial licence granted by the canal owners to the boat owner personally and not because of the boat owner's ownership of the adjoining land.

As the right must be capable of forming the subject-matter of a grant by deed, vague rights such as rights of view or privacy cannot be created as easements.[5] Such rights are essentially negative, operating to prevent a neighbour from using his land in a particular way, *e.g.* by

[2] See Chap. 15. For example, a right to use a fire escape route, which described itself as a licence, was held to be such rather than an easement, as the usual words associated with the grant of an easement had not been used, see *IDC Group v. Clark* [1992] 2 EGLR, 184, C.A.

[3] *London & Blenheim Estates Ltd v. Ladbroke Retail Parks Ltd* [1994] 1 W.L.R 31.

[4] (1863) 2 H. & C. 121.

[5] *Browne v. Flower* [1911] 1 Ch. 219.

building.[6] The only negative easements recognised at law are those of light, air and support,[7] all of which are sufficiently definite to form the subject-matter of a grant. The first two are confined to light or air flowing through particular apertures in the dominant building *e.g.* through a window or skylight. Such easements do not prevent the servient owner from building altogether, but only from materially obstructing that limited access of light or air,[8] through a particular aperture. The easement of support is confined to the support of one building by another, and prevents the servient owner from removing that support.

The category of positive easements, on the other hand, is not closed. There is no difficulty in formulating the grant of a right to use the land of another in a particular way, and the law has recognised as easements a very wide variety of rights, provided always that they comply with the four conditions mentioned above. In the leading case of *Re Ellenborough Park*[9] a right to use an adjoining park for recreational purposes was purportedly granted as an easement to the purchasers of houses on a new estate. At the end of an exhaustive analysis of the nature of an easement, the Court of Appeal arrived at the perhaps unsurprising conclusion that the right was indeed capable of being an easement.[10] Problems have arisen, however, where a right claimed as an easement has been held to be too extensive, amounting virtually to possession of the land (to the exclusion of the servient owner), rather than mere use of the land. As an example, different decisions have been reached by the courts on the question of whether a right of storage can exist as an easement,[11] depending on the degree of use.[12]

It must however be emphasised, at this stage, that there are good reasons why the category of easements, whether positive or negative, should be extended further only reluctantly. Like any other interest in land an easement can be granted expressly. However, unlike the grant of other interests, the grant of an easement also may be implied or presumed. As will be seen later the grant of an easement may be implied by law where an owner disposes of part of his land and retains the remainder. A grant will be presumed where a right in the nature of an easement has been exercised for a long period with the apparent acquiescence of the servient owner. The law is almost bound to

[6] Restrictive covenants are the most effective means of creating such rights, see p. 173.

[7] See *Phipps v. Pears* [1965] 1 Q.B. 76 (no easement of protection from weather).

[8] Compare *Cable v. Bryant* [1908] 1 Ch. 259, *Bryant v. Lefever* (1879) 4 C.P.D. 172.

[9] [1956] Ch. 131.

[10] Another modern example of an easement is the right to park a car in a car park, *London & Blenheim Estates Ltd v. Ladbroke Retail Parks Ltd* [1992] 1 W.L.R. 1278.

[11] Compare *Copeland v. Greenhalf* [1952] Ch. 488, *Grigsby v. Melville* [1972] 1 W.L.R. 1355, *Wright v. Macadam* [1949] 2 K.B. 744.

[12] This test was confirmed in *London & Blenheim Estates Ltd v. Ladbroke Retail Parks Ltd* concerning the right to park a car (see note 10).

recognise as an easement a right which has been expressly granted as such by agreement. However, much greater resistance might be expected where the right is very extensive, encroaching seriously on the servient owner's freedom to enjoy his own property, and is claimed merely on the basis of an implied grant or, even more questionably, a presumed grant.[13]

Easements and natural rights

An easement is an acquired right, *i.e.* it must have been created by a grant of the right made by the owner of the servient tenement. A natural right is one that a landowner has automatically as a result of his ownership of the land. Most natural rights are rights which a man has with respect to his own land, *i.e.* the right to walk about it.[14] There is, however, a natural right of support which gives to every landowner the right to have his land supported laterally by the soil of his neighbour's land. If this support is withdrawn and as a consequence the surface of his land subsides, the landowner will have an action for damages[15] against his neighbour. Damages can be recovered for any resulting damage to buildings, unless the weight of the building contributed to the subsidence, in which case *no* action can succeed for breach of the natural right. Apart from the natural right to support, a landowner may have an easement of support, but like every easement, this can only be acquired by a grant. Such an easement of support can give a landowner the right to have buildings on his land supported by neighbouring land or a neighbouring building.

Extent of easements

The commonest easements are rights of light and rights of way. However, a problem often arises as to the extent to which these may be exercised against the servient land.

There is no natural right of light, and in general a landowner cannot be prevented from obstructing the flow of light to his neighbour's land. The only exceptions are where the neighbour has acquired an easement of light, or some other right (such as a restrictive covenant against building).[16] As has been seen, an easement of light does not extend to the whole of the light flowing from

[13] As in *Copeland v. Greenhalf* (see note 11).
[14] As to riparian rights, see pp. 16–17.
[15] See *Redland Brick Ltd v. Morris* [1970] A.C. 652, in which a mandatory injunction was refused on the ground that the cost of restoring support would greatly exceed the loss caused by subsidence.
[16] As to restrictive covenants, see pp. 173–177.

the servient land, but is confined to the light flowing through a particular window or aperture in a building on the dominant land. It gives the right only to sufficient light for use of the building for ordinary domestic or business purposes.[17] An obstruction of the flow of light which substantially reduces the amount of light reaching the windows of a building will not necessarily constitute an infringement of an easement of light. The question is not how much light has been taken away, but how much light is *left*. Therefore, if there is sufficient light still for ordinary domestic or business purposes there will be no interference with the easement.[18]

The extent of a right of way, *i.e.* whether it is for all purposes and at all times, or is subject to certain limitations (such as access by foot only), depends upon how it was acquired. If it was expressly granted the question is one of construction of the terms of the grant, and for this purpose the *contra proferentem* rule applies, *i.e.* any doubt as to the meaning of the terms will be resolved against the grantor and in favour of the grantee. Accordingly, a right of way granted in general terms will not be confined to the purposes for which the land was used at the time of the grant.[19] (The rules determining the extent of rights of way and other easements acquired by implied grant and by prescription are discussed below.[20])

In the absence of contrary agreement or special circumstances,[21] it is for the grantee of the way, not the grantor, to maintain and repair it.

Acquisition of easements

Commonly an easement may be acquired by a landowner over his neighbour's adjoining land or, where a landowner decides to sell part only of his land and to retain the rest. In the latter situation, the purchaser of part of the land will want to be granted rights of way or drainage over the retained land or an easement of light, for example, to enable him to enjoy the land which he has bought. Equally, the seller may wish to reserve for himself similar easements over the land sold.

As previously mentioned, wherever an easement is acquired it must have its origin in a grant which may be express, implied or presumed (presumed grant is also known as *prescription*). Let us consider each of these possible methods of acquisition separately.

1. Express grant or reservation

A, the fee simple owner of Blackacre, may expressly grant to B, the fee simple owner of Whiteacre, an easement (*e.g.* a right of way) over

[17] Including use as a greenhouse (*Allen v. Greenwood* [1980] Ch. 119).
[18] *Colls v. Home and Colonial Stores Ltd* [1915] A.C. 599.
[19] *British Railways Board v. Glass* [1965] Ch. 538.
[20] At pp. 144–152.
[21] See *Liverpool C.C. v. Irwin* [1977] A.C. 239.

Blackacre. The easement so expressly created will be a legal easement if and only if (a) it is granted for an interest equivalent to an estate in fee simple absolute in possession or a term of years absolute[22] and (b) it is granted by deed.[23] It follows, therefore that an easement granted for the life of a person cannot be a legal easement, although it can exist as an equitable easement. Also, an easement created otherwise than by deed is void at law, although if there is a specifically enforceable agreement to grant it, this too may give rise to a valid equitable easement.[24]

A legal easement is also commonly created by express *reservation*. If a landowner sells part of his land to another person he may expressly reserve for the benefit of the land retained by him an easement (*e.g.* a right of way) against the land sold. The reservation of an easement in a conveyance of land creates a legal easement after 1925.[25]

2. Implied reservation or grant

(i) In favour of the grantor of land

If A grants part of his land to B the law is reluctant to imply the reservation of any easement in favour of the land retained by A against the land granted to B. A claim by A to any such easement is an attempt by him to derogate from his grant *i.e.* to detract from the land he grants to B. It is a general principle of the law that a grantor may not derogate from his grant.[26] In such a case the law is prepared to imply the reservation only of two types of easements namely, *easements of necessity* and *intended easements.*

An easement of necessity is one "without which the property retained cannot be used at all, and not one merely necessary to the reasonable enjoyment of the property."[27] An easement of light will never be implied in favour of the grantor of land, because a building is still usable without the benefit of natural light. However, on the sale of part, the reservation of an easement of way against the land sold will be implied in favour of the seller if he would have no other means of access to the land retained by him. Nevertheless, the law implies the reservation of such an easement grudgingly, and accordingly an easement of necessity can be used only to satisfy the needs of the dominant tenement as they were at the date of the grant. For example, if at the date of the grant the dominant tenement was used

[22] LPA 1925, s.1(2) (see p. 33).
[23] *Ibid.*, s.52 (see p. 27). In the case of registered land it must also be registered, see p. 222.
[24] See p. 27.
[25] LPA 1925, s.65. As to the extent of such an easement, see *St. Edmundsbury and Ipswich Diocesan Board of Finance v. Clark (No. 2)* [1975] 1 W.L.R. 468.
[26] See p. 113.
[27] *Union Lighterage Co. v. London Graving Dock Co.* [1902] 2 Ch. 557.

for agricultural purposes, a right of way impliedly reserved as an easement of necessity cannot be used to carry building materials across the servient tenement for some non-agricultural purpose.[28]

An intended easement is one which it appears in the circumstances the parties must mutually have intended to create. For example, on the sale of a terrace house the grant and reservation may be implied of mutual easements of support as between the house sold and an adjoining house retained by the vendor.

(ii) In favour of the grantee of land

When a landowner conveys part of his land to another person the law is much readier to imply the grant of an easement against the land retained by the grantor, for the benefit of the land sold, than it is to imply a reservation in favour of the land retained. There can be an implied grant of an easement of necessity[29] and of an intended easement[30], but there are also two other possible methods of implied grant, under i) the rule in *Wheeldon v. Burrows*[31] and ii) *section 62 of the Law of Property Act 1925.*

Under the doctrine of *Wheeldon v. Burrows,* on the sale of part, the grantee of the land acquires as easements i) all "continuous and apparent" rights which are capable of becoming easements (called *quasi-easements*) or all those easements which are necessary to the reasonable enjoyment of the land granted and ii) which were in fact used by the owner of the whole of the land at the time of the grant, for the benefit of the part granted.

For example, if there is a house on the land conveyed which before the conveyance enjoyed the flow of natural light across the land retained by the grantor, there will be an implied grant of an easement of light for the benefit of the house. The word "continuous" means regularly exercised, rather than strictly continuous. A right is "apparent" for this purpose if its existence will be revealed by an inspection of the land: a right of way, for example, is apparent if a visible track can be seen.

The rule in *Wheeldon v. Burrows* also applies when a landowner simultaneously disposes of all parts of his land to different persons, *e.g.* if he makes devises of the land to different devisees by his will. In such a case the grantee of what we may call the quasi-dominant plot

[28] *Corporation of London v. Riggs* (1880) 13 Ch.D. 798.

[29] See *e.g. Liverpool C.C. v. Irwin* [1977] A.C. 239. The grant of a way of necessity will generally be implied on the basis either of public policy or of the presumed intention of the parties, if the property conveyed would otherwise be land-locked *(Nickerson v. Barraclough* [1981] Ch.426).

[30] See *Wong v. Beaumont Property Trust Ltd* [1965] 1 QB 173 and *Stafford v. Lee* (1992) 65 P. & C.R. 172 (where intention was inferred from the plans attached to the conveyance).

[31] (1879) 12 Ch.D.31.

(*e.g.* the land with the house on it in the above example) will get the *Wheeldon v. Burrows* easements against the quasi-servient plot.[32] The two plots will then become truly dominant and servient tenements.

There is some overlap between the common law doctrine of *Wheeldon v. Burrows* and section 62 of the Law of Property Act 1925. (The latter section is known as the "general words" section because it implies into every conveyance the words generally used by conveyancers, with the object of shortening the traditional form of clause used in conveyances of land. However, the section does not apply where a contrary intention is expressed in the conveyance). By section 62(1), a conveyance of land shall be deemed to include and shall operate to convey with the land "all buildings, erections, fixtures . . . *privileges, easements, rights and advantages whatsoever,* appertaining or reputed to appertain to the land, or any part thereof, or, at the time of conveyance . . . enjoyed with or reputed or known as part or parcel of or appurtenant to the land or any part thereof."

The effect of this provision is to pass to the grantee of the land all the existing easements which already benefit the land sold. As such, the section merely reflects what was previously the position under general land law principles. However, what is surprising is that, as judicially interpreted, it also operates to convert a mere personal "privilege" into an easement and an irrevocable right of property.[33] For example, in *Wright v. Macadam*[34] a landlord allowed his tenant to store his coal in a coal-shed belonging to the landlord, although the terms of the lease did not give such a right to the tenant. When the lease expired the landlord granted a new lease to the tenant, which again made no mention of the right to store the coal in the landlord's coal-shed. This new lease, however, was a "conveyance"[35] within the terms of section 62, and the court held that the lease had to be read as if it expressly conferred upon the tenant the right to store the coal in the landlord's coal-shed. The privilege which, during the earlier lease was merely precarious and could be withdrawn by the landlord at any time, had now become an easement.

Although an easement may arise by implied grant on the sale of part, both under section 62 and under *Wheeldon v. Burrows,* there are important distinctions between the two. In particular, section 62 applies only to a "conveyance" of land, *i.e.* where there is an instrument effective to create or transfer a legal estate in the land. *Wheeldon v. Burrows* is wider and can apply, not only to a legal

[32] *Schwann v. Cotton* [1916] 2 Ch. 120 and 459.

[33] Unless the right fails to satisfy the conditions of an easement: see *Phipps v. Pears,* note 7; *Regis Property Co. Ltd v. Redman* [1956] 2 Q.B. 612; *Green v. Ashco Horticulturist Ltd* [1966] 1 W.L.R. 889.

[34] Note 11.

[35] Including a merely written lease for three years or less which is effective as a legal lease even though not created by deed (see pp. 99–100).

disposition of land, but also to a disposition which creates an equitable interest in the land, such as an informal lease for more than three years.[36] Further, *Wheeldon v. Burrows* applies to rights that have been enjoyed *by* the common owner of the quasi-dominant and quasi-servient plots, before the sale of part. However, it is now clear that section 62 applies only to rights or privileges that have been exercised *against* the landowner prior to the division of land *e.g.* by his tenant.[37] There must therefore be separate occupation of the land by different persons, prior to the disposition. On the other hand section 62 is wider in that it applies to rights generally, not just those that are "continuous and apparent."[38]

Nevertheless, in either case, it must be remembered that no grant can be implied if the conveyance expresses a contrary intention.[39]

3. Prescription or presumed grant[40]

Long user (*i.e.* the long term enjoyment of a right) may give rise to the presumed grant of a legal easement, otherwise known as an easement by *prescription*. For example, if the owners of Blackacre have been in the habit of using a path across Whiteacre as a convenient means of access to Blackacre, and they have done this for a sufficiently long time, the law may presume that at some time in the past the fee simple owner of Whiteacre granted an easement of way across Whiteacre for the benefit of Blackacre.

Prescription is based upon the acquiescence of the fee simple owners of the servient tenement to the assertion of a right against that land by the fee simple owners of the dominant tenement. The law infers the grant of an easement as the only possible explanation of this long-continued acquiescence. To justify this inference the user of the land must have been as of right (*nec vi, nec clam, nec precario*)[41] and there must be evidence that the fee simple owners of the servient tenement have acquiesced in it.

Acquiescence must be distinguished from permission. Acquiescence by the servient owners to the open and continuous assertion of a right

[36] *Borman v. Griffith* [1930] 1 Ch. 493, and see p. 100.

[37] *Sovmots Investments Ltd v. Secretary of State for Environment* [1979] A.C. 144 affirming *Long v. Gowlett* [1923] 2 Ch. 177. The easement of light is an exception (*Broomfield v. Williams* [1897] 1 Ch. 602).

[38] It accordingly applies to profits, as well as to easements: *White v. Williams* [1922] 1 K.B. 727. See p. 153.

[39] A conveyance may be rectified to accord with such an intention (*Clark v. Barnes* [1929] 2 Ch. 368).

[40] Radical proposals for reform were made by the Law Reform Committee in its 14th Report (1966).

[41] "Not by force, in secret, nor by permission," but by the grant of the right. The use cannot be as of right if it is unlawful under statute, see *Hanning v. Top Deck Travel Group Ltd* (1994) 68 P. & C.R. 14, C.A.

by the dominant owners is the essence of prescription.[42] However, permission goes against the existence of any right, and precludes any prescriptive claim, as it provides an alternative explanation as to the acquisition of the right.[43] There can be no acquiescence without the servient owner having knowledge of user[44] and the power to prevent it. Thus, a prescriptive claim will normally fail if the servient owner was unaware of the user and could not with reasonable diligence have discovered it,[45] or if the period of user was during a time when the servient tenement was leased to a tenant.[46]

The user must have been continuous,[47] but this condition still will be satisfied if the right has been exercised from time to time as circumstances require, provided that the intervals are not excessive.[48] An easement acquired by prescription will be confined to user of the kind that has in fact been enjoyed (*e.g.* a right of way for foot passengers only), although a mere increase in user at some later time will not be excluded.[49]

An easement can be acquired by prescription both at common law and by statute.

(i) At common law

The common law has two modes of prescription. Under the earlier doctrine the grant of an easement is presumed if it appears that there has been user as of right since the beginning of legal memory (which by a fiction is fixed at A.D. 1189). On proving user for a minimum period of 20 years the law presumes that there has been user since 1189, but this presumption is rebuttable. For if it can be proved that user in fact began later than that date the claim will fail. In practice it is generally a matter of no great difficulty to prove that user began at a date after 1189. For example, when an easement of light is claimed, if it is proved that a building was first erected on that spot at some date later than 1189 then no easement by prescription through the windows in that building can be acquired.

The common law has a great reverence for rights, which have in fact been enjoyed over a long period of time, and therefore a second

[42] *Dalton v. Angus* (1881) 6 App.Cas. 740.

[43] But user may cease to be *precario, i.e.* permissive, if permission is not continually sought: see *Healey v. Hawkins* [1968] 1 W.L.R. 1967.

[44] As to knowledge of an agent, see *Diment v. N.H. Foot Ltd* [1974] 1 W.L.R. 1427.

[45] *Union Lighterage Co. v. London Graving Dock Co.* [1902] 2 Ch. 557.

[46] See pp. 150–151. Conversely, user by a lessee of the dominant tenement benefits the fee simple owner of the dominant tenement.

[47] See *Davis v. Whitby* [1974] Ch.186, in which an agreed variation of the route of a right of way did not break continuity, nor make the user thereafter permissive.

[48] *Hollins v. Verney* (1884) 13 Q.B.D. 304.

[49] *British Railways Board v. Glass* [1956] Ch. 538, *Woodhouse & Co. Ltd v. Kirkland Ltd* [1970] 1 W.L.R. 1185. As to the effect of *excessive* user resulting from alterations to the dominant tenement, see note 67.

theory of prescription was invented to supplement the first. This second mode of prescription at common law is known as the doctrine of the *lost modern grant,* whereas the earlier method is known, somewhat inappropriately, as *common law* prescription — it would more aptly be called the doctrine of the lost ancient grant. To establish a claim under the doctrine of the lost modern grant the claimant again must show that there has been user as of right for a minimum period of 20 years. The court may then presume the grant of an easement at some time before user began, which it is assumed has since been lost. This mode of prescription has its own disadvantage, namely that of uncertainty. All one can say is that upon proving at least 20 years' user the court may be prepared to infer a grant. Whether the court will do so depends upon all the circumstances of the particular case, and upon the likelihood or otherwise of a grant having been made.[50] In view of the conceptual difficulties arising from these two common law doctrines, parliament has intervened with the Prescription Act 1832, which provides a third and alternative ground upon which a claim by prescription may be based.[51]

(ii) The Prescription Act 1832

Easements other than light. The Act provides that a claim to an easement other than light may be based upon proof of user for either 20 years or 40 years. In both cases the user must be again *as of right.* Moreover, the user must be for 20 years or 40 years *without interruption* and *next before action (i.e.* the user must be immediately preceding some court action in which the right to the easement is brought into question). It will be seen that user alone does not give rise to an easement under the provisions of the Act. The right is only in its formative stage until some court action is begun, in which the claim to the easement is brought into question. However, the action may be brought by either side. Thus, the dominant owner may start court proceedings by issuing a writ claiming a declaration that he has acquired an easement under the Act. Alternatively the right may be brought into question in an action brought by the servient owner, claiming an injunction to restrain the dominant owner from continuing to exercise the right, in answer to which the dominant owner claims that he has acquired an easement under the Act.

User must have been *without interruption,* but the Act provides that nothing ranks as an interruption unless the dominant owner has

[50] It seems, however, that a claim cannot be defeated by proof that no such grant has in fact been made *Dalton v. Angus* (see note 42), *Tehidy v. Norman* [1971] 2 Q.B. 528.

[51] It is normal practice to plead all three modes of prescription, as a claim might fail under the Act yet succeed on the basis of lost modern grant. (See *Hulbert v. Dale* [1909] 2 Ch. 570; *Pugh v. Savage* [1970] 2 Q.B. 373.)

acquiesced to it for a full year[52] after becoming aware of it and of the person responsible for it. For this reason it is often stated that user for 19 years and one day is as good as user for 20 years. This is a half-truth. It is not possible after user for merely 19 years and a day to issue a writ claiming an easement, because it will not then be possible to prove user for the requisite period of 20 years. What is meant is that after user for 19 years and a day it is too late for the servient owner to interrupt, as long as the dominant owner does not submit to an interruption for more than 364 days. If, in this example, on the 364th day of the interruption the dominant owner immediately issues his writ, he will be able to establish user for 20 years for the purposes of the Act, and the interruption, having lasted for less than a full year, will not rank as an interruption for the purposes of the claim. Any action commenced after that day claiming an easement would fail. The above rules are the same whether the claim is based upon the shorter or the longer period of user. There are differences, however, as to the other conditions which must be fulfilled when claiming under the shorter or longer period. Some of these appear to arise out of the obscure drafting[53] of the Act. The following points should be noticed.

Disabilities. If the claim is based upon the shorter period of user, section 7 of the Act requires that there shall be deducted from the period of user any periods during which the servient owner has been an infant, lunatic, or tenant for life. The claim will not succeed unless there still remains a period of 20 years after these deductions have been made.

If the claim is based upon the longer period of user no deduction is to be made under section 7. However, section 8 of the Act provides that if the claim is to a right of "way or other convenient watercourse or use of water" there shall be deducted from the period of 40 years user any periods when the servient tenement has been held under a tenancy for life or a lease for a term exceeding three years (subject to certain conditions mentioned below). Obviously something has gone wrong with the wording of the Act, because a right of way is not a watercourse, whether convenient or inconvenient. It is therefore doubtful whether section 8 applies to all easements other than light, or only to rights of way and water. Even when the section applies, deduction is not to be made unless the claim to the easement is resisted by a reversioner within three years after the determination of the tenancy for life or lease. Moreover the word "reversioner"[54] has

[52] If the dominant owner has made strong protests to the servient owner against interference with the exercise of the right, failure for a year to make further protests will not necessarily amount to acquiescence during that period: see *Davies v. Du Paver* [1953] 1 Q.B. 184.

[53] Or printing errors might account for some anomalies.

[54] More accurately "person entitled to any reversion."

been strictly construed and, it has been held, not to include a remainderman.[55] Thus, if Whiteacre is settled on A for life with remainder to B in fee simple and the tenant of an adjoining property, Blackacre, uses a way across Whiteacre for upwards of 40 years, there can be no deduction of the period of A's tenancy for life from the period of user because B is a remainderman, not a reversioner. But if during the period of user Whiteacre had been held under a lease for more than three years, the period of the lease would have had to be deducted from the period of user, provided that the landlord of Whiteacre had resisted the claim to the easement within three years after the end of the lease. The landlord is a reversioner.

Strange as it may seem, it sometimes pays to base a claim upon the shorter period of user, even if the longer period can be proved, because there is no provision for deduction of leases when the claim is based upon the shorter period, as there is when it is based upon the longer period. If, however, the servient tenement was let when user began, then, even if the claim is based on the shorter period, the period of the lease will generally have to be deducted under the general principle that prescription is founded upon acquiescence of the fee simple owner of the servient tenement. In this situation the fee simple owner was not then in a position to prevent the user. (The position is quite different if the lease was granted *after* user began: the servient owner has then, by his own act, ensured that it is out of his power to prevent further user.)[56]

Consents. If permission for the exercise of the right has been sought from the servient owners from time to time the claim to an easement will generally fail. The user is not in such a case "as of right," as the Act requires. There is, however, one exception to this rule. If user for the longer period is established, a merely oral consent given *before* the user began will not defeat the claim. This is because the Act provides that a claim based on the longer period of user shall be indefeasible unless the right has been enjoyed by written consent or agreement. Again this reference to written consent is another example of the ill-drafted and seemingly contradictory provisions of the Act.

The easement of light. The Act provides that a claim to an easement of light may be founded upon proof of actual enjoyment of light for a period of 20 years without interruption and next before some court action in which the right is brought into question. Proof that user was by virtue of written consent given by the servient owner will defeat the claim, but in other respects user need not have been as

[55] *Symons v. Leaker* (1885) 15 Q.B.D. 629.
[56] *Palk v. Shinner* (1852) 18 Q.B. 215; *Pugh v. Savage* [1970] 2 Q.B. 373.

of right. Further, it does not need to be by or on behalf of one fee simple owner against another;[57] it is actual user which is important. As a result, a lessee can acquire an easement of light under the Act over land which is occupied by another tenant of his own landlord or which is occupied by the landlord himself. This is possible only in the case of the easement of light and only when the claim is brought under the Act. No provision is made for deduction of periods of disability of the servient owner.[58]

After the Second World War there was much derelict land, especially in the inner cities, and the acquisition of an easement of light over such land was of particular concern. In order to prevent neighbours from acquiring an easement of light by long user, which would hinder the future development of such derelict sites, landowners would erect hoardings on the land. To curb this practice the Rights of Light Act 1959 was enacted, which provides instead for the registration of a light obstruction notice, as a local land charge,[59] specifying the size and position of a notional obstruction, in order to prevent the acquisition of an easement. This has the same effect as if there was an actual obstruction, so that, for example, a dominant owner may sue for a declaration that he has already acquired an easement which is being interfered with by this notional obstruction. The Act provides that in such an action the claimant may treat his user as having begun a year earlier than in fact it did.

PROFITS

A profit is similar to an easement in that it is also a right against the land of another. However, a profit gives the right to take something from another's land which is either part of the soil itself (*e.g.* a right to take gravel) or part of the produce of the soil (*e.g.* a right to graze one's cattle on a neighbour's land or to take fish from his stream). An easement, in contrast, is said to be a right without profit. Nevertheless, a right to take water from another's stream is an easement, not a profit, because the water is not regarded as being part of the soil or of its produce.

A profit may be a *several profit* or a *profit in common* (or a common). A several profit gives to the owner the right to take the subject-matter, *e.g.* the fish, from another's land to the exclusion of everyone else, including the servient owner himself. A profit in

[57] In contrast with other easements by prescription which must be claimed by or on behalf of a fee simple owner against another fee simple owner, see pp. 147–148.

[58] A further distinction between the provisions of the Act, with regard to the easement of light and those relating to other easements, is that only the latter bind the Crown.

[59] See p. 235.

common gives the right to take the subject-matter in common with others. It depends upon the terms of the grant whether a profit is a several profit or a profit in common, but several profits are comparatively rare: so the term "common" is often used as a synonym for profits.[60]

Profits may also be divided into *profits appurtenant* and *profits in gross.* In the case of a profit appurtenant, the benefit of the profit is annexed by the grant to a dominant tenement. It therefore resembles an easement, and indeed a profit appurtenant must comply with the four conditions of an easement.[61] Therefore, it is not possible to claim as a profit appurtenant a right to fish in another's stream for commercial purposes. Such a right does not accommodate the dominant tenement as the amount of fish caught does not relate to the requirements of the dominant tenement.[62] A profit in gross, however, is one which is given to the grantee personally, *i.e.* irrespective of his ownership or occupation of land: there is no dominant tenement.

Mention should also be made of the profit *pur cause de vicinage.* This is a right which arises where there are two adjacent commons[63] and the commoner's cattle may be allowed to stray on to the neighbouring common.

Modes of acquisition

The ways of acquiring a profit are similar to the modes of acquiring an easement, and it is simplest to notice the main differences:

(i) An easement can be acquired both under section 62 of the Law of Property Act 1925 and under the doctrine of *Wheeldon v. Burrows,* but only the former applies to profits.[64]

(ii) A profit in gross cannot be claimed by prescription under the Prescription Act 1832, although it can be claimed under the other modes of prescription.

(iii) If a profit appurtenant is claimed under the 1832 Act the periods of user provided by the Act are 30 years and 60 years, instead of the periods of 20 years and 40 years provided for easements. Mostly, the same differences apply

[60] Rights of common are registerable with the appropriate local authority under the Commons Registration Act 1965 and the Common Land (Rectification of Registers) Act 1989, and cannot be exercised unless so registered.

[61] See pp. 139–142.

[62] *Harris v. Earl of Chesterfield* [1911] A.C. 623.

[63] *I.e.* (in this context) land subject to a right of common.

[64] See note 38.

as for easements between claims founded on the shorter and those founded on the longer period. For example, if the claim is founded on the shorter period a deduction will have to be made for any periods when the servient owner has been under one of the disabilities mentioned in section 7 of the Act. But section 8 of the Act, which applies to a claim to an easement based on the longer period of user, has no application when a profit is claimed on the ground of user for 60 years. There is, therefore, no provision for the deduction of the periods of leases of the servient tenement; but such leases may have to be taken into account in deciding whether there has been that acquiescence by the fee simple owners of the servient tenement which is normally essential to prescription.[65]

EXTINGUISHMENT OF EASEMENTS AND PROFITS

An easement or profit may be extinguished by being given up or *released*, which may be done either expressly or impliedly. To be effective at law an express release must be by deed, but an informal agreement to release may be effective in equity if the servient owner has given consideration or has acted to his detriment on the faith of the agreement.

Release may be implied if there is evidence of an intention on the part of the dominant owner to abandon the easement.[66] Non-user of itself does not necessarily show such an intention; so the release of an easement of way cannot be inferred from non-user during a period when the owner of the easement of way temporarily enjoyed a more convenient means of access to his property. Again, if a house enjoys the benefit of an easement of light, knocking down the house will not show an intention to abandon the easement if the owner intends to re-build the house and the house when re-built has windows which enjoy substantially the same light. The question is always whether an intention to abandon can properly be inferred from all the circumstances of the particular case.[67]

An easement or profit also becomes extinguished if the same person becomes both the owner and in possession of the dominant

[65] *Davies v. Du Paver* [1953] 1 Q.B. 184.

[66] *Moore v. Rawson* (1824) 3 B. & C. 332; distinguish *Cook v. Mayor & Corporation of Bath* (1868) L.R. 6 Eq. 177.

[67] An easement may be extinguished if alterations are made to the dominant tenement which would excessively increase the burden on the servient tenement: see *Ankerson v. Connelly* [1907] 1 Ch. 678, *Ray v. Fairway Motors (Barnstaple) Ltd* (1968) 20 P. & C.R. 261.

and the servient tenements, provided that he holds the two tenements in the same capacity.

OTHER SIMILAR RIGHTS

There are various other rights which are similar, but distinct from easements and profits, which should be considered briefly.

Public rights of way

A public right of way is different from an easement as, rather than being granted to individual owners of a dominant tenement, it is enjoyed by any member of the public regardless of whether he is a landowner. Apart from those created by special statutory provision, a public right of way must be dedicated as a right of way to the public by the land-owners concerned, and accepted as such by the public. Dedication may be express or it may be presumed from user of the way by the public, as of right, with the knowledge of the land-owner or land-owners concerned. Dedication may be presumed from long user by the public, either at common law (in which case no particular period of user is prescribed by the law), or under the Highways Act 1980. Under the Act dedication is to be presumed by proving uninterrupted user as of right for 20 years next before the right of user is brought into question, unless there is sufficient evidence that there was no intention during the period of user to dedicate a way to the public. The absence of an intention to dedicate may be proved in a number of ways provided by the Act (*e.g.* by displaying a suitable notice), or it may be proved in any other way (*e.g.* a method commonly adopted by landowners to avoid dedication at common law is the closure of the way to the public for one day in each year).

As mentioned above, under the Act the relevant period of user is that of 20 years next before the right of user is "brought into question." The right can be brought into question in any way, *e.g.* by the land-owner turning back the public. It is not a requirement that a court action should be brought by either side, as is necessary for the establishment of an easement under the Prescription Act 1832.

Customary and similar other rights

A right similar to an easement may be claimed by a fluctuating body of persons (other than the public at large). For example, the inhabitants of a particular village may claim the right to pass across private land in order to reach the parish church (a right known as a church-way).[68] Such a right cannot exist as a true easement. This is because, as we have seen,[69] an easement must have its origin in a grant, and a changing body of persons is not a separate legal entity and so is not capable of taking a grant. The right may, however, be established under the doctrine of custom. The main requirements of a valid custom are that the right claimed should be limited to a defined locality known to the law, such as a parish or manor, and that the right should have been enjoyed continuously since 1189. Proof of user for 20 years raises a rebuttable presumption that the right has been enjoyed continuously since 1189.[70]

Further, a fluctuating body of persons cannot directly claim a profit, because a profit, like an easement, must be capable of being granted. Nor is such a body allowed to claim a right in the nature of a profit under the doctrine of custom.[71] But there are two very restricted methods by which the claim may be established. First, if the right has been granted by the Crown, the Crown may incorporate a fluctuating body of persons and so create a separate legal entity.[72] As a corporation, the fluctuating body of persons becomes a competent grantee. Indeed, when the right has been granted by the Crown incorporation may sometimes be presumed. Secondly, if it can be established that from time immemorial the right has been claimed by a local corporation (*e.g.* a borough corporation), as well as by a fluctuating body of persons, the court may presume the grant of a profit to the corporation. Such a profit is held by the corporation upon trust for itself and the fluctuating body, creating a presumed charitable trust.[73]

Access to Neighbouring Land Act 1992

The Access to Neighbouring Land Act 1992[74] may be of assistance where a person needs to enter on to a neighbour's land, for example, in order to do essential repair work to help maintain his adjacent land, but where he has no easement or other right which allows him access to do so. Where a neighbour will not consent to such access, under section 1 of the Act, a person can apply to the county court for an order allowing him access to carry out work which is reasonably necessary for the preservation of the whole or any part of the "dominant land". This is provided that the work cannot be carried out

[68] *Brocklebank v. Thompson* [1903] 2 Ch. 344.
[69] See p. 140.
[70] *Cf.* common law prescription (p. 148).
[71] *Alfred F. Beckett v. Lyons* [1967] Ch. 449.
[72] The Crown has power to confer the status of corporation on any body of persons.
[73] *Goodman v. Mayor of Saltash* (1882) 7 App.Cas. 633.
[74] This came into force on January 31, 1993.

(or would be substantially more difficult to carry out) if entry was refused. For example, the type of work which will be deemed to be reasonably necessary for the preservation of the dominant land includes access to clear or repair drains, sewers or cables, to treat, prune or fell trees or shrubs, or to maintain or repair the structure of a building on the dominant land.[75] Under section 2, if an access order is made, it will state the works to be carried out, the area of the "servient land" affected and the period during which the dominant owner is allowed to enter. The order may also provide for the payment of compensation for loss, damage, injury or inconvenience caused to the servient owner or any other person.[76]

An access order will be enforceable against successors in title to the servient land if, in the case of unregistered land, it is registered as a writ or order affecting land[77] or where land is registered as a notice or caution, since it is a minor interest and not an overriding interest.[78]

[75] S.1(4) of the Act.

[76] S.2(1) of the Act.

[77] S.5(1) of the Act, amending the LCA 1972 s.6(1). See also p. 230.

[78] S.5(2) and (3) of the Act adding s.49(1)(j) and s.64(7) to LRA 1925, and s.5(5) of the Act. See also pp. 223–226.

15. Licences

In its simplest form, a licence is merely a permission to enter the land of another (otherwise such entry would be trespass). In that sense it is distinguished from both a lease and an easement, in that it does not amount to an estate or interest in the land, and so cannot be assigned, and is binding (if at all) on the person who grants the licence *i.e.* the licensor only.[1] A lease on the other hand is assignable, and the burden of the lease runs with the reversion, just as the benefit and burden of an easement run with the tenements of the dominant and servient owners respectively. A licence is further distinguished (a) from a lease, in that normally the person who receives the licence, *i.e.* the licensee, does not have exclusive possession of the land[2] and (b) from an easement, in that a licence may (and generally does) exist in gross, without reference to any dominant tenement.[3] In some cases it may also be necessary to distinguish between a mere licence to reside in property for life and a life interest in the property. If a disposition is held to have created a life interest, the property will be settled land, and the person beneficially entitled for life will have the statutory powers of sale, lease and mortgage under the Settled Land Act 1925.[4]

Another characteristic of a simple licence is that, unlike an interest in property, it can be revoked at any time, in which case the former licensee becomes a trespasser. Here, however, a distinction must be drawn between a simple licence (commonly called a *bare licence*), on the one hand, and on the other a licence arising either under a contract between the parties (*a contractual licence*), or in connection with some legal or equitable interest held by the licensee (a *licence coupled with an interest* and an *equitable licence* respectively), which are each considered further below.

[1] *King v. David Allen & Sons Billposting Ltd* [1916] 2 A.C. 54; *Clore v. Theatrical Properties Ltd* [1936] 3 All E.R. 483.

[2] see p. 98.

[3] see p. 140.

[4] See *Re Carne's Settled Estates* [1899] 1 Ch. 324 (gift by will), *Bannister v. Bannister* [1948] 2 All E.R. 133 and also *Ungurian v. Lesnoff* [1990] Ch. 206 (dispositions *inter vivos* where a constructive trust was used to impose a Settled Land Act trust, see equitable licences below). For a means of avoiding a result which is so far from what may have been intended, see *Griffiths v. Williams* (1977) 248 E.G. 947, where a lease for life was imposed instead, (see p. 103 above).

Bare licence

This is a licence given gratuitously, without consideration, *e.g.* an invitation to a barbecue. It is not coupled with some interest in the land, and is revocable at will.

Contractual licence

A licence for value, such as that implied on the sale of a theatre ticket,[5] is a contractual licence and was regarded at common law as being revocable at will.[6] If it was revoked in breach of contract the licensor would be liable in damages to the licensee, but the revocation was nevertheless effective, and the former licensee had no right to remain on the land. As a result of the intervention of equity, however, such a licence is now regarded as irrevocable between the parties for as long as the parties intended, *i.e.* for any period expressly agreed, or until terminated by giving prescribed notice or, if none is prescribed, reasonable notice.[7]

In some family-type situations the courts may even imply a contractual licence to occupy which is not terminable between the parties or only in certain limited circumstances *e.g.* a contractual licence for as long as the children of the parties are of school age and accommodation is reasonably needed for them.[8]

However, as a contractual licence is not in itself an interest in land, it will not be binding on a third party who acquires an interest in the land.[9]

Licence coupled with an interest

A licence may be coupled with the grant of an interest in land, for example where trees are sold on terms that the purchaser is entitled

[5] *Hurst v. Picture Theatres Ltd* [1915] 1 K.B. 1. Lodging agreements are another example, but these may enjoy some security of tenure (see p. 123).

[6] *Wood v. Leadbitter* (1845) 13 M. & W. 838.

[7] *Winter Garden Theatre (London) Ltd v. Millennium Productions Ltd* [1948] A.C. 173; *Hounslow L.B.C. v Twickenham Garden Developments Ltd* [1971] Ch. 233. The basis of equity's intervention is the equitable remedy of an injunction to prevent a breach of contract. (Compare the role elsewhere of the equitable remedy of specific performance: see p. 27).

[8] *Tanner v. Tanner* [1975] 1 W.L.R. 1346; see also *Hardwick v. Johnson* [1978] 1 W.L.R. 683; and *Chandler v. Kerley* [1978] 1 W.L.R. 693 for examples of other terms. In other circumstances, beneficial co-ownership may arise under a resulting trust, where a party has contributed to the purchase price of property, see pp. 68–70.

[9] See *obiter dicta* comments of the Court of Appeal in *Ashburn Anstalt v. Arnold* [1989] Ch. 1. However, it may be binding if coupled with an equitable interest, see p. 161 below.

to cut down the timber. The sale implies a grant to the purchaser of a licence to enter the vendor's land in order to obtain the timber. The interest may be legal, arising for example from the formal grant by deed of a profit,[10] (*e.g.* a right to fish), or equitable, where there is a specifically enforceable agreement for a grant.[11] The licence is irrevocable so long as the interest to which it is annexed lasts, and unless otherwise agreed it can be assigned together with the interest.

Equitable licences

A licence coupled with an equitable interest in land has gradually acquired increasing importance as the courts have developed the doctrine of equitable or *proprietary estoppel*. Under this doctrine, if a licensee incurs expenditure or acts in some other way to his detriment (*e.g.* by building on the licensor's land)[12] in reliance on the licensor's representations and in the reasonable expectation that the licence will not be revoked, an equitable estoppel may arise in the licensee's favour. The effect of this is that both the licensor himself and persons claiming through him (other than a purchaser without notice)[13] will be prevented or *estopped* from revoking the licence.

The means by which proprietary estoppel will be protected may vary between at one extreme, giving rise to a determinable life interest[14], and at the other to the grant of an interest in fee simple.[15] In some cases, where the licensee has adjoining land and the detriment incurred is in relation to that land, the interest acquired may be in the nature of an easement over the licensor's land rather than a right to possession of that land.[16]

In recent years the courts have also used the vehicle of a *constructive* trust as a means of enforcing a licence against third parties. A constructive trust may arise in varying circumstances, which are often difficult to categorise. Nevertheless, in the simplest terms it generally occurs, in a land law context, where a trust is imposed by the court because a person has acted fraudulently or inequitably. However, it will not be imposed in all cases, but only where the "conscience of the

[10] See pp. 152–154.

[11] Under the principle in *Walsh v. Lonsdale* (1882) 21 Ch. D.9, see pp. 27–28.

[12] *Dillwyn v. Llewelyn* (1862) 4 De G.F. & J. 517; *Inwards v. Baker* [1965] 2 Q.B. 29.

[13] *E.R. Ives Investment Ltd v. High* [1967[2 Q.B. 379.

[14] *Inwards v. Baker,* note 12 above; *Binions v. Evans* [1972] Ch.359 and *Ungurian v. Lesnoff,* note 4 above (from which it appears that the land affected may be settled land) but see *Matharu v. Matharu* (1994) 68 P. & C.R. 93, C.A. where the imposition of a trust was avoided by granting a licence for life.

[15] *Dillwyn v. Llewelyn*, note 12 above; *Errington v Errington and Woods* [1952] 1 K.B. 290; *Pascoe v. Turner* [1979] 1 W.L.R. 431. Another means is by imposing a constructive trust, see below.

[16] *E.R. Ives Investment Ltd v. High*, note 13 above; *Crabb v. Arun D.C.* [1976] Ch. 179

estate owner is affected,"[17] in which case the property will be held on trust for the claimant.[18] For instance, a constructive trust may be imposed where a purchaser buys property with knowledge of a widow's right to occupy the property for her life and he pays a reduced price for the property, having agreed to be bound by the right.[19] It should be noted, in contrast, that simply acquiring property with notice that it is subject to a licence will not of itself necessarily give rise to a constructive trust. Further evidence will often be needed that the purchaser has acted so inequitably that a constructive trust should be imposed.[20] Whilst it is admirable that a licence by estoppel or a licence giving rise to a constructive trust may be used, in particular, to protect informal family-type situations, allowing flexibility and avoiding hardship in this area of the law, this has inevitably led to uncertainty. Indeed in some cases different judges have given different reasons for the same decisions, leading to difficulties in advising a potential litigant. All that can be said to have emerged from a very large and confused body of case law is a trend towards providing a greater degree of protection to a licensee against a third party, in some limited circumstances. It is still true to say that a licence is not in itself an interest in land, but it can no longer be said with the same confidence that no proprietary right arises at all if the licence is supported by an equitable interest.

This leads to further problems as to whether such interests must be registered in order to bind a purchaser of land. In the case of a licence by estoppel arising in respect of unregistered land, this is not registrable under the Land Charges Act 1972 and therefore the old doctrine of notice applies.[21] Where land is registered, the interest should be noted on the register as it is a minor interest (which is not likely to occur) or it may be an overriding interest, if the claimant is in actual occupation or if the right is an easement arising by estoppel.[22] A constructive trust imposed by the court appears to be binding on a purchaser regardless of registration.[23]

17 Per Fox L.J. in the Court of Appeal in *Ashburn Anstalt v Arnold*, see note 9 above, at pp. 25–26

18 See *Bannister v. Bannister*, note 4 above. In some cases, there appears to be some overlap between proprietary estoppel and constructive trusts although proprietary estoppel seems the broader of the two concepts. For instance, one means by which the courts may enforce the estoppel, but not the only one, is by imposing a constructive trust. For further discussion as to the relationship between them see Gray pp. 356–359.

19 Lord Denning's interpretation of the position in *Binions v. Evans* note 14 above, which although a dissenting judgement was approved by the Court of Appeal in *Ashburn Anstalt v. Arnold*, (see note 9 above), at p. 23.

20 See note 17 above.

21 See *E.R. Ives Investment v. High*, note 13 above and p. 35.

22 Under LRA 1925, s.70(1) (g) and (a) respectively, see p. 224, note 7.

23 If, for example, *Lyus v. Prowsa Developments Ltd* [1982] 2 All E.R. 953 is followed, and *Peffer v. Rigg* [1977] 1 W.L.R. 285 (which has been criticised).

Rights in respect of the matrimonial home

It has been held that the right or licence of a deserted spouse to remain in the matrimonial home on the breakdown of marriage (the spouse not being owner or part owner of the house) is enforceable only against the other spouse, and is incapable of binding a third party, such as a purchaser or mortgagee.[24] To overcome the effects of this decision the Matrimonial Homes Act 1983, gives a spouse a statutory right to occupy the former matrimonial home, for so long as the marriage exists (regardless of whether he or she also has an equitable interest in the property). This right of occupation is a charge on the other spouse's estate or interest and is registrable as a Class F land charge, where land is unregistered, or must be noted on the register as it is a minor interest, in the case of registered land.[25]

[24] Attempts to elevate the deserted spouse's rights to the status of an interest in land enforceable against third parties were unsuccessful in *National Provincial Bank Ltd v. Ainsworth* [1965] A.C. 1175.

[25] See pp. 232 and 225–226.

16. Covenants concerning land

A covenant is a promise contained in a deed. Covenants commonly occur in leases, laying down the respective rights and obligations of a landlord and tenant. However, covenants may also be entered into on the sale of land to a purchaser, where the vendor intends to retain land adjoining the part sold. In either case, the rules differ concerning the enforceability of such covenants between the original parties to the covenant or, where they have parted with the land, between their successors in title. The principles therefore in each case must be considered separately.

LEASEHOLD COVENANTS

As between original parties

The original landlord and the original tenant of a lease are bound personally to one another under any covenants which they have entered into in the lease under the doctrine of *privity of contract*. This contractual liability exists throughout the whole term of the lease,[1] notwithstanding the death of either party (*i.e.* in such a case his personal representatives remain liable under his covenants in the lease)[2] and notwithstanding any assignment of the reversion or of the lease.[3] The covenants are usually expressly worded so that the covenantor undertakes liability not only for his own acts and omis-

[1] It is otherwise with the *implied* obligations of landlord and tenant (see p. 113 *et seq.*); the landlord or tenant is liable only for breaches committed while he held the reversion or the lease, respectively. The Landlord and Tenant (Covenants) Bill; H.L. Bill 1994–1995 (70) proposes the abolition of the doctrine of privity of contract in respect of future leases and the rules concerning existing leases will be modified. As to the other proposals of the Bill, see p. 117.

[2] To the extent of the deceased's assets. The same rule applies to a periodic tenancy: the estate of the deceased tenant remains liable for the rent until the tenancy is validly determined by notice (*Youngmin v. Heath* [1974] 1 W.L.R. 135).

[3] The transfer to a purchaser of the leasehold reversion by a landlord or of the unexpired term of a lease by a tenant is effected by a document called an assignment.

sions but also for those of his successors in title and persons deriving title under him. Even where there is no such express provision, under section 79 of the Law of Property Act 1925, any covenant affecting land of the covenantor is *deemed* to be made in these terms unless a contrary intention is expressed.

As between assignees

On an assignment of the landlord's reversion the *benefit of the tenant's covenants* can be (and usually is) expressly assigned with the reversion, and the assignee (*i.e.* the new landlord) can then sue the original tenant under the tenant's covenants in the lease. Similarly on an assignment of the lease the *benefit of the landlord's covenants* can be expressly assigned with the lease, and the assignee (*i.e.* the new tenant) can then sue the original landlord under the landlord's covenants.[4]

However, the doctrine of privity of contract prevents the *burden* of a landlord's or tenant's covenants being assigned with the reversion or the lease and so, in each case, it is the original covenantor who remains liable. The inconvenience of this rule is avoided by the doctrine of *privity of estate,* which treats the relationship of landlord and tenant as subsisting between the owner of the reversion for the time being and the owner of the lease for the time being, *i.e.* the current landlord and tenant. In such circumstances, under this doctrine, the assignee of the reversion has the benefit of the tenant's covenants and the burden of the landlord's covenants where those covenants "have reference to the subject matter of the lease" under sections 141–142 of the Law of Property Act 1925.[5] The assignee of the lease has the benefit of the landlord's covenants and the burden of the tenant's covenants in the lease as far as they "touch and concern the land" under the rule in *Spencer's Case.*[6] In either circumstances the covenants are said to run with the reversion or lease respectively.

A covenant touches and concerns[7] the land if it regulates the position of the landlord and the tenant in their capacities as landlord and tenant, as distinct from merely their personal capacities.[8] Most covenants commonly found in leases do touch and concern the land,

[4] The benefit may also pass, even without express assignment, under the principle discussed at pp. 171–173.

[5] The rule was first enacted in 1540.

[6] (1583) 5 Co.Rep. 16. The rule does not apply to equitable leases, see *Marquis Camden v. Batterbury* (1860) 7 C.B.N.S. 864.

[7] The term is synonymous with the expression "have reference to the subject matter of the lease" used in LPA 1925, ss.141–2.

[8] See a further definition in *P&A Swift Investments v. Combined English Stores Group Plc* [1989] A.C. 632.

e.g. a landlord's covenant for quiet enjoyment,[9] or to maintain the exterior of the premises in repair, or to renew the lease at the tenant's option;[10] or a tenant's covenant to pay the rent, to maintain the interior of premises in repair, or not to use the premises for certain purposes. An example of a provision that does not touch and concern the land is a tenant's option to purchase the reversion on the lease. Such a provision does not regulate the relationship of landlord and tenant, but contemplates its determination by the exercise of the option.[11]

There is an important distinction between liability under privity of contract and liability under privity of estate. As we have seen, each of the original parties remains liable by privity of contract on his covenants *throughout the term of the lease*.[12] However, a landlord or tenant who is liable solely under privity of estate is liable only for breaches of covenant committed by him while he held the reversion or the lease, as the case may be. For example, suppose that L is the original landlord and T the original tenant, and that T has assigned the lease to A and A in his turn has assigned the lease to B. Suppose further that the lease contains a tenant's covenant that he repair the interior of the premises and that B breaks this covenant.

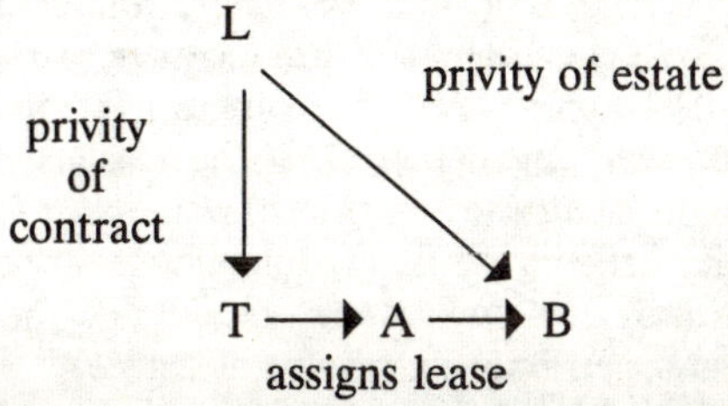

L may sue T, who cannot excuse himself by claiming that he had assigned the lease before the breach of covenant occurred. T is liable by privity of contract and remains liable for breach of tenant's covenants committed *at any time* during the lease. Alternatively, L may sue B, the tenant who in fact committed the breach of covenant: B is liable by privity of estate as the tenant for the time being.

9 *I.e.* that the tenant can enjoy the land free from disturbance, uninterrupted by other claimants.

10 The inclusion of this covenant is anomalous. An option for renewal is registrable as an estate contract under LCA 1925, in the case of unregistered land, (see *Beesley v. Hallwood Estates Ltd* [1960] 1 W.L.R. 549); it is a minor interest or possibly an overriding interest under LRA 1925, s.70(1)(g), where land is registered see p. 223–226.

11 Such options are enforceable on the basis discussed at p. 27.

12 Law Commission Report No. 174 (1988) criticised this continuing liability. As to proposed reform see note 1, above.

However, L cannot sue A; A was liable only by privity of estate and ceased to be liable for future breaches of tenant's covenants when he parted with the lease.

Under the principles mentioned above, there is no privity of contract or estate between an assignee of the reversion and the original tenant if the tenant has already assigned the lease before the new landlord acquired the reversion. For example, suppose L is the original landlord and T the original tenant and T assigns his lease to A, and L subsequently assigns his reversion to X.

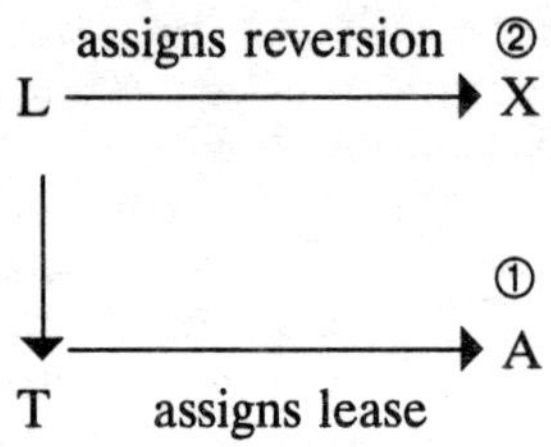

There is no privity of contract or estate under the above rules between X and T. Nevertheless, it has been held that under section 141 of the Law of Property Act 1925, in respect of covenants which have reference to the subject matter of the lease, the assignee of the reversion (X) acquires *all* the rights of the assignor (L), including the right to sue the original tenant (T) (whose contractual liability, continues indefinitely), as well as the tenant for the time being (A) (whose liability is based only on privity of estate).[13] Further, it seems that the same principle should apply, for instance, where an assignee of the lease (A) seeks to enforce a landlord's covenant to repair the exterior of the premises against the original landlord (L) after the latter has assigned the reversion. There is no privity between the parties, but the original landlord remains liable indefinitely, and the benefit of his covenant would pass to the assignee of the lease (A), either by express assignment or under section 78 of the Law of Property Act 1925 (discussed below).[14]

[13] Furthermore, the assignee of the reversion can sue for breach of a tenant's covenant committed whether before or after the assignment as on assignment of the reversion the original landlord loses the right to sue. (*Re King* [1963] Ch. 459; *London and County (A. & D.) Ltd v. Wilfred Sportsman Ltd* [1971] Ch. 764; *Arlesford Trading Co. Ltd v. Servansingh* [1971] 1 W.L.R. 1080).

[14] At pp. 171–173. The benefit does not pass under *Spencer's Case*, above, which applies only where there is privity of estate.

Indemnities

If the original tenant is sued for breach of a tenant's covenant committed after he had parted with the lease, he may claim indemnity from the assignee of the lease who in fact committed the breach. Thus, in the first illustration above, if L sued T in respect of the breach committed by B, T could claim indemnity from B. This is a common law right.[15] It will be observed that T could not claim indemnity from A under this common law right. The common law right of indemnity is, therefore, potentially defective, in that B may prove to be not worth suing, *e.g.* because he is in financial difficulties. Therefore it became the practice of conveyancers to insert into an assignment of a lease an express covenant by the assignee to indemnify the assignor against liability for any breach of a tenant's covenant committed after the assignment, whether by the assignee himself or by a later assignee. Such an indemnity covenant is now implied by section 77 of the Law of Property Act 1925, in an assignment for value. As a result, in our illustration, if L sued T and such an express or implied indemnity covenant was included in the assignment of the lease by T to A, T could claim indemnity from A in respect of the breach committed by B. It should be noted, however, that T can only recover once and T would therefore, not be able to claim from A if he has already recovered from B under the common law rule.

On an assignment of the reversion there is no statutory provision implying an indemnity covenant. An express covenant of indemnity should, therefore, be included in the conveyance.

As between lessor and sub-lessee

If L grants a lease to T and T grants a sub-lease for a lesser term to S, there is no privity of contract or estate between L and S, as there is no direct relationship of landlord and tenant between them.

L
↓ head-lease for *e.g.* 25 years
T
↓ sub-lease for *e.g.* 15 years
S

[15] *Moule v. Garrett* (1872) L.R. Ex. 101.

It follows that L cannot enforce T's covenants in the head-lease directly against S. It should not be supposed, however, that there is no basis on which liability can arise between L and S. Thus, if S's use of the land is inconsistent with a negative or *restrictive covenant* in the head-lease, he may be liable directly to L under the doctrine of *Tulk v. Moxhay*[16] (discussed below). Also, if the head-lease contains a right of re-entry in the event of breach of T's covenants, L may be able to forfeit the head-lease, whereupon the sub-lease will also end.[17] By the same token, if the head-lease contains a landlord's repairing covenant, it seems that S may be able to enforce this directly against L.[18]

OTHER COVENANTS

Covenants other than those between landlord and tenant are commonly referred to as vendor and purchaser covenants, because they are commonly entered into on the sale by a vendor of part of his land. In such a case, the purchaser may enter into a covenant with the vendor (*e.g.* to use the land bought for the purposes of a private dwelling-house only), and the vendor may perhaps enter into a similar covenant with the purchaser.

Blackacre	Whiteacre
V	V → P
V covenants with P to use the retained land, Blackacre, for use as a dwelling house only.	P covenants with V to use the purchased land, Whiteacre, for use as a dwelling house only.

[16] See p. 173 *et seq.* It is immaterial whether the covenants were taken for the benefit of other land owned by the landlord: his reversion on the lease is a sufficient interest for this purpose *(Regent Oil Co. Ltd v. J.A. Gregory (Hatch End) Ltd* [1966] Ch. 402).

[17] See p. 110.

[18] This is by virtue of LPA 1925, s.78, under which the benefit of a covenant relating to the covenantee's land runs with the land, as such a covenant is deemed to be made with a person deriving title under the covenantee, which includes a sub-lessee. See *Williams v. Unit Construction Co. Ltd* (1951) 19 Conv. (N.S.) 262, and note 24.

Such covenants are sometimes also referred to as freehold covenants (to distinguish them from covenants in a lease), but it should be noted that the same principles apply whether the land sold is freehold or leasehold. If the vendor is a lessee, and sells part of the land held under the lease to a purchaser (the assignee of part of the lease) any covenants entered into between them on the sale are still between vendor and purchaser, not between landlord and tenant.[19]

The enforcement of such covenants is subject to different rules at common law and in equity.[20]

At common law

As between the original covenantor (the person who has the obligation to perform the covenant) and the original covenantee (the person who receives the benefit of the covenant) there is privity of contract, and to that extent the rules are similar to those governing covenants in a lease. Thus, unless the covenant is specially worded, the original covenantor remains *liable* for any breach, even if in the meantime he has parted with the land affected, *i.e.* he is liable for breaches committed by subsequent owners of the land.[21] Further, under section 56 of the Law of Property Act 1925, the covenant can be *enforced* not only by the original covenantee himself, but also by any other person with whom it purports to be made (*e.g.* an adjoining owner at the time that the covenant was entered into), even though that other person was not himself a party to the covenant. This section effectively extends the definition of the original covenantee to include such persons.[22]

The *benefit* of a covenant can be expressly assigned with the land to which it relates, in which case the assignee will have the same right of action against the covenantor as the covenantee would have had. In the absence of express assignment, if the covenant is taken for the benefit of land owned by the covenantee, the benefit of the covenant may pass without express assignment on a transfer of the land. This is a common law rule of some antiquity,[23] applying equally to positive

[19] See, *e.g. Shiloh Spinners Ltd, v. Harding* [1973] A.C. 691.

[20] Fundamental reforms are proposed by Law Commission No. 127 (1984).

[21] LPA 1925, s.79, see p. 165. This provision merely extends the liability of the covenantor: it does not impose liability on his successors (see *Tophams Ltd v. Earl of Sefton* [1967] 1 A.C. 50).

[22] However, in order to come within LPA 1925, s.56, such persons must be clearly identifiable, when the covenant is made. Future purchasers do not obtain the benefit of the covenant under this section (but it may pass to them under the normal common law rules discussed below). The limited scope of this exception to the common law doctrine of privity of contract was established in *Beswick v. Beswick* [1968] A.C. 58.

[23] *The Prior's Case* (1368) Co.Litt. 385 a.

and to negative covenants, and it does not require that the covenantor should have retained any land for the covenant to be enforceable against him. Originally the covenantee had to have a legal estate in the land, and his successor in title had to possess the same estate. For covenants made after 1925 this rule has been somewhat relaxed by section 78 of the Law of Property Act 1925, which enables persons claiming under the original covenantee to enforce the covenant even if they do not hold the same estate as the covenantee. For example, a covenant may be enforced not only by successors in title, but also by lessees of the covenantee.[24]

At common law the *burden* of the covenant cannot pass with the land of the covenantor, even though the covenant is clearly intended to regulate the use of the land.[25] Therefore, although at common law a transferee of the covenantee's land may be able to enforce the covenant against the original covenantor (as the benefit automatically passes to the transferee at common law and the original covenantor is liable under the principles discussed above),[26] neither the original covenantee nor a transferee of his land can enforce the covenant against a subsequent owner of the covenantor's land (as the burden does not pass to the subsequent owner). The covenant can be enforced only against the original covenantor (or his personal representative after his death).

Although at common law a subsequent owner of the covenantor's land cannot be made directly liable on the covenants, there are nevertheless some circumstances in which he may in effect become indirectly liable. For example, i) a chain of indemnity may be created, whereby the original covenantor, on disposing of his land, takes an indemnity[27] from his purchaser against any loss he may incur as a result of his continuing personal liability on the covenants, and similar indemnities are taken on subsequent dispositions; or ii) a right of re-entry may be reserved by the covenantee allowing forfeiture of the estate of any subsequent owner of the covenantor's land if there is breach of covenant by such a subsequent owner[28]; or iii) the covenantor may undertake not to dispose of the land without ensuring that a new owner enters into direct covenants with the covenantee and his successors on the same terms as the original covenants.[29] Another

[24] *Smith v. River Douglas Catchment Board* [1949] 2 K.B. 500 or a sub-lessee, see note 18 above.

[25] *Austerberry v. Corporation of Oldham* (1885) 29 Ch.D. 750; reaffirmed by the House of Lords in *Rhone v. Stephens* [1994] 2 WLR 429.

[26] See p. 171.

[27] There is no *implied* right of indemnity: *cf.* p. 169.

[28] This is an equitable right and so relief against forfeiture may be granted, (see *Shiloh Spinners Ltd v. Harding*, note 19). Sometimes a rentcharge is also reserved for this purpose, in which case a supporting right of re-entry is legal (see pp. 33, 179).

[29] For breach of such an undertaking the covenantee may have remedies against both the covenantor and his assignee (see *Esso Petroleum Co. Ltd v. Kingswood Motors (Addlestone) Ltd* [1974] K.B. 142).

indirect exception to the common law rule derives from the principle of "benefit and burden," under which one who claims the benefit of a grant must accept its burdens. For example, it was held in *Halsall v. Brizell*[30] that if a purchaser is given the right to use roads which pass across another's land subject to the obligation to contribute to the cost of maintaining the roads, he may not use the roads without making the contribution, and a subsequent owner of the purchaser's land is in the same position.[31]

In equity: the doctrine of *Tulk v. Moxhay*[32]

Under this doctrine, equity allows both the benefit and the burden of negative or *restrictive covenants* to run with the land of the covenantee and covenantor respectively.

If a restrictive covenant affecting the covenantor's land is taken for the benefit of land belonging to the covenantee, equity is prepared, on certain conditions, to treat the covenant as creating an interest in the covenantor's land. This is analogous to a negative easement, and equity may enforce the covenant by its' own remedy of an injunction. The covenantee's and covenantor's land may then be regarded as in the nature of a dominant and servient tenement respectively.[33] Accordingly, not only will the *benefit* of the covenant pass with the covenantee's land,[34] but also (of much greater importance) the *burden* will pass on a transfer of the covenantor's land, and a subsequent owner of that land will be bound by the covenant as if it were a negative easement.

Since the interest arising under this doctrine is merely equitable, it is subject to the usual rules which govern whether such an interest binds a purchaser of the land. In respect of unregistered land, the old doctrine of notice still applies to a covenant created before 1926 and the burden of the restrictive covenant cannot be enforced against a subsequent purchaser for value of the legal estate in the covenantor's land who acquires the land without notice, actual or constructive, of the covenant. However, a restrictive covenant created after 1925 (and not being in a lease) is registrable as a land charge under the Land Charges Act 1972.[35] In accordance with the usual rule, registration of

[30] [1975] Ch. 169. See also *E.R. Ives Investment Ltd v. High* 2 Q.B. 379, and *Tito v. Waddell (No. 2)* [1977] Ch. 106.

[31] This case was approved by Lord Templeman in *Rhone v. Stephens* (see note 25 above), at p. 437, but it was stressed that this doctrine only applies in limited circumstances where the burden is relevant to exercising the right *i.e.* where there are reciprocal benefits and burdens.

[32] (1848) 2 Ph. 774. The case itself was decided on very broad principles of equity: the doctrine evolved gradually through subsequent decisions.

[33] See pp. 139–140.

[34] This, as we have seen, is also permitted by the common law.

[35] See p. 231.

the interest will constitute actual notice of its existence to anyone who afterwards acquires the covenantor's land, and failure to register the interest will render it void against a subsequent purchaser of that land (even if he has actual notice of the interest).[36] In the case of registered land a restrictive covenant (not between a lessor and lessee) must be protected by a notice or caution[37] entered in the charges register of the servient land, as it is a minor interest. If there is no such entry, on a disposition for valuable consideration, a transferee will take free from the burden of the covenant.[38]

The analogy between restrictive covenants and negative easements is not complete, and there are some important differences. Restrictive covenants are more flexible and more extensive than negative easements. Since all easements must be capable of being the subject matter of a grant by deed[39] they must be clearly definable with the result that their subject matter is necessarily limited, and negative easements in particular are confined to rights of light and air flowing to windows or apertures in the dominant building.[40] Restrictive covenants, on the other hand, are not so limited and there is nothing to prevent the "servient" owner from covenanting not to build *at all*, or covenanting not to carry on a wide range of other activities on his land. Two further important differences are, first, that a restrictive covenant is enforceable only in equity, whereas an easement can (and normally does) constitute a legal interest.[41] Secondly, a restrictive covenant can only be entered into expressly, whereas an easement can arise both by implied grant and by prescription, as well as by express grant.[42]

There are certain conditions that must be satisfied in order that a covenant may be enforced under the doctrine of *Tulk v. Moxhay*.[43]

First, the doctrine applies only to restrictive covenants: both at law and in equity the burden of a positive covenant falls on the original covenantor alone.[44] The test for determining whether the covenant is positive or negative is the substance, not the form, of the covenant, and the question is whether performance of the covenant requires expenditure of work or money. Thus, a covenant to use premises for

[36] LPA 1925, ss.198–199 and LCA 1972, s.4.
[37] LRA 1925, s.50 and p. 225–226.
[38] LRA 1925, ss.20 and 23.
[39] See p. 140.
[40] The easement of support is also in effect negative.
[41] See pp. 143–144.
[42] It is principally for this reason that the law is reluctant to extend the category of negative easements: see *Phipps v. Pears* [1965] 1 Q.B. 76 and pp. 140–141.
[43] The equitable doctrine is irrelevant where a covenant is enforced against the original covenantor: his liability is contractual, and is enforceable at common law (see p. 171).
[44] Subject to the qualifications concerning indirect methods of enforcement, noted at p. 172.

the purposes only of a private dwelling-house is a restrictive or negative covenant, but a covenant not to allow a building to fall into disrepair is a positive covenant.

Secondly, the covenant must have been taken for the benefit of land retained by the covenantee and be capable of being so benefited[45] *i.e.* it must touch and concern the land.[46] The plaintiff (*i.e.* the person suing on the covenant) must own some interest in that land[47] and it follows that even the original covenantee cannot rely on the equitable doctrine once he has parted with his land.[48]

Thirdly, if the plaintiff is not the original covenantee, but a subsequent owner of the land, he must prove that the benefit of the covenant has passed to him. This he may do in any of three ways:

1. Assignment

The benefit of the covenant may have been assigned to him, expressly or by necessary implication,[49] at the time when he acquired the dominant land.

2. Annexation

If the terms of the covenant[50] or the surrounding circumstances[51] indicate that the benefit was intended to be taken not only by the original covenantee, but also by subsequent owners of the land, the benefit will have passed to the plaintiff without express assignment. Where the plaintiff acquires part only of the original covenantee's land the courts have been curiously reluctant to hold that he can enforce the covenant[52] (without express assignment) unless it is worded so as to annex the benefit expressly to each part of the land, rather than merely to the land as a whole. It seems now, however, that such annexation can be implied, because under section 78 of the Law of Property Act 1925 a covenant relating to the covenantee's land is deemed to be made with the covenantee and his successors in title. It

[45] *Re Ballard's Conveyance* [1937] 1 Ch. 473 (where the estate was too large for the covenant to benefit the whole). *Cf. Earl of Leicester v. Wells-next-the-sea* U.D.C. [1973] Ch. 110 (on the facts it was found that the covenant did benefit the estate as a whole).

[46] See p. 166.

[47] *Formby v. Barker* [1903] 2 Ch. 539, *London County Council v. Allen* [1914] 3 K.B. 642.

[48] *Chambers v. Randall* [1923] 1 Ch. 149.

[49] *E.g.* it passes by operation of law automatically on the death of the original covenantee to his personal representatives, who hold on trust for the beneficiary. See *Earl of Leicester v. Wells-next-the-Sea U.D.C.,* note 45 above.

[50] *Rogers v. Hosegood* [1900] 2 Ch. 388; *cf.* the common law rule, p. 171.

[51] *Marten v. Flight Refuelling Ltd* [1962] Ch. 115, (which has been criticised for leading to uncertainty).

[52] See note 45 above.

has been held that this provision acts as a form of statutory annexation, permitting successors in title to part of the original covenantee's land to sue.[53]

3. Scheme of development

When land is developed, *e.g.* by the building of a housing estate, the developer usually requires each purchaser of a plot to enter into restrictive covenants designed to maintain the general character of the estate and the value of the property. In accordance with principles first stated definitively in *Elliston v. Reacher,*[54] which have since been considerably extended,[55] these covenants then operate as a form of local law enforceable by any plot-owner against any other plot-owner, irrespective of the dates on which they acquired their respective plots. In order for the scheme to operate it must cover a defined area, which has been laid out in plots prior to sale. The purchasers must enter into the same type of restrictive covenants with a common vendor and each purchaser must buy on the basis that he will be bound by and can enforce the same defined set of restrictions. In such a case, the benefit of the covenants is regarded as running in equity with each plot sold under the scheme, in order to give effect to the common intention and interest of the vendor, the purchasers and their successors. The technicalities mentioned above requiring assignment or annexation of the benefit are thus removed. It must not be overlooked, however, that the running of the *burden* of the covenants depends on registration. There is no exemption from this requirement for building scheme covenants, and therefore on the sale of each plot the purchaser's covenants must be registered in order to ensure that his successors will be bound.[56]

Discharge of restrictive covenants

The general rule is that restrictive covenants can exist indefinitely, but there are various statutory provisions under which restrictive covenants may be discharged or modified. In particular, by section 84 of the Law of Property Act 1925[57] the Lands Tribunal has power to

[53] *Federated Homes Ltd v. Mill Lodge Properties Ltd* [1980] 1 W.L.R. 594, applying LPA 1925, s.78 (p. 172 above). The predecessor to this section will not assist where the covenant is made pre 1926, see *J. Sainsbury Plc v. Enfield London Borough Council* [1989] 1 W.L.R. 590.

[54] [1908] 2 Ch. 665.

[55] *Baxter v. Four Oaks Properties Ltd* [1965] Ch. 654; *Re Dolphin's Conveyance* [1970] Ch. 654; *Brunner v. Greenslade* [1971] Ch. 993. (This is so even if a purchaser buys part of a plot.)

[56] Failure by the covenantee (*i.e.* the developer) to register might render him liable to purchasers of other plots.

[57] Applying both to freehold land and to leaseholds if the lease was made for more than 40 years, at least 25 of which have expired. See LPA 1925, s.84 (12).

modify or discharge a restrictive covenant, with or without the payment of compensation, on the various grounds which are set out in the section. For example, one ground is that by reason of changes in the character of the neighbourhood or other circumstances the covenant has become obsolete or would impede some reasonable user of the land.

Apart from these statutory provisions, equity may also refuse to grant an injunction for breach of a restrictive covenant if it appears that the covenant is obsolete, or that the plaintiff, by acquiescing in previous breaches, has waived his rights[58] or in general that it would be inequitable to enforce the covenant.[59]

Where the fee simple of land having the benefit and burden of covenants becomes vested in one person, any restrictive covenants are extinguished unless the common owner recreates them.[60]

[58] *Chatsworth Estates Co. v. Fewell* [1931] 1 Ch. 224 (where permission given to other covenantors to use land other than as a private dwelling did not prevent the plaintiff, from obtaining an injunction restraining the defendant's breach of such a covenant.)

[59] *Wrotham Park Estate Co. Ltd v. Parkside Homes Ltd* [1974] 1 W.L.R. 798 (houses constructed in breach of covenant: damages awarded in lieu of mandatory injunction requiring demolition).

[60] *Re Tiltwood, Sussex Barrett v. Bond* [1978] Ch. 269.

17. Rentcharges

A rentcharge is a rent charged on land, not being a rent payable to a landlord under a lease (a rent payable to a landlord is known as a *rent service*). To be a legal rentcharge it must be in possession and either perpetual or for a term of years absolute (*i.e.* for a freehold or leasehold estate) and it must be created by deed.[1] Any other rentcharge is equitable only.

Legal rentcharges used sometimes to be created on the sale of land, when the purchaser, instead of paying the purchase price as a lump sum, would covenant to pay an annual sum of money for a fixed term of years or in perpetuity, and the obligation to pay this sum would be charged on the land. Now, however, the Rentcharges Act 1977 prohibits the creation of any new rentcharge whether at law or in equity, subject to two main exceptions. First, an equitable rentcharge may be created affecting settled land, *e.g.* a widow's annuity charged on the land under a strict settlement.[2] Secondly, an "estate rentcharge," can still arise. This is a rentcharge created either i) for the purpose of making covenants enforceable against the owner for the time being of that land or ii) to be performed by the owner of the land affected by the rentcharge, for the purpose of meeting or contributing towards the cost of the provision of services or the carrying out of repairs or maintenance by the rent owner to the land charged.[3] It is a useful means of enforcing positive freehold covenants relating to housing developments,[4] for instance.

REMEDIES FOR RECOVERY

The owner of a rentcharge has the following remedies for the recovery of the rent if it is not paid.

[1] See pp. 27, 33 and registered as a registered interest in the case of registered land, see p. 222.

[2] This is where the land is charged with an annual payment for the maintenance of the settlor's widow or perhaps another member of his family. See pp. 40, 52.

[3] Rentcharges Act 1977, s.2(4).

[4] See p. 172.

1. Action on the covenant

The original covenantee, if still the owner of the rentcharge, may sue the original covenantor under his covenant to pay in the deed creating the rentcharge. Such an action against the original covenantor may also be brought by an assignee of the rentcharge if the benefit of the covenant was also expressly assigned to him.[5]

2. Action against terre tenant

At common law the freehold tenant in possession of the land (the *terre tenant*) is personally liable for the rent to the owner of the rentcharge for the time being, and this is so even if the amount of the rent exceeds the current income from the land. Moreover, at common law, if the land has been split up, the *terre tenant* of any part of the land is liable for the whole of the rentcharge unless the owner of the rent has agreed to its being apportioned. Under sections 4 to 7 of the Rentcharges Act 1977, however, the Secretary of State now has the power to order apportionment on the application of any person whose land is affected.

3. Statutory remedies

By section 121 of the Law of Property Act 1925, the owner of a rentcharge is given three statutory remedies for its recovery. First, if the rent or any part of it is 21 days in arrears, the owner of the rentcharge can distrain[6] for it. Secondly, if the rent or any part of it is 40 days in arrears, he may enter and take possession of the land and take the rent and profits from the land until he has raised all the arrears. Thirdly, if the rent or any part of it is 40 days in arrears, the owner of the rentcharge may grant a lease of the land to a trustee upon trust. The trustee may then raise the arrears by mortgaging the leasehold term or any other reasonable means.

4. Re-entry

If the instrument creating the rentcharge so provides, but not otherwise, the owner of a rentcharge which has fallen into arrears may re-enter on to the land and claim the *fee simple* (or any other estate of the grantor of the rentcharge).[7]

Section 122 of the Law of Property Act 1925, provides that a rentcharge may be charged on another rentcharge, rather than land

[5] *Grant v. Edmondson* [1931] 1 Ch. 1.
[6] See p. 105.
[7] See p. 172.

e.g. where a rentcharge of £100 is charged, in turn with a payment of a rentcharge of £40. The owner of the sub-rentcharge may appoint a receiver of the main rent if the sub-rentcharge or any part of it falls 21 days into arrears. Such a receiver will then obtain payment of the main rent (*e.g.* £100) and out of it pay to the owner of the sub-rent what is due to him and the receiver's costs and expenses, returning any balance to the main owner.

EXTINGUISHMENT AND REDEMPTION

Section 3 of the Rentcharges Act 1977 provides for the extinguishment of all existing rentcharges (save for those exceptions mentioned above[8] which can still be created) at the expiry of 60 years either i) after the passing of the Act (*i.e.* July 22, 2037) or ii) after the date on which the rentcharge first became payable, whichever is the later.

The Act also contains provisions[9] whereby a landowner may obtain the discharge of a rentcharge to which his land is subject on payment of a lump sum to the owner of the rentcharge, representing the capital value, determined in accordance with a prescribed formula.

[8] See p. 179.
[9] ss.8–10, replacing LPA 1925, s.191.

18. Mortgages

A mortgage of land is a transaction by which a borrower of money (the mortgagor) gives land as security for the repayment of a loan to his lender (the mortgagee). The mortgagee then has certain rights against the land (*e.g.* a power of sale), by which he may raise any sums that become due to him if the borrower defaults in repaying the loan. Therefore the mortgagee, is not restricted to merely suing for the debt in a personal action against the borrower, although he does have that right, as well as his remedies against the land itself.

Mortgages are most commonly entered into on a purchase of property, when the purchaser borrows the purchase money from a lender such as a building society or a bank. The conveyance or transfer by the vendor to the purchaser, and the mortgage by the purchaser to the lender, will both be executed simultaneously on completion of the purchase (and often the money advanced by the purchaser's mortgagee will be paid, not to the vendor, but to the vendor's own mortgagee, in order to pay off the loan with which the vendor himself purchased the property). Second (and other subsequent) mortgages may be created if further sums are borrowed using the same property as security, whether the loan is to pay for improvements to the property or for collateral purposes.

Most mortgages are of a legal estate in land—they are made by the freeholder or by a leaseholder. However, an equitable interest in land may also be mortgaged; for example if land is settled on A for life, with remainder to B in fee simple, it is possible for B to raise a loan for money by mortgaging his equitable interest in remainder under the settlement. However, it may be assumed that the discussion in the following pages is of mortgages of a legal estate unless otherwise stated.

The general rules concerning mortgages apply to both registered and unregistered land. Nevertheless, there are some special provisions relating to mortgages of registered land, in particular concerning their creation and priority between such mortgages, which are best dealt with in the final chapter on registration. Cross references to these provisions will be made where necessary in this chapter.

METHODS OF MORTGAGING

Since 1926, if a mortgage is to be a legal mortgage it must be a mortgage of a legal estate created by deed[1] and be made either by *demise* or by *legal charge*.[2] If a freehold is being mortgaged by demise, the mortgagee will be granted a long lease, usually for a long term of 3,000 years, with *a proviso for cesser on redemption, i.e.* a qualification that the lease is to end when the mortgage is paid off. The corresponding method of mortgaging a leasehold is by sub-demise with a similar proviso. In this case, the mortgagee is granted a sub-lease for a term of years less by, at least one day, than that of the leasehold which is being mortgaged. In practice the sub-lease is usually for 10 days less than the leasehold mortgaged.

Both freeholds and leaseholds may be mortgaged by legal charge (or, to give its full title, by a "charge by deed expressed to be made by way of legal mortgage"). This is a new form of mortgage introduced by the Law of Property Act 1925. Such a charge gives to the mortgagee the same rights and remedies as if he had a mortgage by demise or sub-demise. The mortgagor charges his land, by way of legal mortgage, with repayment of the loan but he does not technically give to the the mortgagee an estate for a term of years in the land. Nevertheless, the legal charge has certain advantages over a mortgage by demise or sub-demise. For example, a mortgage of a leasehold created in this way will not be a breach of a tenant's covenant not to sub-let the premises, whereas a mortgage by sub-demise would be.

It will be noticed that whichever method of mortgaging is adopted, the mortgagor is left with his legal estate in the land. He may, therefore, create second and subsequent legal mortgages to secure any further loans that may be raised on the same land. Until 1926 this was not possible, because a mortgage of land usually took the form of a conveyance of the mortgagor's whole legal estate in the land to the mortgagee, subject to a proviso for reconveyance on redemption of the mortgage. The Law of Property Act 1925, however, now prohibits this method of mortgaging a legal estate.

An equitable mortgage in land may be created in a number of ways including where there is i) an informal mortgage of a legal estate or, ii) an equitable interest is mortgaged.[3] In the past, an informal

[1] As to the further conditions which must be complied with for the creation of mortgages in registered land, see pp. 227–228.

[2] LPA 1925, ss.85–87. The term mortgage is commonly used whatever the method of creation.

[3] Another type is an equitable charge, see M & W p. 929. The Law Commission have proposed a new system of land mortgages creating two types of mortgages, formal and informal mortgages, which could apply to legal and equitable interests in land, see Law Commission Report (1991) No. 204.

mortgage has arisen where there is a contract to create a mortgage of a legal estate or, alternatively, by a deposit of title deeds. In the first case, such a mortgage, which is not made by deed, will be a valid equitable mortgage if it constitutes a specifically enforceable contract to grant a mortgage.[4] To be a specifically enforceable contract, the loan must have been made and, where the mortgage is entered into on or after September 27, 1989, it must comply with section 2 of the Law of Property (Miscellaneous Provisions) Act 1989, as it is a disposition of an interest in land. Thus, the mortgage must be in writing, incorporate all the terms in one document and be signed by the parties.[5] Another traditional method of informally mortgaging property is by the borrower giving up the title deeds to his property to the lender (or the Land Certificate in the case of registered land) as security for the loan. In particular, this method may be used when a lender makes a temporary loan *e.g.* where he requires security for providing an overdraft facility. For those mortgages created before September 27, 1989, section 40 of the Law of Property Act 1925[6] still applies. In such circumstances, a mere oral agreement between the parties, supported by a deposit of title deeds with the mortgagee, may be sufficient to create an equitable mortgage as long as there is enough evidence to show that the intention of the deposit is to provide security, and not some other reason. This is because, under section 40, there is an enforceable contract if there is evidence in writing of an agreement or a sufficient act of part performance. It has been held that a deposit of title deeds is such an act of part performance.[7] However, for mortgages entered into on or after September 27, 1989, to which the 1989 Act applies, as well as taking a deposit of title deeds, a mortgagee must ensure that there is a deed or, at least a written contract, containing the mortgage terms and signed by the parties (commonly referred to as a *memorandum of deposit)*, otherwise the mortgage will be void.[8]

A mortgage of an equitable interest can only create an equitable mortgage. An example of such an equitable mortgage includes a mortgage of a life or remainder interest under a trust. Unlike a legal mortgage of a legal estate created after 1925, a mortgage of an equitable interest is created by actually assigning the equitable interest to the mortgagee, subject to a proviso for re-assignment on redemption. The assignment must be in writing and signed by the assignor, or his authorised agent,[9] and notice of the assignment should be served by the mortgagee on the trustees of the legal estate.

[4] See p. 27 and this is similar to the position with informal leases, see p. 100.

[5] LPA 1925 s.40 applies to mortgages created before September 27, 1989, see below.

[6] See pp. 93–94.

[7] *Russel v. Russel* (1783) 1 Bro. C.C. 269.

[8] The memorandum must comply with the 1989 Act, s.2, see p. 95 and also *United Bank of Kuwait Plc v. Sahib* [1995] 2 W.L.R. 94.

[9] LPA 1925, s.53(1)(c). See further p. 199.

REDEMPTION OF MORTGAGES

In the mortgage deed, the mortgagor covenants to repay the principal money (*i.e.* the loan) with interest on a date specified in the deed. This is called the contractual or *legal date of redemption*. At common law once this date has passed the mortgagor has no right to redeem his property *i.e.* to repay the loan and the mortgagee can in principle take the property for himself (called *foreclosure*).[10] Equity, however, compels the mortgagee to allow redemption at any time after the contractual date has passed, provided that he is paid the "price of redemption," *i.e.* the principal money, arrears of interest[11] and his costs of discharging the mortgage. This equitable right of redemption, which arises once the contractual date has passed, was developed by equity into an equitable interest in the land, called the *equity of redemption.* The mortgagor is regarded as having the equity of redemption from the moment the mortgage deed is executed, and it comprises of the mortgagor's entire beneficial interest in the property subject to the mortgage, including not only his equitable right to redeem, but also his general rights of ownership.

It has become the practice to choose a contractual date of redemption which is soon after the date of execution of the mortgage (generally six months).[12] Thereafter, the mortgagor must rely on his equitable right to redeem. Equity does not attach any time limit to the exercise of this right, but there are various events which will extinguish the right.[13] For example, if the mortgagee sells the land under his power of sale, the purchaser will acquire the mortgagor's legal estate free from the equity of redemption. Again, if the mortgagee takes possession of the land and remains in possession for 12 years without acknowledging the mortgagor's title, the equitable right of redemption will become extinguished.[14] As we shall see later, equity itself, in foreclosure proceedings, may put a time limit on the period during which the equitable right of redemption may be exercised.[15]

Notice of intention to redeem

One of the equitable maxims is that "he who seeks equity must do equity". Therefore, equity will not allow the mortgagor to exercise his

[10] See p. 195.

[11] All arrears must be paid, even though statute-barred; see *Holmes v. Cowcher* [1970] 1 W.L.R. 834, and p. 213 below.

[12] Mainly because the mortgagee's statutory powers arise only when the contractual date has passed and so the mortgage money has become due (see pp. 192–196).

[13] See p. 213.

[14] See p. 213.

[15] See pp. 195–196.

equitable right of redemption in an unfair manner. If the mortgagor was free to repay the mortgage money without prior notice to the mortgagee, the money might be uninvested for a considerable time before the mortgagee found a suitable new investment. Equity, therefore, requires the mortgagor to give reasonable prior notice to the mortgagee of his intention to exercise his equitable right of redemption, or to pay additional interest instead. For a formal legal mortgage six months' notice will usually be required. However, the giving of notice, or the payment of additional interest in lieu, is not necessary if the mortgagee has already shown that he wants his money, *e.g.* by giving notice requiring repayment.

CONSOLIDATION

Another application of the principle "he who seeks equity must do equity" is the doctrine of consolidation. In its simplest form this means that if the same person, by separate mortgages, mortgages two different properties to the same mortgagee, and then seeks to exercise his equitable right to redeem one of the properties, the mortgagee can require him to redeem both or neither. If this was not the case, the mortgagor might be able to redeem the property that was a more than adequate security for the loan made on it, leaving the mortgagee with the property that was an inadequate security for the loan made on that property. The right to consolidate has now been abolished by section 93 of the Law of Property Act 1925, unless the right is reserved in at least one of the mortgages. This is often done by providing expressly that section 93 shall not apply. Moreover, the right does not exist unless the contractual date of redemption has passed in both cases.

The right to consolidate exists not only in the simple case mentioned above, but also whenever the following conditions are satisfied[16]:

(i) originally both mortgages were made by the same mortgagor and
(ii) either (a) the equities of redemption (*i.e.* the properties, subject to the mortgages) are in one person's hands and the mortgages in another single person's hands, or (b) the position described in (a) has existed at some time in the past, since when the equities of redemption have become separated.

Some examples will illustrate the operation of these rules.

[16] *Pledge v. White* [1896] A.C. 187.

Example 1

A mortgages Blackacre to B.
A mortgages Whiteacre to C.
B and C transfer their mortgages to D.
If A then seeks to redeem one of the two properties, D can consolidate, *i.e.* he can require A to pay off the mortgages on both properties or not to redeem at all.
Rule (ii) above is satisfied here, under (ii)(a).

Example 2

A mortgages Blackacre to B.
A mortgages Whiteacre to C.
A sells Blackacre, subject to the mortgage, to X.
B and C transfer their mortgages to D.
If X or A seeks to redeem his property (Blackacre or Whiteacre, respectively) D cannot consolidate. Rule (ii) above is not satisfied because there has never been a moment of time when both the properties have been in the hands of one person and both the mortgages in another single person's hands. The properties had become separated before the mortgages fell into one person's hands.

Example 3

A mortgages Blackacre to B.
A mortgages Whiteacre to B.
A sells Blackacre, subject to the mortgage, to X.
If X or A seeks to redeem his property B can consolidate because rule (ii) is satisfied under (ii)(b). It can be seen that in this case, as a condition of paying off the mortgage on his own property, X or A can be required to pay off the mortgage on the other property. That mortgage will not then be discharged, but will be transferred to the person making the payment off (*i.e.* X or A, as the case may be).[17]

PRESERVING THE EQUITY OF REDEMPTION

Equity has developed a series of rules for the protection of the equity of redemption, which may be regarded as falling under the general principle "once a mortgage always a mortgage." Equity is concerned to ensure i) that a mortgage shall provide security and nothing more, ii) that it shall not be made irredeemable, and iii) that

[17] See p. 201.

the mortgagee shall not in any way bring improper pressure to bear on the mortgagor.[18]

It should, perhaps, be borne in mind that equity's jurisdiction in these matters was established largely at a time when money-lending was regarded as a suspect and undesirable activity. Social and economic circumstances have changed, and it is difficult now to reconcile equity's traditional attitude to mortgages with the transactions into which the vast majority of house-buyers enter so readily with their building society or bank. A further point to note is that the leading cases in which equity's jurisdiction over mortgages developed were, almost without exception, cases concerning mortgages of commercial property. The principles applied may be the same as with mortgages of domestic property, but the matters in issue are scarcely comparable.

The main rules are as follows:

1. The substance not the form

Equity will treat as a mortgage, any transaction which is in substance intended to provide security for the loan of money, whatever name the parties may give to the transaction. For example, if the lender of money insists upon the transaction being expressed as a conveyance of the property to the lender, with an option to the borrower to re-purchase the property at an enhanced price within a certain time (the difference in price being in fact the interest on the loan), equity will treat this transaction as a mortgage in order to preserve the mortgagor's right of redemption. The mortgagor will then have the right to redeem, even after the end of the fixed period specified in the deed.[19]

2. Provisions repugnant to the equity of redemption

In equity any restrictions on the mortgagor's right to redeem will not be acceptable and this is referred to as the rule that there must be "no clogs on the equity of redemption."[20] Equity will treat as void any provision in a mortgage which would, or might, destroy the equity of

[18] Under contractual principles the courts may set aside a mortgage if there was undue influence or misrepresentation by the mortgagee or his agent, particularly in family-type situations. See *Barclay's Bank plc v. O'Brien* [1993] 3 W.L.R. 786 (where a wife was a guarantor of her husband's mortgage); contrast with *C.I.B.C. Mortgages Plc v. Pitt* [1993] 3 W.L.R. 802. As an example of the steps that may be taken by a mortgagee to counteract a claim of undue influence, see *Banco-Exterior v. Mann, The Independent*, December 8, 1994, C.A.

[19] *Waters v. Mynn* (1850) 15 L.T. 157.

[20] *Samuel v. Jarrah Timber Corporation* [1904] A.C. 323. The same rule applies if the option is granted to a transferee on a transfer of the mortgage (*Lewis v. Frank Love Ltd* [1961] 1 W.L.R. 261).

redemption. For example, if the mortgage purports to give to the mortgagee an option to purchase the property, the grant of the option is void. If this was not the case, by exercising the option the mortgagee could destroy the mortgagor's right of redemption. Once the mortgage has been created, however, the mortgagor, by an independent transaction, may validly grant an option to purchase the property to the mortgagee.[21]

3. Postponing the right of redemption

Prima facie, in the absence of evidence of fraud or oppression by the mortgagee, the parties can make what bargain they like as to the earliest possible date of redemption of the property.[22] They are not bound to follow the usual practice, by which the contractual date of redemption is made six months after the date of the execution of the mortgage. Nonetheless, equity disallows a postponement which would make the right of redemption simply nominal or illusory, *e.g.* when a leasehold is mortgaged, a provision postponing the right of redemption until the lease itself has almost expired.[23] If a postponement is coupled with some *tie* between the mortgagor and the mortgagee which is void, as being in restraint of trade,[24] it seems that the postponement will also be void. For example, where the owner of a petrol station mortgages it to an oil company and agrees to be tied to taking all his supplies from the company throughout the term of the mortgage, and not to redeem the mortgage for 21 years.[25]

4. Other clogs on the equity of redemption

Any provision in a mortgage is void to the extent that it would prevent the mortgagor on redemption from getting back his property in substantially the same condition as it was in when he mortgaged it. For example, if the owner of a free public-house (*i.e.* a public-house where the owner is free to sell any brewer's beers) mortgages it to a brewer, any provision in the mortgage requiring the mortgagor to sell only the mortgagee's beers will be void, so far as the restriction purports to continue after the mortgagor has paid off the loan. Otherwise, were this not the case, having mortgaged a free public-house, the owner would get back a tied one, where he was compelled to purchase the former mortgagee's beer.[26]

[21] *Reeve v. Lisle* [1902] A.C. 461.
[22] *Knightsbridge Estates Ltd v. Byrne* [1939] Ch. 441 (affirmed on different grounds [1940] A.C. 613).
[23] *Fairclough v. Swan Brewery Co. Ltd* [1912] A.C. 565.
[24] This is a common law doctrine based on grounds of public policy.
[25] *Esso Petroleum Co. Ltd v. Harper's Garage (Stourport) Ltd* [1968] A.C. 269.
[26] *Noakes & Co. Ltd v. Rice* [1902] A.C. 24.

5. Collateral advantages

In the absence of evidence of fraud or oppression by the mortgagee, equity has no objection to a provision in the mortgage giving to the mortgagee some collateral advantage, *i.e.* some advantage over and above repayment of the loan with interest.[27] Thus, there is no objection to a provision in the mortgage of a free public-house which requires the mortgagor to sell only the mortgagee's beers *so long as the mortgage lasts.*[28] Nevertheless, if the advantage operates as a clog on the equity of redemption, it will be void. Therefore, if the mortgage provides that the property can only be redeemed on payment of a premium, and the amount of the premium is excessive, equity will allow the mortgagor to redeem on repaying the principal, plus a reasonable rate of interest.[29]

MORTGAGEE'S REMEDIES

In addition to his right to sue the mortgagor personally for any money that becomes due to him, the mortgagee has (or may have) the following main remedies: i) a right to take possession of the land; ii) a right to sell the land; iii) a right to appoint a receiver of the rents and profits of the land; and iv) a right to foreclose. Generally, a mortgagee's remedies are cumulative, so the fact that he has exercised one of the remedies does not prevent him from making use of another, if part of the mortgage monies still remain outstanding.[30] Each of these remedies must be considered separately.

1. Possession

From the moment that a mortgage is created, a legal mortgagee, whether his mortgage is by demise or by charge, has the right to take possession of the land.[31] By this means the mortgagee can obtain the rents and profits from the land and can, if necessary, grant leases of the land.[32] In principle a mortgagee is entitled to possession regardless of whether the mortgagor is in default.[33] However, in practice he

[27] *Kreglinger (G. & C.) v. New Patagonia Meat and Cold Storage Co. Ltd* [1914] A.C. 25: *cf. Multiservice Bookbinding Ltd v. Marsden* [1979] Ch. 84 (provisions in respect of interest were "imprudent" but valid, since they were not unconscionable).

[28] *Biggs v. Hoddinott* [1898] 2 Ch. 307. But note the *Esso* case, note 25 above.

[29] *Cityland and Property (Holdings) Ltd v. Dabrah* [1968] Ch. 166. Under the Consumer Credit Act 1974, ss.137-140, the court has power to relieve any debtor from an "extortionate credit bargain."

[30] Subject to an exception in the case of foreclosure proceedings, see p. 196.

[31] An equitable mortgagee probably has a similar right: see M & W. pp. 951–952.

[32] See p. 196.

[33] See *Western Bank Ltd v. Schindler* [1977] Ch. 1. *(Quennel v. Maltby* [1979] 1 W.L.R. 318, in which doubt is cast on this principle, can be regarded as confined to its special facts. This was an attempt by mortgagor and mortgagee in collusion to evict the mortgagor's statutory tenant).

will not normally exercise this right except either as a preliminary step to selling the property, or as a means of recovering interest on the mortgage debt, (by for instance letting the property).[34] In either case it will usually be necessary for him to bring a court action for possession against the mortgagor. If the mortgage is of a dwelling-house, the court now has a power to adjourn such proceedings or to suspend or postpone the possession order, if it appears that the mortgagor is likely within a reasonable period to pay the amount due or remedy any other default.[35]

Any sums received by a mortgagee in possession must, of course, be set off against the mortgage debt. Further, a mortgagee who does take possession is responsible to the mortgagor for any loss suffered as a result of wilful default. This means that he is accountable to the mortgagor, not only for any profits that he does make, but also for any further profits that he *ought* to have made. For example, suppose the property is a free public-house and the mortgagee is a brewer, and the mortgagee takes possession of the premises and then grants a lease containing a term which requires the lessee to sell only the mortgagee's beers. The mortgagee will be accountable to the mortgagor for the higher rent he could have obtained if he had let the premises without any such tie.[36] Due to this principle of strict accountability, a mortgagee will generally prefer to appoint a receiver of the rents and profits, rather than to take possession himself, as he will not then be accountable in this way.

2. Sale

The two principal statutory remedies are the power of sale and the power to appoint a receiver. Both apply by section 101 of the Law of Property Act 1925 to every mortgagee whose mortgage is by deed. So, every legal mortgagee has these powers, and an equitable mortgagee enjoys them if his mortgage is by deed, *e.g.* if it was created by deposit of title deeds accompanied by a memorandum of deposit made by deed.[37] The statutory powers may be varied or extended by the mortgage.

The power of sale *arises* as soon as the contractual date for redemption has passed or, in cases where the principal sum is repayable by instalments, as soon as any instalment is due and

[34] On application by the mortgagor under LPA 1925, s.91 the court has the power to order a sale instead, see *Palk v. Mortgage Services Funding Plc* [1993] Ch. 330 (where a sale was ordered even in a depressed market).

[35] Administration of Justice Act 1970, ss.36-39. The Administration of Justice Act 1973, s.8, extends this power to cases where the mortgagor appears likely to bring payment of instalments up to date.

[36] *White v. City of London Brewery Co.* (1889) 42 Ch.D. 237.

[37] See p. 185.

unpaid.[38] Nonetheless, it does not become *exercisable* until one of three events occurs[39]:

(i) the mortgagee has served a notice requiring payment of the mortgage money and default in payment has been made for three months after service of such notice;
(ii) some interest under the mortgage is in arrears for two months after becoming due;
(iii) there has been a breach of some other provision contained in the mortgage deed or in the Act which is to be observed by the mortgagor, *e.g.* a failure to repair the mortgaged property.

A purchaser from the mortgagee is concerned to see that the power of sale has arisen, but not that it has become exercisable. The purchaser will get a good title, even if the power has not become exercisable,[40] but the mortgagee will then be liable in damages to the mortgagor.

A mortgagee is not a trustee of his statutory power of sale[41] and, in general, he need not ensure that he gets the best possible price for the property. However, he must act in good faith and take reasonable care to obtain a fair and reasonable price in all the circumstances.[42] This appears to be a duty arising in equity as a result of the relationship of mortgagor and mortgagee.[43] Therefore, the mortgagee must not deliberately sell at a lower price than he can readily obtain, and he must make a genuine sale. It follows that he may not sell to himself, directly or indirectly, whether by private sale or at public auction.[44] Further, under this duty, a mortgagee may be liable in damages for any loss suffered, when exercising his power of sale, if through his negligence the property is sold for less than it ought to have realised.[45] The duty is owed not only to the mortgagor himself,

38 *Payne v. Cardiff R.D.C.* [1932] 1 K.B. 241.

39 LPA 1925, s.103.

40 LPA 1925, s.104.

41 *Kennedy v. De Trafford* [1897] A.C. 180 and *Cuckmere Brick Co. Ltd v. Mutual Finance Ltd* [1971] Ch. 949.

42 *Palk v. Mortgage Services Funding Plc,* see note 34 above. Building societies, however, are under a statutory duty to obtain the best price reasonably obtainable, see the Building Societies Act 1986, Sched.4.

43 *Downsview Nominees Ltd v. First City Corporation Ltd* [1993] A.C. 295. In the view of some this is akin to a fiduciary duty, but other cases seem to indicate it is a duty of care in tort, see *Cuckmere Brick Co. Ltd v. Mutual Finance Ltd,* see note 41 above.

44 A sale to a company in which the mortgagee is the majority shareholder is not necessarily objectionable, provided that he otherwise acts reasonably *(Farrar v. Farrars Ltd* (1888) 40 Ch.D.: *cf. Tse Kwong Lam v. Wong Chit Sen* [1983] 1 W.L.R. 1349).

45 See the *Cuckmere Brick Co. Ltd* case, note 41 above, where the mortgagee failed to notify prospective purchasers of the full extent of the planning permission obtained for the land.

but also to a guarantor of the mortgage debt. However, it appears that the duty does not extend, for example, to a beneficiary of trust property which has been mortgaged.[46]

When the mortgagee of a freehold or leasehold sells the land under his statutory power of sale, he conveys to the purchaser the mortgagor's fee simple, or leasehold term as applicable. The conveyance to the purchaser takes effect subject to any rights which rank in priority over the mortgage (unless they are discharged out of the proceeds), but free from the mortgagor's interest and all estates interests and rights over which the mortgage has priority.[47] The mortgagor's equity of redemption and later mortgages are therefore overreached,[48] as is any interest created out of the mortgagor's equity of redemption, such as a contract of sale made previously by him,[49] and the purchaser takes free from these.

The mortgagee is a trustee of the proceeds of sale, which are paid to him and he must distribute these in a certain order.[50] First, any prior mortgagees must be paid off, for example, if the power of sale has been exercised by a second mortgagee. Thereafter, the costs and expenses of the sale will be paid and then the seller-mortgagee's own mortgage is paid off and after that any subsequent mortgages. Any remaining monies (if any) will be passed to the mortgagor.

A mortgagee, whose mortgage is not by deed, does not have the statutory power of sale, but on receiving an application by him (or by anyone interested in the equity of redemption, *e.g.* the mortgagor) the court may order a sale.[51] An equitable mortgagee has the statutory power if his mortgage is by deed.[52] It is generally thought, however, that he cannot pass a legal estate to the purchaser unless there is some conveyancing device in the mortgage which enables him to do this, *e.g.* an irrevocable power of attorney given by the mortgagor to the mortgagee for this purpose.

3. Receiver

As soon as the contractual date for redemption has passed, a mortgagee, whose mortgage is by deed, has the statutory power to

[46] *Parker-Tweedale v. Dunbar Bank Plc* [1991] ch.12., as it arises from the relationship of mortgagor and mortgagee.

[47] LPA 125, ss.88, 89, 104.

[48] *Ibid.* s.2(1)(iii).

[49] Whether or not protected by registration (*Duke v. Robson* [1973] 1 W.L.R. 267; contrast *Lyus v. Prowsa Developments Ltd* [1982] 1 W.L.R. 1044, in which the sale by the mortgagee was expressly subject to rights created by the mortgagor's contract see p. 37).

[50] LPA 1925, s.105.

[51] LPA 1925, s.91.

[52] *Ibid* s.101.

appoint a receiver of the income of the mortgaged property. The power is not to be exercised, however, until the power of sale has become exercisable.[53] The role of the receiver is to manage the property, in order to raise income from the property to repay the loan, or to deal with the property in order to sell it and recover the sums due. For example, this remedy may be used where the mortgaged property consists of business premises let on long commercial leases. A receiver is deemed to be the agent of the *mortgagor*, who, therefore, is to be solely responsible for the receiver's acts or defaults, unless the mortgage otherwise provides. It is for this reason that a mortgagee, who wishes to obtain the profits of the land, will generally prefer to appoint a receiver rather than take possession of the land himself. If he appoints a receiver he escapes liability on the basis of wilful default.[54]

After paying various outgoings and his own commission, the receiver must apply any money received by him in payment of the interest due under the mortgage, and, if directed to do so in writing by the mortgagee, towards the discharge of the principal money.[55] Any residue is to be paid by him to the person who, but for the possession of the receiver, would have been entitled to receive the income. This will be normally the mortgagor.

A mortgagee whose mortgage is not by deed may apply to the court for the appointment of a receiver.[56]

4. Foreclosure

Foreclosure is a court procedure whereby the mortgagor's estate is vested in the mortgagee. The right of the mortgagee to apply to court for foreclosure arises as soon as the contractual date for redemption has passed.[57] In such proceedings the court will initially make an order called a *foreclosure order nisi*, giving to the mortgagor a fixed period (usually six months) within which he must repay the monies due under the mortgage. If he fails to do so within the period, the order will be made *absolute,* the mortgagor will lose his right of redemption and the mortgagee will become the beneficial owner of the property (even though the amount of the outstanding mortgage debt may be much less than the value of the property). This is therefore a drastic remedy and it is for this reason that foreclosure is rarely used

[53] *Ibid,* ss.101, 109 and see p. 193. A person paying money to a receiver need not be concerned whether the receiver is authorised to act, see s.109(4).

[54] See p. 192.

[55] LPA 1925, s.109.

[56] Supreme Court Act 1981, s.37 and *Meaden v. Sealey* (1849) 6 Hare 620.

[57] Or, it seems, if the mortgagor is in breach of some other condition in the mortgage, *e.g.* as to payment of interest, even though the principal sum is not due: see *Twentieth Century Banking Corporation Ltd v. Wilkinson* [1977] Ch. 99.

nowadays. Indeed, the court has power to order sale instead of foreclosure,[58] and will generally do so unless it appears that the value of the property is equivalent to the mortgage debt.

By the equitable remedy of foreclosure equity takes away from the mortgagor the very interest which it has created, *i.e.* the equity of redemption. Therefore, foreclosure is the mortgagee's counterblast to the mortgagor's equity of redemption. A foreclosure order absolute vests the mortgagor's legal estate in the mortgagee, free from the equity of redemption and free from any subsequent mortgages, which are extinguished.[59] If there are subsequent mortgages, each subsequent mortgagee must be given the right to pay off the plaintiff's mortgage and take a transfer of it, failing which the subsequent mortgagee will lose his security when the order absolute is made. It follows that subsequent mortgagees must be joined with the mortgagor as co-defendants in the mortgagee's foreclosure action. Prior mortgages are unaffected and remain attached to the land.

In exceptional circumstances, an application may be made to the court by the mortgagor to re-open the foreclosure, even though an order absolute has been made, and the court may restore to the mortgagor his equity of redemption. Moreover, the foreclosure will automatically be re-opened if after the foreclosure absolute, the mortgagee sues the mortgagor for the mortgage debt. For this reason, if a mortgagee, who has obtained a foreclosure order absolute, sells the property afterwards, he cannot sue the mortgagor to recover the mortgage debt, as he is not now in a position to allow the mortgagor to redeem the property. This is an exception to the general rule that a mortgagee's remedies are cumulative.

The equitable remedy of foreclosure is available to all mortgagees, legal or equitable.

The power of leasing

Section 99 of the Law of Property Act 1925, gives the power to grant leases of mortgaged land which will be binding on all persons interested in the land. This power is given to the mortgagor, unless the mortgagee has taken possession or has appointed a receiver, in which case the power belongs to the mortgagee. A mortgagee who has appointed a receiver may delegate the power of leasing to the receiver. The type of leases which the section authorises are agricultural or occupation leases for any term not exceeding 50 years, and

[58] LPA 1925, s.91. The power to order sale under this provision also applies to other actions brought in respect of mortgaged property, see *Arab Bank Plc v. Mercantile Holdings Ltd* [1994] 2 W.L.R. 307 and *Palk v. Mortgage Services Funding Plc*, see note 34 above.

[59] *Ibid.* ss.88(2), 89(2).

building leases for any term not exceeding 999 years. The lease must reserve the best rent that can reasonably be obtained, no fine may be taken, and certain other conditions are laid down by the Act.[60]

With the exception of mortgages of agricultural land,[61] the statutory power of leasing can be excluded by the mortgage, and in practice the mortgagor's power is usually excluded. Alternatively, the statutory power may also be extended by the mortgage.

Quite apart from the statutory power, if either party to the mortgage grants a lease, that lease will be binding on him, although it is not binding on the other party to the mortgage.

PRIORITY OF SUCCESSIVE MORTGAGES

Where several successive mortgages of the same land have been created, and the security proves inadequate, the question of the priority of those mortgages becomes crucial. It is, therefore, necessary to determine the order in which the rights of these mortgagees are to take effect. The position varies depending on whether the land is registered or unregistered. The rules set out below apply to unregistered land and the provisions concerning the priority between mortgages relating to registered land are discussed in the last chapter on registration.

1. Mortgages of a legal estate

These principles relate to both legal and equitable mortgages of a legal estate. The general rule is "first in time, first in right", *i.e.* priority follows the order in which the mortgages are created. However, there are variations to this rule and in order to understand these it is necessary to consider first a mortgagee's right to take a deposit of title deeds[62] and secondly the rules concerning the registration of mortgages. A first mortgagee (including a mortgagee of a charge by way of legal mortgage), has a statutory right to retain the title deeds to the mortgaged property.[63] The rationale behind this provision is that, otherwise, it would be possible for the mortgagor to fraudulently sell or further mortgage the property, without the mortgagee's knowledge. In the case of a mortgage of the legal estate which is not protected by a deposit of title deeds, the mortgagee's

[60] *Ibid.* s.99(5) to (11).
[61] Agricultural Holdings Act 1986, Sched. 14, para. 12.
[62] Which is separate from the mortgagee taking a deposit of title deeds as a means of creating an equitable mortgage, see p. 185.
[63] See LPA ss.85(1), 86(1) and 87(1), reflecting the position pre 1926 when the mortgagee held the title deeds to the property as the legal estate was conveyed to him.

position must be protected by registering the mortgage under the Land Charges Act 1972. Therefore, even a second or other subsequent *legal* mortgage is registrable and this is an exception to the general rule that only equitable interests are registrable under the Act. If the subsequent mortgage is a legal mortgage, it is registrable as a *puisne* mortgage; if it is an equitable mortgage of a legal estate it is also registrable, but as a *general equitable charge*.[64]

We may now consider the two exceptions to the general rule, first in time, first in right.

(i) If the earlier mortgage is an equitable mortgage protected by deposit (and so not registrable) and the later mortgage is a legal mortgage, and the legal mortgagee took his mortgage in good faith and without notice, actual or constructive, of the equitable mortgage, the legal mortgage will rank first. This is not because of any misconduct on the part of the equitable mortgagee, but because the old doctrine of notice applies and in general an equitable interest does not bind a subsequent bona fide purchaser for value of a legal estate (including a legal mortgagee) without notice of the equitable interest. The position of the earlier equitable mortgagee is not, however, as precarious as might at first sight appear. This is because the fact that the title deeds have been deposited with him will usually ensure that any subsequent mortgagee has notice, actual or constructive, of the equitable mortgage. If the later mortgagee asks for the title deeds, he will generally discover the existence of the equitable mortgage, and if he does not request them, he will be fixed with constructive notice of the mortgage, as he ought reasonably to have inspected them. However, if the legal mortgagee did ask for the title deeds and was given a false, but credible, explanation of the mortgagor's inability to produce them, he would *not* be fixed with notice of the equitable mortgage, and would have priority.[65]

(ii) If the earlier mortgage, whether legal or equitable, is registrable, and has not been registered when the later mortgage is *created*, the later mortgage will have priority according to the provisions of section 4 of the Land Charges Act 1972. This states that failure to register the earlier mortgage renders it void against a subsequent "purchaser" of any interest in the land; the later mortgagee (whether legal or equitable) is within the statutory definition of a "purchaser," for these purposes and it follows that he gains priority, even if he has actual notice of the earlier mortgage.[66]

There is, however, a possible conflict between section 4 of the Land Charges Act 1972, and section 97 of the Law of Property Act 1925, which provides that a registrable mortgage shall rank in priority

[64] As a Class C(i) and C(iii) land charge respectively, see p. 231.
[65] *Hewitt v. Loosemore* (1851) 9 Hare 449; *Oliver v. Hinton* [1899] 2 Ch.264.
[66] LPA 1925, s.199.

according to the date of its *registration* as a land charge. According to section 97, if there are two successive mortgages, both of which are registrable, the earlier will rank first, if *registered* first (even though it had not been registered when the later mortgage was created). The conflict has yet to be resolved, but it seems that the provisions of the Land Charges Act 1972 ought to prevail, on the basis that once a charge is void it cannot later be revived (at least not without an express provision to that effect). Therefore, on this interpretation, the earlier mortgage must be registered before the later mortgage is created.

Nevertheless, it should be noted that, for the purposes of the Land Charges Act 1972, if the second mortgage is registrable, nothing turns on *its* registration, when determining whether it takes priority to the first mortgage. This is because failure to register a registrable interest merely makes it void against a *later* purchaser (*e.g.* a third mortgagee), but its priority in relation to the first mortgagee would not be affected by its non-registration.

2. Mortgages of an equitable interest

The priority of successive mortgages of an equitable interest in any property, real or personal, is governed by the rule in *Dearle v. Hall,*[67] as amended by section 137 of the Law of Property Act 1925. Under this rule, priority generally follows the order in which the respective mortgagees have given written notice of their mortgages to the trustees of the settlement or trust under which the mortgaged interest exists. For example, suppose by means of a strict settlement, or a trust for sale, land is settled on A for life, with remainder to B in fee simple, and B mortgages his equitable remainder, first to X and then to Y. The priority of the two mortgages will generally follow the order in which X and Y give written notice of their mortgages to the trustees of the settlement or trust for sale. The first to give notice will rank first, but there is an exception. If Y, when he took his mortgage had actual or constructive notice of the existence of X's mortgage, he cannot gain priority by being the first to give notice, as it would be fraudulent for Y to claim priority in those circumstances.[68]

Mortgages of a beneficial interest under a settlement or trust for sale are not registrable under the Land Charges Act 1972, nor is priority affected by the deposit of documents of title.

Tacking

Sometimes the rules of priority between mortgages are affected by the doctrine of *tacking*, the right of a mortgagee to attach a further

[67] (1823) 3 Russ. 1.
[68] *Re Holmes* (1885) 29 Ch.D. 786.

mortgage to an existing mortgage and so obtain priority over intermediate mortgages. After 1925, only one form of tacking is permitted, namely, the tacking of further loans, which is now governed by section 94 of the Law of Property Act 1925.[69] Where land is unregistered, if two successive mortgages of the same land are made to A and B, respectively and A then makes a further loan to the borrower on the same security, A may sometimes add or *tack* this further advance to his original loan, and so claim priority for both his loans over B's mortgage. A prior mortgagee has the right to tack in three cases:

(i) with the agreement of the intervening mortgagee;

(ii) if he had no notice of the intervening mortgage (*e.g.* B's mortgage) at the time when he made the further advance;

(iii) whether or not he had such notice, if under his mortgage there was an obligation to make the further advance.

It will be observed that in case (ii) notice of the intervening mortgage will be fatal to the right to tack. In general, if the intervening mortgage was registered under the Land Charges Act 1972 at the date of the further advance, registration itself will constitute sufficient notice to prevent tacking. However, there is an exception if the prior mortgage was made expressly for securing a current account or any further advances as might be made. In such a case registration under the Land Charges Act 1972 is not sufficient notice to prevent the prior mortgagee from tacking. The prior mortgagee must have *actual notice* of the intervening mortgage (*e.g.* by actually searching the register when he makes the further advance) to prevent him from tacking. For this reason, when a prior mortgage is expressly made to secure a current account (*e.g.* an overdraft facility) or any further advances that may be made, a later mortgagee should always give express notice of his mortgage to the prior mortgagee (*e.g.* by letter) and so prevent tacking.

DISCHARGE OF MORTGAGES

Once the mortgagor has repaid the mortgage monies, and thus redeemed the mortgage, he will want evidence that the mortgage is discharged. In the case of unregistered land, it is usual practice to note or *endorse* a receipt on the mortgage deed, or to attach such a receipt to the mortgage. Under section 115 of the Law of Property Act 1925, such a receipt should state the name of the person who pays the money and be signed by the mortgagee. This will then operate to discharge any mortgage, if payment is made by the mortgagor.[70]

[69] This provision does not apply to registered land, where the position is governed by L.R.A. 1925, s.30, see p. 229.

[70] There are special rules regarding building societies, see Building Societies Act 1986, Sched. 4., para. 2.

However, if a person not entitled to the immediate equity of redemption, *e.g.* a second or subsequent mortgagee, makes the payment, an endorsed receipt will not discharge the mortgage, but will (with certain exceptions) transfer it to the person making the payment.[71]

[71] See p. 188 note 17. As to the position concerning registered land see p. 229.

19. Disabilities

There are special land law rules relating to those persons who are regarded as being under a disability, who include: i) infants and ii) persons suffering from a mental disorder.

INFANTS

After 1925 an infant or *minor i.e.* a person below the age of 18 years old[1] cannot hold a legal estate in land, although he may in general own other property, including an equitable interest in land under a trust for sale or a strict settlement. Further, an infant cannot make a binding disposition of the property which is vested in him and any purported disposition is voidable by the infant during his minority or within a reasonable time of him reaching 18 years of age.

If there is a disposition to an infant of a fee simple or term of years absolute the land will be deemed to be settled land,[2] even though the disposition is to him absolutely and there is no succession of interests. Therefore, any purported conveyance or transfer of a legal estate in land to an infant alone, or to two or more persons jointly, both or all of whom are infants, for his or their own benefit, operates only as an agreement for valuable consideration to execute a settlement. This is the case whether consideration has in fact been given or not. A trust instrument must be executed in favour of the infant or infants by the grantor and in the meantime the land is held on trust for the infant or infants.[3] The legal estate must be vested by vesting deed or assent in the statutory owners[4] who will normally be those persons appointed as trustees of the settlement (as an infant cannot be a tenant for life as he is not of full age). The statutory owner has all the powers of disposition of a tenant for life under the Settled Land Act 1925 and

[1] Family Law Reform Act 1969, ss.1, 12. Before January 1, 1970, the age of majority was 21.

[2] Settled Land Act 1925, s.1. See p. 40 note 2.

[3] SLA 1925, s.27.

[4] See p. 43.

this is why the Act makes the land settled land, so that the infancy does not prevent dispositions being made.

On the other hand, a conveyance of a legal estate in land to an infant jointly with one or more other persons of full age operates to vest the legal estate in those who have reached majority on trust for sale, imposed by statute,[5] as is usual in the case of co-ownership. The rents and profits, pending sale, and the net proceeds of sale, after sale, must be held on trust for the person or persons of full age and the infant, therefore preserving the infant's beneficial interest. Similar provisions apply to the grant or transfer of a legal mortgage to an infant solely or jointly with another person.

The appointment of an infant as trustee of any property is void.[6] However, the appointment of an infant as executor is not void, but is suspended during his minority.[7] Other arrangements are then made for someone else, on his behalf, to administer the deceased's estate during the minority, but the infant is entitled to a grant of probate on reaching his majority.

PERSONS SUFFERING FROM MENTAL DISORDER

Under the Mental Health Act 1983 the court has wide powers to dispose of the property of a person who is suffering from mental disorder, and a receiver may be appointed to exercise these powers on the court's behalf.[8] So long as a receiver has been appointed the patient has no power to make an *inter vivos* disposition of his property, although he may make a valid will during a lucid period. If there is no receivership the position regarding a disposition of property by a person suffering from mental disorder is that:

(i) It is *valid* if the disposition is made for valuable consideration and the other party has no notice of the disability.[9]
(ii) It is *voidable* by the insane person, his personal representative, or a receiver when appointed, if it is made for valuable consideration and the other party has notice of the disability.
(iii) It is *void* if the disposition is gratuitous.[10]

[5] LPA 1925, s.19.
[6] *Ibid.* s.20.
[7] Supreme Court Act 1981, s.118.
[8] Mental Health Act 1983, s.99. Applications are dealt with by the Court of Protection.
[9] *Hart v. O'Connor* [1985] A.C. 1000.
[10] *Elliot v. Ince* (1857) 7 De GM&G 475.

OTHER PERSONS AND BODIES

Married women, non-British subjects, convicts, corporations and charities were all formerly subject to particular disabilities. However, with slight exceptions[11] these disabilities have now been abolished by various statutes.

[11] See for example, Charities Act 1960 and Charities Act 1993, s.36-40.

20. Acquisition of title under the Limitation Act 1980

The general policy behind statutes of limitation is to impose a time limit on the period within which legal claims must be pursued, in order to avoid the problem of lack of evidence when bringing stale claims. Different limitation periods, within which claims must be commenced, may be laid down for different causes of action *e.g.* for contract, tort or land claims. However, in each case, after the end of the prescribed period, no legal action can be successfully brought and the action is referred to as *statute-barred.*

As regards actions to recover possession of land, the basic provision is contained in section 15(1) of the Limitation Act 1980. This provides that "no action shall be brought by any person to recover any land after the expiration of 12 years[1] from the date on which the *right of action accrued* to him or, if it first accrued to some person through whom he claims, to that person."

In general, only a person who is entitled to possession himself can bring an action to recover possession from a *squatter i.e.* some other person who has wrongfully taken possession of land. Land, in this context, is widely defined to include any legal or equitable estate or interest and interests under a trust for sale.[2]

Problems may therefore arise where land is subject to a succession of interests under a strict settlement or a trust for sale, as it is the tenant for life or the trustees respectively, in whom the legal fee simple is vested, who are usually entitled to sue prior to the expiry of the limitation period. Therefore, as we shall see, the Act also contains detailed provisions governing the rights of action of those persons who are not immediately entitled, and whose interests might be prejudiced by the inactivity of the owner in possession.

Under the Act, the effect of the lapse of time on the ability to recover possession of land is twofold. First, the title of the former

[1] Or under Sched. 1. para. 10 and 11 of the 1980 Act, 30 years when the action is brought by the Crown or certain corporations sole (see p. 10.) and 60 years for actions by the Crown to recover the foreshore, see p. 16.

[2] S.38(1)

owner is extinguished, in the case of unregistered land, or held on trust for the squatter, where land is registered.[3] Secondly, the squatter acquires title to the land based on possession.[4] In considering both these negative and positive aspects, however, it must be remembered that title to land in England means title to a particular estate or interest. It follows that where several persons own different estates or interests in the same land, separate rights of action to recover possession of the land may accrue, at different times, to different owners of these estates and interests, *e.g.* a remainderman. Further, the nature and extent of any title acquired by a squatter can only be determined by reference to the particular estate owner whose claim has become statute-barred.[5]

It is, of course, rare for one person actively to dispossess another of his land. Questions are most likely to arise under the Limitation Act 1980, where there is a misunderstanding as to the correct boundaries of land, and one person takes possession of part of another's land in the mistaken belief that it is his own.

It can be seen from the above that we must consider separately: i) when the right of action to recover land accrues to a particular owner of an estate or interest, in order to determine ultimately when the limitation period expires and ii) how the squatter acquires title by adverse possession.

ACCRUAL OF RIGHT OF ACTION

Interests in possession

Where the person bringing an action to recover land (*i.e.* the plaintiff) has an interest in possession, his right of action is deemed to have accrued when two conditions are fulfilled: i) when he has been dispossessed or has discontinued possession of the land *and* ii) when adverse possession has been taken by another person.[6] This means that where the plaintiff has been dispossessed by a squatter entering onto the land, the right of action accrues on the date when he was dispossessed. However, if he has merely discontinued his possession and the land is unoccupied, the right of action does not accrue unless and until *adverse possession* has been taken by some other person. In either case, it will be appreciated that the overall effect of these provisions is that if the owner is to recover the land, and prevent his

[3] S.17 (unregistered land) and LRA 1925, s.75(1) (registered land). See p. 219.

[4] With registered land this is an equitable interest until the squatter is registered as proprietor of his estate, see Ruoff & Roper, 29–02 and p. 219 below.

[5] See, for example, p. 211 as to the position where a tenant rather than a landlord is dispossessed.

[6] Sched. 1, paras. 1, and 8.

title being ended, he must bring his action within 12 years from the date on which adverse possession was obtained. The Act is vague as to what will amount to adverse possession, defining it as where "land is in the possession of some person in whose favour the period of limitation can run,"[7] but there is considerable case law on this point which is discussed later in this chapter.[8]

Future interests

If a succession of interests exists in land and adverse possession is taken during a preceding interest, the owner of a future interest may generally bring an action to recover the land within either: i) 12 years from the date when adverse possession was taken or, ii) six years from the date when his future interest falls into possession, whichever period is longer.[9] For example, suppose land is settled on A for life, with remainder to B in fee simple, and adverse possession of the land is taken by a squatter during A's life interest. When A dies B may bring an action against the squatter within 12 years from the date when the squatter took possession of the land or six years from the death of A, whichever is longer.

This special rule has no application if adverse possession has been taken before the future interest is created. For example, in the above illustration, if adverse possession had been taken by the squatter before the land was settled on A and B, neither A nor B could bring an action to recover the land from the squatter after the expiration of 12 years from the date when the squatter took possession. This is because the right of action accrued to the settlor, as he was entitled to possession at the time of dispossession by the squatter. The creation of the settlement, after the right has accrued, does not alter this and A and B only have the right to claim through the settlor, whose claim is now statute-barred.

Again, the special rule has no application to the owner of an interest which falls into possession on the determination of an entailed interest.[10] For example, if land is settled on A in tail, with remainder to B in fee simple, and S takes adverse possession of the land during the period of the entailed interest, B must bring his action within 12 years from the date when adverse possession was taken. Yet B cannot himself sue until his remainder falls into possession and prior to that he can only claim through A. If A fails to sue, the limitation period may well have expired before B has any chance to sue.

[7] Sched. 1, para. 8.
[8] See p. 216.
[9] S.15(2); Sched. 1, para. 4.
[10] S.15(3). As to entailed interests see pp. 5 and 17–20.

Finally, the Act also deals with the situation where a person is entitled to an interest in possession and at the same time he is also entitled to a future interest in the same land. In such a case, if that person's right to recover the interest in possession becomes barred under the Act, no action may be brought by him, or by any person claiming through him, in respect of the future interest unless, in the meantime, possession of the land has been recovered by a person entitled to an intermediate interest.[11] For example, suppose land is settled on A for life, with remainder to B for life, with remainder to A in fee simple, and S takes possession of the land and holds it for 12 years during A's lifetime. Once his claim is statute-barred A cannot take action in respect of his life interest nor the fee simple in remainder. After A's death, no action can be brought on behalf of his estate, in respect of the fee simple remainder, unless possession of the land has been recovered on behalf of B. Time of course only begins to run against B once his interest vests in possession.

Settled land and land held on trust

The provisions of the Act apply to equitable interests in land (including interests in the proceeds of sale of land held on trust for sale), just as they apply to legal estates.[12]

Therefore, for the purposes of determining the limitation period under the Act, a right of action to recover the land is deemed to accrue to a person entitled to an *equitable interest in possession* in the same way as it would have accrued if his interest had been a legal estate in the land. However, as we have seen, in practice it is usually the holder of the legal estate who must bring the action on behalf of the beneficiaries. It is therefore necessary for the Act to protect future beneficiaries' claims as otherwise their rights would be lost when the trustees' or tenant for life's right to recover the legal estate becomes statute-barred. This is achieved by providing that the title of a tenant for life or statutory owner to the *legal estate* under a strict settlement is not extinguished until the right of action to recover the land of every person entitled to a beneficial interest has become statute-barred.[13] Similarly, when land is held on trust, including a trust for sale, the right of the trustees is not to be extinguished as long as the right of action of any beneficiary to recover the land has still to accrue or has not been barred.[14] This means that the statutory owner or trustees can still sue on behalf of the beneficiaries whose claim is not statute-barred,[15] although not on their own account if their own right of action is barred.

[11] S.15(5).
[12] S.18(1).
[13] S.18(2).
[14] S.18(3).
[15] S.18(4).

For example, suppose land is settled on A for life, with remainder to B in fee simple, and S takes adverse possession of the land and holds it for 12 years during A's lifetime. A's right to the beneficial life interest will become extinguished, but his title to the legal estate (vested in him as the "tenant for life" under the Settled Land Act 1925) will not, because no cause of action has yet accrued to the remainderman B.[16]

Also, under the Act,[17] the fact that a beneficiary (who is not a sole absolute owner) is in possession of settled land, or land held on trust for sale, does not bar the title of a tenant for life, statutory owner, or trustee, or of any remainderman. Similarly, trustees cannot acquire a squatter's title against their own beneficiaries.[18] A somewhat curious consequence of these provisions is that, where there is co-ownership of land, and so a statutory trust for sale[19] arises (where the co-owners are the trustees and beneficiaries), one co-owner cannot, by ousting his fellow owners, acquire a squatter's title to the land.[20]

Leaseholds generally

If a squatter takes possession of land after a lease has been granted, the landlord may sue the squatter to recover the land within 12 years after the determination of the lease. For example, if shortly after the fee simple owner has granted a lease for 50 years to a tenant, a squatter takes possession of the land and holds it for 12 years, the tenant will be statute-barred from recovering possession. The squatter will be entitled to remain in possession of the land for the rest of the lease, but the landlord will have 12 years from the determination of the lease within which to sue the squatter for recovery of the land.[21]

A lessee, under a lease for a fixed term, cannot acquire a squatter's title against his own landlord by virtue of his possession of the land during the period of the lease, as this is not adverse. If, for example, shortly after a lease for 50 years has been granted, the lessee begins to withhold payment of his rent and continues to do so for 12 years, he does not thereby acquire a squatter's title against his landlord. The landlord at any time may require the tenant to pay rent for the remainder of the leasehold term. He may also sue the tenant for arrears of rent, so far as the Act allows.[22] Generally, he may recover up to six years' arrears by court action or distress,[22] but in the case of

[16] B's claim will not be statute-barred until 6 years from A's death, see p. 209.
[17] Sched. 1, para. 9.
[18] S.21 *Re Milking Pail Farm Trusts* [1940] Ch. 996.
[19] See p. 61–62.
[20] *Re Landi* [1939] Ch. 828.
[21] As to the other rights of the landlord, see pp. 217–218.
[22] S.19.

agricultural holdings, the right of distress is limited to one year's rent.[23]

Similarly, a tenant at will cannot acquire a squatter's title against his landlord merely by remaining in possession without paying rent, as time does not begin to run in his favour until the tenancy is determined by the landlord. However, in the case of a tenancy at sufferance (which is not really a tenancy at all and amounts to adverse possession), time begins to run from its commencement.[24] Where a person wrongfully claims to be entitled to the reversion on a lease, which is in writing and at a rent of at least £10 per annum (other than a lease granted by the Crown), if he demands payment of the rent from the tenant, and the tenant pays the rent to that person for 12 years, the person to whom the rent has been paid acquires a possessory title to the reversion.[25]

Periodic tenancies

Normally, if a periodic tenancy is granted in writing, time does not begin to run against the landlord until the tenancy is determined *e.g.* by service of the appropriate notice to quit.

Nevertheless, special rules apply where there is an oral periodic tenancy, but it should be noted that these rules apply only for the purpose of calculating the limitation period. For these purposes, a tenancy from year to year or for any other period, *not* granted in writing, shall be deemed to determine on expiry of the first year or other period of the tenancy *e.g.* at the end of a month in the case of a monthly tenancy. The right of action in respect of such a tenancy then accrues on the date of deemed termination or on the date of the last receipt of rent, whichever occurs last.[26]

If, for example, a tenant under a yearly oral tenancy remains in possession without paying rent for 13 years from the commencement of the tenancy, he will acquire a squatter's title against the landlord. However, the payment of rent, or a written acknowledgement of the landlord's title, before the landlord's claim becomes statute-barred, will start the 12-year period running afresh. In practice this problem may arise where the rent payable in respect of the premises is nominal and so the landlord neglects to recover it.[27]

[23] Agricultural Holdings Act 1986, s.16.

[24] As to tenancies at will and sufferance, see pp. 102–103. Until August 1, 1980 a special rule applied to tenancies at will, but this was abolished by the Limitation Amendment Act 1980, s.3(1).

[25] Limitation Act 1980, Sched. 1, paras. 6, 8(3).

[26] Sched. 1, para. 5.

[27] *Hayward v. Chaloner* [1968] 1 QB 107.

Rentcharges

The Act[28] defines land as including rentcharges and provides more specifically that, in relation to rentcharges, references in the Act to the possession of land shall be construed as references to the receipt of the rent. Further, references to the date of dispossession of land shall be construed as references to the date of the last receipt of rent. As a result of these provisions, if a rentcharge is unpaid for 12 years it becomes extinguished. Moreover, if a person wrongfully claims to be entitled to the rentcharge, and the rent is paid to him for 12 years, the former owner of the rentcharge becomes statute-barred and the claimant acquires a possessory title to the rentcharge.

Mortgages

Both the mortgagor's right of redemption, and the mortgagee's rights to recover the principal and interest due or to foreclose,[29] may be extinguished by lapse of time.

1. Right of redemption

The Act[30] provides that when a mortgagee of land has been in possession of the mortgaged land for a period of 12 years, no action to redeem that land can be brought by the mortgagor or any person claiming through him.

2. Rights of mortgagee

An action to recover any principal sum of money secured by a mortgage on any property, real or personal, must be brought within 12 years from the date when the right to receive the money accrued *i.e.* the contractual date of redemption.[31] In general, a mortgagee may not recover more than six years' arrears of *interest* payable under a mortgage.[32] Similarly, a foreclosure action in respect of land must be commenced within 12 years of the right of action accruing, which once more will be the contractual date of redemption.[33]

[28] S.38.
[29] See p. 195–196.
[30] S.16.
[31] S.20(1) and see p. 186.
[32] S.20(5) and *Barclays Bank plc v. Walters* (1988) *The Times,* 20 October, but see *Holmes v. Cowcher* [1970] 1 W.L.R. 834 (p. 186 above).
[33] S.15(1), s.20(4) and *Purnell v. Roche* [1927] 2 Ch. 142. As to the effect, in the above cases, if the debt is acknowledged after the right of action has accrued, see p. 214.

Disabilities

If on the date when a right of action accrues, the person to whom it accrues is under a disability (*i.e.* is an infant or of unsound mind), the action may be brought at any time before the expiry of six years from the date when either i) the person ceased to be under disability or ii) he died, whichever occurs first. This is notwithstanding that the period of limitation has expired. However, it should be noted that the extension of time only applies where the relevant person is under a disability at *the date the right of action accrues.*[34] Further, there is a proviso that in any event no action to recover land or money charged on land can be brought after 30 years have expired from the date on which the right of action accrued.[35]

Where a right of action accrues to a person under a disability who dies (still under a disability) and is succeeded by another person who is also under a disability, time still runs from the death of the first person.[36] No further extension of time is to be allowed by reason of the disability of the second person. However, successive disabilities without a break of the *same* person, rank as one disability, *e.g.* where someone is an infant at the date of the accrual of the cause of action to him and later becomes of unsound mind before reaching his majority. He or his personal representatives will have six years from his becoming of sound mind, or his death, to sue.

Acknowledgement and part-payment

If a person in adverse possession acknowledges the title of the person to whom the right of action has accrued *e.g.* the fee simple owner, the right is deemed to have accrued on, and not before, the date of the acknowledgement.[37] Thus, the limitation period within which the true owner may bring proceedings starts anew from that date. The same rule applies where a right of action has accrued for the recovery of a debt, *e.g.* rent, and the claim is subsequently acknowledged or part payment is made by the person liable, *e.g.* the tenant.[38] Further, where in an action by a mortgagee (including foreclosure), the person in possession of the land makes any payment in respect of the mortgage debt, whether principal or interest, the right is deemed to accrue on the date of payment and not before.[39] For example, if a mortgagor in possession of the mortgaged land

[34] S.28(1) and (2).
[35] S.28(4).
[36] S.28(3).
[37] S.29(2)(a).
[38] S.29(5).
[39] S.29(3).

makes a payment of interest to the mortgagee, the mortgagee may bring a foreclosure action within 12 years from the date of that payment. He is not limited to 12 years from the contractual date of redemption, as he otherwise would have been.[40]

On the other hand, as regards a mortgagor's right of action, where a mortgagee is in possession of the mortgaged land, and the mortgagee either receives a sum in respect of the principal or interest due under the mortgage or he acknowledges the title of the mortgagor, an action to redeem the land may be brought by the mortgagor at any time before the expiration of 12 years from the date of the payment or acknowledgement.[41]

For the above purposes, an acknowledgement must be in writing and signed by the person making the acknowledgement. Any such acknowledgement, and any such payment mentioned above, may be made by the agent of the person by whom it is required to be made. Also, it must be made to the person whose title or claim is being acknowledged or his agent.[42] There are detailed provisions as to the effect of acknowledgement or part-payment on persons other than the maker or recipient, *e.g.* where one of two or more mortgagees in possession gives an acknowledgement of the mortgagor's title.[43]

It must be stressed that in all the cases mentioned above, however, once the right of a person to bring an action to recover land or a debt has become statute-barred, no acknowledgement or payment given or made thereafter will revive his right to recover the land or debt.[44]

Fraud and mistake

In a case where either i) the action is based on the fraud of the defendant, or ii) any fact relevant to the right of action has been deliberately concealed from the plaintiff by the defendant, or iii) the action is for relief from the consequences of mistake, the period of limitation does not begin to run until the plaintiff has discovered the fraud or mistake or could with reasonable diligence have discovered it.[45] References to the defendant include the defendant's agent and any person through whom the defendant claims and his agent.

The above provision, however, has no application to an action against an innocent purchaser for value of property who was not a party to any fraud and did not at the time of the purchase know or have reason to believe that any fraud or mistake had occurred.[46]

40 See p. 232.
41 S.29(4).
42 S.30.
43 S.31.
44 S.29(7).
45 S.32(1).
46 S.32(3) and (4).

ADVERSE POSSESSION

Having considered the effect of expiry of time on the original owner's title, we must now consider the acquisition of title by the person wrongfully in possession.

The essence of the acquisition of title under the Limitation Act 1980 is adverse possession. To amount to adverse possession, first, the squatter's acts must be such as to in fact *exclude* the true owner and secondly, it must be clear that the squatter has the necessary *intention* to dispossess the true owner.[47] Under the first limb, factual possession by the squatter will be shown by an appropriate degree of physical control. For example, usually the most obvious evidence of this is the enclosure of the land by fencing.[48] At the other extreme, however, casual acts of trespass from time to time are insufficient to show adverse possession.[49] Under the second head it must be the squatter's clear intention to exclude everyone from the land, including the true owner. Thus, a squatter will lack the necessary intention if he accepts the owner's right to restrict the squatter's activities on the land.[50]

One problem area is where the owner has no present use for the land, but has future plans for it and, in the meantime, another person occupies the land. One example of this is where a local authority has acquired land for road development in the future, but in the meantime the land is standing idle. In these circumstances, it may be difficult to decide whether acts done by a squatter in relation to that land, amount to adverse possession. Previously it had been held that the true owner was not dispossessed in this situation, as for dispossession to take place, it must be shown that the acts of the squatter are inconsistent with the owner's use of the land. This is not the case where the true owner has no current use for the land, but only future plans.[51] However, it now appears that there is no such special rule in these cases and that the usual principles of actual possession and intention apply; although strong evidence of possession by the squatter and intention is necessary to demonstrate adverse possession in such circumstances.[52]

47 *Powell v. McFarlane* (1977) 38 P.&C.R. 452, approved in *Buckingham County Council v. Moran* [1990] Ch.623.

48 See *Williams v. Usherwood* (1983) 45 P.&C.R. 235, but this will not always amount to adverse possession; note *George Wimpey & Co v. Sohn* [1967] Ch. 487 (fencing intended to exclude the public) and *Marsden v. Miller* (1992) P. & C.R. 239 (where land was only fenced for a short period).

49 See for example, *Tecbild Ltd v. Chamberlain* (1969) 20 P.&C.R. 633.

50 *Morrice v. Evans* (1989) *The Times,* 27 February (where an owner put restrictions on the use of a greenhouse by the squatter), *R v. Secretary of State for the Environment ex. p. Davies* (1990) 61 P.&C.R. 487 (where the squatter offered to pay rent).

51 *Leigh v. Jack* (1879) 5 Ex. D. 264.

52 *Buckingham County Council v. Moran*, see note 47 above, (where there was total enclosure of the land and the only access was via the squatter's adjoining property), disapproving *Leigh v. Jack, ibid.*

Another approach adopted by the courts to overcome the problem where the true owner had no present use of the land, was to deem that the squatter's possession must be with the implied licence of the owner and therefore was not adverse.[53] However, following the Limitation Amendment Act 1980,[54] such a licence to occupy shall not be implied as a matter of *law* in all cases where, on the facts, occupation by the squatter is consistent with the owner's present or future plans for the land. Nevertheless, this does not prevent any finding of *fact* that a person's occupation of land is by implied permission of the owner.[55]

NATURE OF POSSESSORY TITLE

Titles to land are relative; the owner of land being the person with the best right to possession, until some other person can prove a better title to the land. It follows that if the only person who can prove a better title to the land is statute-barred, *i.e.* the fee simple absolute owner, the possession of the squatter gives a title to the land which is good against the whole world. It is on this principle that the squatter's title depends; there is no notional statutory transfer, under the Act or otherwise, of the title of the former owner to the squatter. The squatter's title, based on possession, is a separate interest. Thus, the squatter is not a purchaser for value of the land and cannot claim to be entitled as such to take free from equitable interests (such as restrictive covenants) of which he has no notice.[56] Again, if a squatter takes possession of land which has been let under a lease and acquires a squatter's title against the lessee, the landlord cannot directly sue the squatter upon the tenant's covenants in the lease, as the squatter is not an assignee of the lease.[57] However, as long as the squatter has not obtained title by adverse possession against the landlord, the estate between the *landlord and tenant* is not destroyed. During the remaining term of the lease, if the landlord has a right to re-enter for breach of the tenant's covenants in the lease, the landlord may forfeit the lease and the squatter has no right to relief from forfeiture.[58] The squatter, therefore, may see it as wise to perform the covenants, in order to escape dispossession by the landlord.

The position is different where the squatter is estopped from denying that he has the burden of the covenants in the lease. For

[53] *Wallis's Cayton Bay Holiday Camp Ltd v. Shell-Mex and B.P. Ltd* [1975] Q.B. 94.
[54] S.4., inserted into the Limitation Act 1980, Sched. 1, para. 8(4).
[55] *Ibid.*
[56] *Re Nisbet and Potts' Contract* [1906] 1 Ch. 386 and he would also be bound by an unregistered post 1925 covenant.
[57] *Tichborne v. Weir* (1892) 67 L.T. 735.
[58] *Tickner v. Buzzacott* [1965] Ch. 246.

example, if the lease provides for the payment of a reduced rent, if the tenant performs the tenant's covenants in the lease, and the squatter chooses to take the benefit of this provision, and pays the rent at the reduced rate, he may then be estopped from denying his liability on the other covenants in the lease.[59]

Where a squatter obtains a squatter's title against a lessee, and the lessee later acquires the reversion, he can at once obtain possession from the squatter. The lease has become merged in the freehold and the former tenant is now claiming possession by virtue of his right of action as the freeholder, which accrued on merger.[60] Equally, where land is unregistered, if, prior to expiry of the term, the tenant surrenders the lease to his landlord, the landlord can at once oust the squatter, as his right of action accrues on the termination of the lease.[61]

Even before possessory title has been completed, *i.e.* before the former owner has become statute-barred, a squatter who takes possession of another's land at once acquires an interest in it, which he can assign *inter vivos*, or dispose of by his will, and which will pass to his statutory next of kin on his intestacy. A successor in title to a squatter can add his own period of possession to that of his predecessors, and the title of the former owner will become extinguished after a total of 12 years.[62] Moreover, if a squatter is himself ousted by another squatter, the second squatter, in defending an action brought by the *former owner* of the land, can add to his own period of possession, that of the squatter whom he has ejected. The first squatter could, however, recover the land from the second squatter if he brought an action against him before the expiration of 12 years from the date when the second squatter took possession, as prior to that, the second squatter does not have an undefeatable title. The second squatter cannot plead that the land belongs to someone else, other than the first squatter, as a defence.[63]

If a squatter abandons possession, and after an interval a second squatter takes possession, the second squatter has no right to add to his own period of possession that of the first squatter.[64]

As has been seen, where the limitation period has expired a former owner's title to unregistered land is automatically extinguished.[65] Generally, the Limitation Act 1980 applies to registered land in the

[59] *Ashe v. Hogan* [1920] I.R. 159.

[60] *Taylor v. Twinberrow* [1930] 2 K.B. 16.

[61] *Fairweather v. St. Marylebone Property Co.* [1963] A.C. 510. As to the position concerning registered land see below.

[62] *Asher v. Whitlock* (1865) L.R. 1 Q.B. 1., *Mount Carmel Investments Ltd v. Peter Thurlow Ltd* [1988] 1 W.L.R. 1078.

[63] See M. & W., pp. 103–104, 1036.

[64] Limitation Act 1980, Sched. 1, para. 8(2), as during the gap there is no adverse possession; as there is nothing in the way of the true owner's rights.

[65] See p. 208.

same manner and to the same extent as unregistered land.[66] However, if land is registered, the Land Registration Act 1925 also applies. This provides that where a registered proprietor's claim to recover land is statute-barred, the estate is not extinguished, but held by the registered proprietor on trust for the squatter, but without prejudice to the interests of any persons whose estate, or interest, is not extinguished by the Limitation Acts.[67] The squatter can then apply to be registered as the proprietor of the title acquired by adverse possession[68] and, in the meantime, the rights acquired, or in the course of being acquired under the Limitation Acts, are overriding interests.[69] If the squatter's application is successful the squatter will become the first registered proprietor of a new title,[70] but any estate or interest, which is not statute-barred and which was protected by an entry on the old register, will be entered onto the new register.[71]

One result of this procedure is that where a registered proprietor of a long leasehold title is dispossessed and the squatter has been registered as proprietor of a leasehold title acquired under the Limitation Acts, the former tenant and proprietor of the leasehold estate cannot purport to surrender his lease, to ensure that an immediate right of action accrues to his landlord, as he no longer has an estate to surrender.[72]

66 LRA 1925, s.75(1).

67 *Ibid.*

68 LRA 1925, s.75(2).

69 LRA 1925, s.70(1)(f) and *Bridges v. Mees* [1957] Ch. 475. See p. 224.

70 LRA 1925, s.75(3). This may be absolute, good leasehold, qualified or possessory title, see p. 222–223, but it does not have to be the same type of title as previously held by the registered proprietor who was dispossessed.

71 LRA 1925 s.75(3) and see Ruoff & Roper 29–02.

72 *Spectrum Investment Co. v. Holmes* [1981] 1 W.L.R. 221. (but see E. Cooke: (1994) 14 L.S.I., where it is argued that the case is peculiar to its' facts and does not reflect the general principles which usually apply). Compare with unregistered land, see note 61 above.

21. Registration

The underlying land law principles discussed in this book are generally the same whether title to the land is registered or unregistered, subject to a few minor exceptions. Nevertheless, for conveyancing purposes, so that the purchaser can ascertain the nature and extent of the rights to which he is subject, it is necessary to understand the form of registration and the different entries on the register of title at Her Majesty's Land Registry (with registered land) and the register of commercial incumbrances at the Land Charges Registry (where the land is unregistered).

REGISTRATION OF TITLE TO LAND

As mentioned previously under the registered land system the whole title to land, including the legal estate and incumbrances and rights affecting land, must be registered at HM Land Registry, where the register is maintained by the Chief Land Registrar and his staff. The land is allocated an individual title number and the name of the owner of the land is entered on the register as the *registered proprietor* of the title. Two types of legal estate are capable of registration with separate title, under a specific title number, and these are: a) a legal fee simple absolute in possession, called *freehold* and b) a term of years absolute granted for more than 21 years, called *leasehold*.[1]

The title of the registered proprietor is in effect guaranteed by the state in that, should any error occur in the register, an application may be made for rectification of the register *i.e.* by substituting the

[1] Application must be made for first registration of title to land on the first conveyance *on sale* of freehold land, or grant or assignment *on sale* of a lease for an unexpired term of more than 21 years, following an area becoming a compulsory registration area. If registration is not applied for within 2 months of such a transaction it becomes void, as regards the conveyance of grant of the legal estate, (L.R.A. 1925, s.123(1)). All areas of England and Wales are now compulsory registration areas (Registration of Title Order, S.I. 1989 No. 1347). However, as registration will not take place until one of the above transactions occurs some land still remains unregistered, although this will gradually decrease.

true owner's name as the registered proprietor. Also, compensation is payable out of public funds in respect of any loss caused by rectification.

The register of title

This is divided into three parts:

(i) The property register, which describes the land and the estate (*e.g.* the fee simple), the title to which is registered, and any interests, such as easements, which are known to belong to the land.

(ii) The proprietorship register, which states the kind of title[2] (*e.g.* absolute) which has been granted and the name and address of the proprietor; it also contains a note of any *cautions, inhibitions* or *restrictions* which have been entered, affecting his powers of disposition.[3]

(iii) The charges register, which consists of entries of mortgages and *notices* of other interests adverse to the land.[4]

Rights in registered land

Rights in land, the title to which has been registered, fall into three classes, namely *registered interests, overriding interests* and *minor interests,* (although some rights may fall into more than one class).

Registered interests

These are the *legal* estates which have been substantively registered under the Land Registration Act 1925 *i.e.* they have been registered with an individual title number. The only estates in respect of which separate title may be registered are the legal estates of: a) the fee simple absolute in possession and b) the term of years absolute (but not, if the lease was granted for a term of 21 years or less or it is a mortgage term with a subsisting right of redemption).[5] Those other interests capable of existing at law under section 1(2) of the Law of Property Act 1925, *e.g.* the grant of a legal easement, are registrable against the title to which they relate.

[2] See below.
[3] See pp. 225–226.
[4] See pp. 227 and 225.
[5] LRA 1925, ss.2, 3 (xi), 8

1. Nature of title

Upon application for registration of the title to a *freehold*, the registrar may grant any one of three titles, namely a) *absolute*, b) *qualified* or c) *possessory* title. If an absolute title is granted, the title of the proprietor to the fee simple is guaranteed, subject only to interests entered on the register, overriding interests (unless the register states that there are no such interests affecting the land) and, where the proprietor is not entitled for his own benefit, minor interests of which he has notice. Registration with qualified title has the same effect, subject to some possible adverse interest which is *specified* in the register. Registration with possessory title also has the same effect, except that no guarantee at all is given as to the absence of adverse interests subsisting at the date of first registration. Possessory title may be registered, for instance, where title deeds have been lost or where title has been acquired through adverse possession.

Leasehold title may be a) *absolute,* b) *qualified,* c) *possessory* or d) *good leasehold*. Absolute, qualified and possessory titles have the same effect as the corresponding freehold titles, except that the registered proprietor is, of course, subject to all the obligations of the lease. Absolute leasehold title guarantees the title of the landlord to grant the lease, as well as the title of the leasehold proprietor to the lease itself. When good leasehold title is granted no guarantee is given with regard to the landlord's right to grant the lease, but in other respects the title is the same as absolute title.

2. Conversion of title

The registrar has power to upgrade titles, and on application by the proprietor must upgrade:

(i) good leasehold to absolute title, if satisfied as to the freehold and any intermediate leasehold title;
(ii) possessory to absolute or good leasehold title, if satisfied as to the title, or if the land has been registered with possessory title for at least 12 years and the proprietor is in possession;
(iii) qualified to absolute or good leasehold title, if satisfied as to the title.

Overriding interests

These are interests, which are not required to be noted on the register, but which will bind a purchaser of the land, whether or not he has notice of their existence. All registered land is deemed to be subject to any overriding interests relating to the land and falling within the categories listed in section 70 of the Land Registration Act 1925. The most important overriding interests are set out in the following paragraphs of section 70(1):

- *(a)* easements, profits, public rights, etc;
- *(f)* rights acquired or in the course of being acquired under the Limitation Acts;
- *(g)* the rights of every person in actual occupation of the land or in receipt of the rents and profits thereof, save where inquiry is made of such person and the rights are not disclosed;
- *(k)* leases granted for a term not exceeding twenty-one years.

Paragraph (a) includes easements arising by prescription, under *Wheeldon v. Borrows* or under section 62 of the Law of Property Act 1925,[6] but not equitable easements.[7]

Paragraph (g) also calls for further comment. The rights to which it refers are confined to those of a proprietary character, and do not include personal rights, such as those created by a mere licence, which are not binding on third parties.[8] Interests arising through adverse possession or under a contract of sale, or an informal lease, or an option or a right of pre-emption, are included.[9] The result is that whereas in the case of unregistered land, such rights would not bind the land unless they were registered under the Land Charges Act 1972, they will be binding as overriding interests if the title to the land is registered, provided that the person entitled is in *actual occupation.*[10] The rights of a beneficiary in actual occupation under a trust may also constitute an overriding interest under this paragraph[11] notwithstanding that the Land Registration Act 1925, expressly provides that persons dealing with a registered estate shall not be affected with notice of a trust express, implied or constructive.[12] However, such interests under a trust still may be overreached under section 2 of the Law of Property Act 1925, thus ensuring that a purchaser takes free.[13]

[6] As to these methods of acquiring an easement see pp. 144–152.

[7] Unless *Celsteel Ltd v. Alton House Holdings Ltd* [1985] 1 W.L.R. 204 is followed.

[8] *Strand Securities Ltd v. Caswell* [1965] Ch. 958; *National Provincial Bank Ltd v. Ainsworth* [1965] A.C. 1175.

[9] *Bridges v. Mees* [1957] Ch. 475; *Woolwich Equitable B.S. v. Marshall* [1952] Ch. 1; *Webb v. Pollmount Ltd* [1966] Ch. 584; *Kling v. Keston Properties Ltd* (1985) 49 P. & C.R. 212.

[10] If he is not in actual occupation, they will constitute minor interests only, and as such require protection by notice or caution, see p. 225.

[11] *Hodgson v. Marks* [1971] Ch. 918; *Williams & Glyn's Bank v. Boland* [1981] A.C. 487.

[12] S.74. With respect to beneficial interests under a strict settlement, however, s.86(2) provides that these shall take effect as minor interests *and not otherwise* — see p. 225.

[13] *City of London B.S. v. Flegg* [1987] 2 W.L.R. 1266 (see p. 71. above).

For the purposes of paragraph (*g*) "actual occupation" is a matter of fact, although it usually involves a degree of permanent, continual, physical presence[14] (albeit through an agent). The relevant date by which the person must be in actual occupation, for the purposes of this paragraph, is the date of execution of the transfer or the date of completion of the mortgage deed, rather than the date of registration of the disposition.[15]

Only *legal* leases for a term not exceeding 21 years constitute overriding interests under paragraph (k)[16] the policy being that such short term leases need not be registered. These include leases not exceeding three years, granted orally or in writing, and taking effect in possession under section 54(2) of the Law of Property Act 1925. It should be noted, however, that unlike paragraph (g), this paragraph is not dependent on occupation or the receipt of rent or profits, although usually a legal lease for less than 21 years will be overriding under both provisions.

Minor interests

These comprise all interests in registered land, other than registered interests and overriding interests. They take effect in equity and fall into two classes:

(a) interests, such as those of beneficiaries under a settlement or trust for sale, which (as in the case of unregistered land) are capable of being overreached;

(b) interests which are not overreachable and resemble those interests registrable under the Land Charges Act 1972, such as those created by estate contracts or restrictive covenants.

Minor interests must be protected by an entry on the register[17] otherwise they are void against a purchaser for valuable consideration. The rule regarding a volunteer is that he takes subject to any minor interests which were binding on the transferor.[18]

Minor interests may be protected by the entry of a restriction, notice, caution or inhibition on the register. Despite this, if those interests within category (a) are overreached, they will not bind a purchaser, even if they have been protected by some kind of entry on the register.

Restrictions are appropriate to protect any minor interest in class (a) above. They are entered at the request of the registered proprietor

[14] *Hodgson v. Marks* and *Williams & Glyn's Bank v. Boland* (see note 11 above) and *Abbey National Building Society v. Cann* [1991] 1 A.C. 56.

[15] *Abbey National Building Society v. Cann, ibid.*

[16] Because of the use of the word "grant" in the paragraph.

[17] Although this must be distinguished from, and is not the same as, actual registration of the interest itself, as in the case of registered interests.

[18] LRA 1925, s20(1) and (4).

in the proprietorship register and indicate, *e.g.* that capital money is to be paid to the trustees of the settlement or trust for sale, so that overreaching can take place.

A *notice* appears in the charges register and any subsequent dealing takes subject to the right protected. This is the primary method of protecting interests in class (b) above and which, in the case of unregistered land, would be registrable under the Land Charges Act 1972. A notice is sometimes referred to as a *friendly* entry as, for the entry to be made, it requires the co-operation of the registered proprietor. He must submit the Land Certificate to the H.M. Land Registry, so that the entry can be made on the Land Certificate as well as the register itself. (This need for compliance will not be a problem if the land is subject to a registered charge, as in such cases the Land Certificate is retained by the registry, whilst the mortgagee is issued with a Charge Certificate.)

A *caution* against dealings with the land may be lodged in the proprietorship register by any person interested in registered land. This entitles the cautioner to be notified by the registrar of proposed dealings with the land, and to object within a specified period. A caution is frequently lodged as a means of protecting a minor interest, such as that of a purchaser under an estate contract,[19] where the cautioner is unable to register a notice because the registered proprietor has not furnished his Land Certificate. Therefore, it is often regarded as a *hostile* entry.

An *inhibition* may be entered in the proprietorship register, in pursuance of an order of the court or of the Registrar, in circumstances such as the bankruptcy of the registered proprietor. Its effect generally is to prevent all dealings with the land until further order.

An official search of the register can be made to ascertain the entries made in respect of minor interests. Obtaining an official search certificate gives a purchaser priority, for a 30 working day period, over any other entries made during that period, provided that the purchaser also applies for registration of his disposition within that period.[20]

Dispositions of registered land

Ownership of a legal estate in registered land is vested in the proprietor by virtue of registration, and his powers of disposition are those conferred by the Act, including such powers to transfer the legal

[19] It may also be used to protect the interest of a person beneficially entitled under a trust for sale (*Elias v. Mitchell* [1972] Ch. 652.). The caution merely gives the cautioner the right to be given notice of a proposed dealing and does not of itself give him a right to priority, see *Clark v. Chief Land Registrar,* [1994] 3 W.L.R. 593.

[20] Land Registration (Official Searches) Rules 1990 (No. 1361) and 1993 (No. 3276).

estate and to grant leases, easements and other rights over the land as ordinarily attach to estate ownership of unregistered land.[21] A disposition of registered land requires completion by registration, otherwise it will create a minor interest only, which takes effect only in equity and requires protection by a notice or caution.[22] Thus, the transfer of the freehold of registered land must itself be registered, to confer the legal estate.[23]

A disposition for value of registered land, when registered, confers on the transferee or grantee, the legal estate or interest disposed of, together with all rights belonging thereto. It is however, subject to any incumbrances and other entries appearing on the register, and to any overriding interests, but free from all other estates and interests whatsoever.[24] As we have seen, minor interests are thus overridden by a registered transfer, or other disposition for value of registered land, (whether or not the purchaser has express, implied or constructive notice of them),[25] unless they are protected by some entry on the register, such as a restriction (in the case of beneficial interests under a trust), or a notice or caution (in the case of other minor interests). It must, however, be remembered that if, a person entitled to a minor interest is in actual occupation of the land, his interest will also constitute an overriding interest, and accordingly have the protection afforded by section 70(1)(g) of the Land Registration Act 1925, regardless of any entry on the register.[26]

Mortgages of registered land

1. Types of mortgages in registered land

Mortgages may be effected in any of three ways:

(i) Registered charge.

This is the usual way of creating a mortgage of registered land and it may be in any form permitted for unregistered land (*i.e.* by demise or a charge by way of legal mortgage).[27] However, it must be by deed and must be registered in the charges register in order for the legal interest to arise, as such it is in a category of its own as it is not a registrable interest, a minor interest nor an overriding interest. The

[21] LRA 1925, s.18 (freeholds), s.21 (leaseholds).
[22] *Ibid* s.101.
[23] See p. 222.
[24] LRA 1925, s.20 (freeholds), s.23 (leaseholds). Dispositions in the latter case are also subject to the obligations contained in the lease.
[25] *Ibid*. s.59(6) except in cases of fraud, see p. 37.
[26] See pp. 223–225.
[27] See pp. 184–186.

Land Certificate is deposited at the registry (until the mortgage is redeemed); the chargee's name is entered on the register as the proprietor of the charge and a Charge Certificate is issued to the chargee.

A registered chargee has all the powers of a legal mortgagee including, for example, the right to possession and the power of sale.[28]

(ii) Unregistered mortgage.

This is where registered land is mortgaged in the same way as if it were unregistered land, including informally where there is a contract to create a mortgage.[29] Further, an unregistered mortgage will arise where it was intended to create a registered charge, but this failed as the charge has not been registered. Such mortgages are equitable, only taking effect as minor interests and require protection by the entry of a notice or caution. The powers of such mortgagees do not include the power of sale.

(iii) Deposit of Land Certificate.

As has been seen, the Land Certificate takes the place of title deeds, and so a lien (a right to retain property), or a mortgage may be created if the registered proprietor deposits the Land Certificate with a lender of money, as security for the loan.[30] The deposit of the Land Certificate will give rise to an equitable mortgage, as long as there is an agreement to provide the certificate as security. As this method of creating a mortgage is contract-based, nowadays, there must also be a written memorandum of mortgage, incorporating all the mortgage terms and signed by, or on behalf of all the parties, otherwise the mortgage will be void.[31]

This method of mortgaging gives protection, since without the Land Certificate no disposition of the land can be registered, but the mortgagee may also be protected, as this is a minor interest, by the entry of a notice or caution. The advantage of this type of mortgage is that it is cheaper to create than a registered charge, but one disadvantage is that the mortgagee has no power of sale.

2. Priority of mortgages in registered land

The priority of successive registered charges depends on their order of registration, rather than creation, unless otherwise provided.[32]

[28] See pp. 191–197 for remedies available to mortgages generally.
[29] See pp. 184–185.
[30] This is comparable with an informal mortgage by deposit of title deeds in unregistered land, see p. 95 and pp. 184–185.
[31] Complying with LP(MP)A 1989, s.2(1). See *United Bank of Kuwait Plc v. Sahib* [1995] 2 W.L.R. 94 and pp. 95–96.
[32] LRA 1925, s.29.

Unregistered mortgages which are protected as minor interests by the entry of a notice, or caution, or deposit of a Land Certificate, will take priority over any later mortgage, including a registered charge. If there is no entry protecting the minor interest, or deposit of the Land Certificate, a later registered charge will take priority over the earlier mortgages, unless they are overriding interests. If, however, the two mortgages of the legal estate vying for priority are equitable, the traditional rule applies, *i.e.* that the first in time prevails, even though the second mortgage has been protected as a minor interest, whilst the first has not.[33] Finally, where the mortgages are equitable mortgages of an equitable interest in registered land, the rule in *Dearle v. Hall* applies.[34]

3. Tacking

This can only apply to registered land if a registered charge is made for the purpose of securing further advances, or the registered proprietor of the charge is under an obligation to make further advances. A notice must be given by the Registrar to the proprietor of the charge before he authorises an entry which affects the priority of a further advance under the charge.[35]

4. Discharge

A registered charge is discharged by sending the Charge Certificate and a form of discharge to the Registrar, who will remove the charge from the register.

Rectification and indemnity

As we have seen, the title of the registered proprietor arises not from any conveyance or transfer to him but from registration, and the title so registered is guaranteed by the state. Clearly, however, provision must be made for cases in which it subsequently appears that the wrong person has been registered as proprietor, or in which adverse claims are held to prevail over his title. Accordingly, the Act provides that in certain circumstances the register may be rectified, and that an indemnity may be paid out of state funds to any person who suffers loss when rectification is either granted or, notwithstanding some error or omission in the register, refused.

The register may be rectified, pursuant to an order of the court or by the registrar, subject to an appeal to the court, in, for example, the

[33] *Mortgage Corporation Ltd v. Nationwide Credit Corporation Ltd* [1994] Ch. 49.
[34] See p. 199.
[35] See LRA 1925 s.30. For the rules relating to unregistered land see pp. 199–200.

following cases: i) where the court has decided that any person is entitled to any estate, right or interest in the land; or ii) an entry has been obtained by fraud; or iii) in any other case where by reason of an error or omission in the register it may be deemed just to rectify it.[36] Where the registered proprietor is in possession, however, rectification will not be ordered[37] (except to give effect to an overriding interest or an order of the court), unless the proprietor has caused or substantially contributed to the error or omission by fraud or lack of proper care, or unless for some other reason it would be unjust not to rectify the register against him.[38]

Any person who suffers loss as a result, either of the register being rectified, or of some error or omission in the register which is not rectified, is entitled to be indemnified under the Act.[39] No indemnity can be recovered, however, if either the applicant or a person from whom he derives title has caused or substantially contributed to the loss by fraud or lack of proper care.[40] It has also been held that a proprietor is not entitled to an indemnity if the register is rectified merely to give effect to an overriding interest which is in any event binding on him, such as rights acquired by adverse possession prior to his acquisition.[41]

The amount of the indemnity recoverable under the Act, in respect of the loss of an estate or interest, is its value at the time of rectification or, where the register is not rectified, at the time when the error or omission which caused the loss was made. The period within which a claim to an indemnity must be brought is six years. For the purposes of the Limitation Act 1980, time does not start to run until the claimant knows, or ought to know, of the existence of his claim. However, subject to certain exceptions, if the claim arises from the registration of land with an absolute or good leasehold title, it must be brought within six years from the date of such registration.[42]

THE CENTRAL LAND CHARGES REGISTER

Provision is made by the Land Charges Act 1972[43] for the registration of certain rights against unregistered land, in five registers kept by the Land Charges Department of the Land Registry. These are the

[36] LRA 1925, s.82(1) and (2).
[37] And see *Freer v. Unwins Ltd* [1976] Ch. 288 (rectification is not retrospective).
[38] LRA 1925, s.82(3).
[39] *Ibid.* s.83(1) and (2).
[40] *Ibid.* s.83(5).
[41] *Re Chowood's Registered Land* [1933] Ch. 574.
[42] As to the consequences where rectification is refused, despite an error in the register, see *Epps v. Esso Petroleum Co. Ltd* [1973] 1 W.L.R. 1071.
[43] This repealed and re-enacted most of the provisions of the Land Charges Act 1925.

registers of: i) *pending actions* (including bankruptcy petitions and other court proceedings affecting land), ii) *annuities (i.e.* certain annuities, (the right to receive payment of an annual sum), created before 1926), iii) *writs and orders affecting land* (such as writs of execution enforcing court orders or judgments), iv) *deeds of arrangement* executed by debtors (commonly to avoid bankruptcy) and v) *land charges.* Of these, the last-mentioned are by far the most important category for our purposes.

Register of land charges

Land charges comprise six classes, A–F, of which mention need be made only of classes C, D and F.

Class C

(i) Puisne mortgage, i.e. a *legal* mortgage not protected by deposit of title deeds with the mortgagee.[44]

(ii) Limited owner's charge, i.e. a charge given by statute to a tenant for life or statutory owner who discharges inheritance tax or certain other liabilities.

(iii) General equitable charge, i.e. any equitable charge which is not registrable in any other class, is not protected by deposit of title deeds, and does not arise, or affect an interest arising, under a trust for sale or strict settlement. A common example is an equitable mortgage of a legal estate in land, (*e.g.* created in writing, not by deed) which is not protected by deposit of title deeds.[45] On the other hand, a mortgage or other charge of an equitable (*i.e.* beneficial) interest under a trust for sale or settlement, is not registrable.

(iv) Estate contract, i.e. a contract to convey or create a legal estate, made by a person who at the date of the contract owns a legal estate, or is entitled to have such an estate conveyed to him. This important class includes contracts of sale, agreements for a lease, options to purchase and similar rights.[46]

Class D

(i) Inland Revenue charge, i.e. a charge on land for inheritance tax.

[44] See pp. 197–198.
[45] *Ibid.*
[46] As to the nature of equitable interests arising under such transactions, see pp. 27–28.

(ii) Restrictive covenant, i.e. a covenant (other than one between lessor and lessee) restricting the use of land and entered into after 1925.

(iii) Equitable easement, i.e. an easement, right or privilege over land, created after 1925 and being merely an equitable interest[47] because *e.g.*, it is an easement for life or an easement created in writing, rather than by deed.

Class F

A spouse's statutory right to occupy the matrimonial home, which is a charge affecting any land by virtue of the Matrimonial Homes Act 1983.[48]

Registration and failure to register

In general, registration of a registrable interest constitutes actual notice of the interest to all persons who acquire the land or any interest in it.[49] Failure to register the interest renders it void against a subsequent "purchaser,"[50] and where an interest is void by reason of non-registration a purchaser "shall not be prejudicially affected" by notice of it.[51]

The definition of a "purchaser" differs with the type of land charge. For the purposes of Class C land charges (other than estate contracts entered into after 1925) and Class F land charges, "purchaser" means purchaser for value (which includes marriage consideration) of any interest in the land, whether legal or equitable. For the purposes of Class D land charges, and estate contracts entered into after 1925, "purchaser" means a purchaser of a *legal* estate for money or money's worth (which does not include marriage consideration). In either case a mortgagee or lessee is a "purchaser" for this purpose; but, if the second, narrower definition applies, only if he obtains a legal estate. Notably, there is no requirement under the Land Charges Act 1972 that the purchaser must act in good faith.[52]

[47] Distinguish this with *E.R. Ives Investments Ltd v. High* [1967] 2 Q.B. 379 (proprietory estoppel) and *Shiloh Spinners Ltd v. Harding* [1973] A.C. 691 (an equitable right of re-entry, not between a landlord and tenant) which were held not to be registrable rights under this class, see p. 35 and pp. 161–162.

[48] See p. 163.

[49] LPA 1925, s.198.

[50] LCA 1972, s.4.

[51] LPA 1925, s.199.

[52] See *Midland Bank Trust Co. Ltd v. Green* [1981] A.C. 513, in which the House of Lords held that an unregistered option was void against a "purchaser", although the transaction had the sole collusive purpose of defeating the option, and was at a gross undervalue (land worth £40,000 was "sold" to the owner's wife for £500).

The above provisions have been applied rigorously by the courts, and the consequences of failure to register are likely to be drastic. They can be understood by considering a basic example. Suppose that L, by an instrument in writing but not a deed, has leased land at a rent to T for seven years. The purported lease is void at law,[53] but it constitutes a valid equitable lease[54] enforceable not merely against L personally (whose liability is contractual), but also against anyone acquiring the land from L, except a purchaser without notice. Suppose that L now sells and conveys the land to P, expressly subject to T's lease (and probably at a lower price because P is not getting vacant possession). Under general principles P should be bound by the lease, and he will be, if T has registered it as an estate contract. However, if T has failed to register it, the lease will be void against P, and the fact that P had notice of it will not prejudicially affect him. If P then evicts T, and T sues L for breach of contract, L has no defence to T's action and is liable in substantial damages.[55] This is notwithstanding that T's loss was caused, on one view, by his own default[56] in failing either to require the lease to be made by deed, or to register it (if there is no deed); or, on another view, by P's default in breaking his agreement with L to take the property subject to the lease.[57]

The result can scarcely be regarded as either just, expedient or even necessary. It could be avoided if P were held directly liable to T on either or both of two well recognised grounds. The first is that P became a constructive trustee for T when he acquired the land *expressly* subject to T's interest[58]; the second, is that an injunction lies against P to restrain him from wrongfully causing a breach of contract between L and T.[59] Neither of these solutions is inconsistent with section 4 of the Land Charges Act 1972 or with section 199 of the Law of Property Act 1925. The fact that T's equitable lease is void as an estate contract should not prevent its enforcement on some other ground or by some other means.

If P did not purchase expressly subject to T's lease, he would in any event have *constructive* notice of the lease,[60] but that of itself would be insufficient to raise a constructive trust of the kind suggested. P

[53] LPA 1925, s.52

[54] Under the principle discussed at pp. 100–101.

[55] *Wright v. Dean* [1948] Ch. 686, *Hollington Bros. Ltd v. Rhodes* [1951] 2 T.L.R. 691 (query as to the measure of damages).

[56] Or that of his solicitor: see *Midland Bank Trust Co. Ltd v. Hett, Stubbs & Kemp* [1979] Ch. 384.

[57] P may be liable to indemnify L if T sues L.

[58] *Binions v. Evans* [1972] Ch. 359 (see p. 162 note 19, *Lyus v. Prowsa Developments Ltd* [1982] 1 W.L.R. 1044 (see p. 194 note 49). But note the constructive trust arises, not by mere notice of the interest, but by P's agreement to take the land subject to T's interest, see below.

[59] See *Swiss Bank Corpn v. Lloyds Bank Ltd* [1979] Ch. 548.

[60] See p. 30 note 14.

accordingly would be protected by section 199 of the Law of Property Act 1925, against the equitable lease. Nevertheless, he would be bound by any *legal* rights which T might have acquired as a periodic tenant, by virtue of his occupation of L's land and payment of rent.[61] Further, of course, if P were himself to accept rent from T, or in any other way to deal with him as a tenant, an estoppel would arise and the equitable lease would be binding despite non-registration.[62]

System of registration

Registration of a registrable interest is against the name of the estate owner of the land affected, and not against the land itself. This is a serious defect in the system; it is not possible to ascertain what interests have been registered in respect of a particular plot of land since 1925 (when interests such as restrictive covenants and equitable easements created after 1925 became registrable), unless the names of all the estate owners for that period are known. Although the deeds produced by a vendor to a purchaser, as proof of title, should reveal charges created during the period for which the title is adduced,[63] and might also refer to earlier charges, there is a very real risk that both vendor and purchaser might be unaware of certain registered charges affecting the title. To meet this difficulty, section 25 of the Law of Property Act 1969, provides for the payment of compensation where a purchaser of any estate or interest has suffered loss by reason that the estate or interest is affected by a land charge[64] of which he had no knowledge (in this case, unusually registration does not constitute actual knowledge). This is provided that the land charge was registered against the name of any estate owner, who was not a party to any transaction comprising the relevant title, or concerned in any event with it. Compensation is payable to the purchaser by the Chief Land Registrar, and is recoverable by proceedings in the High Court.

Searches

Searches of the registers may be made in person, but in practice official certificates of search are generally obtained, by or on behalf of prospective purchasers, by officials of the registry. Such a certificate is conclusive in favour of a purchaser. Moreover, if the purchaser completes his transaction before the expiration of 15 working days, after the date of the certificate, he will not be affected by any entry in

[61] See pp. 99–102.
[62] *Taylor Fashions Ltd v. Liverpool Victoria Trustees Co. Ltd* [1982] Q.B. 133.
[63] See p. 29 note 11.
[64] Other than a local land charge, see p. 235.

the register which is made after the date of the certificate, (unless it is made as a result of a priority notice which had already been entered on the register, before the certificate was issued).[65]

Priority notices

Any person who intends to take an incumbrance which is a registrable land charge, *e.g.* a restrictive covenant, may lodge a priority notice on the register, not less than 15 working days, before the date of creation of the registrable incumbrance. If he then registers his charge, within 30 working days of the entry of the priority notice, the registration will date from the time when the incumbrance was created. The object of this procedure is to ensure that, where the creation of a registrable incumbrance is to be followed immediately by some other transaction, such as a mortgage of the land affected, registration is effective against a party to that other transaction.

LOCAL LAND CHARGES

Local land charges affect both unregistered and registered land. The Local Land Charges Act 1975[66] makes provision for the registration of certain charges in registers kept by local authorities. As defined by the Act, local land charges are generally public rights and include: i) various charges arising by statute in favour of a local authority or other public body, (such as charges for securing money recoverable in respect of highways and sewerage matters) and ii) prohibitions or restrictions on the use of land, imposed by a local authority or government department, *e.g.*, planning permission conditions. They also include any other charge or matter which is expressly made a local land charge by any statutory provision.[67]

Local land charges are registered against the land, and not against the name of the estate owner. Failure to register a charge does not affect its enforceability, but if a purchaser suffers loss by reason of a charge not being registered, or not being disclosed on an official search of the register, he is entitled to compensation payable by the registering authority.

[65] LCA 1972, s.11, as to priority notices see below.
[66] Repealing and replacing provisions in the Land Charges Act 1925.
[67] For an example of a *private* charge, see the Rights of Light Act 1959, s.2, see p. 152.

Index